THE PERDUE CHICKEN COOKBOOK

THE

PERDUE

CHICKEN COOKBOOK

MITZI PERDUE

POCKET BOOKS

New York   London   Toronto   Sydney   Tokyo   Singapore

This book is dedicated to Robbie Robinson and the organization she loves so much, the Business and Professional Women's Clubs. It's said that anyone can count the number of seeds in an apple, but only God can count the number of apples that will come from a seed. Robbie, as a teacher in the BPW Individual Development classes, doesn't just plant seeds. She and her fellow BPW instructors have planted whole orchards.

POCKET BOOKS, a division of Simon & Schuster
1230 Avenue of the Americas, New York, NY 10020

Perdue, Mitzi.
   The Perdue chicken cookbook / by Mitzi Perdue.
      p.   cm.
   Includes index.
   ISBN 0-671-69143-0 : $18.95
   1. Cookery (Chicken)   I. Title.
TX750.5.C45P47   1991
641.6′65—dc20

90-25926
CIP

First Pocket Books hardcover printing June 1991

10   9   8   7   6   5   4   3   2   1

DESIGN: Stanley S. Drate/Folio Graphics Co. Inc.

POCKET and colophon are registered trademarks of Simon & Schuster.

Printed in the U.S.A.

Contents

Acknowledgments

I've often thought that inspiration is one of the greatest gifts one person can give another, and there are several people who were an inspiration in writing this book. Bev Cox, a home economist and food stylist, was an inspiration for her meticulous attention to detail, her enthusiasm, and her unfailing good humor no matter what. Beth Fusaro, who typed most of the recipes in this book, is a Renaissance Woman, who knows not only about food and typing, but also about everything from making pottery to preserving the environment. It's been a privilege to work with Beth. Gretchen Barnes, who assisted Bev Cox in editing, learned a whole new computer program, Word Perfect, in order to get the job done quickly. Sharon Sakemiller, who is already a Word Perfect expert, also helped with typing and retyping recipes. She impressed everyone with how rapidly she could get things done. Anne Salisbury, who is both a home economist and a good friend, provided valuable advice. Connie Littleton, as an editor, colleague, and friend, provided the most inspiration of all.

My sincere thanks to the members of American Agri-Women who over the years have shared their food tips with me. Also, deepest thanks to the U.S. Department of Agriculture's Cooperative Extension. One of Cooperative Extension's major activities is helping to educate consumers, and I am deeply indebted and grateful for the education I've received through their many publications, broadcasts, classes, seminars, meetings, and personal contacts. The following Cooperative Extension members— many of whom are good friends as well as professional colleagues—have been invaluable resources for food tips and food knowledge: Dorothy

Thurber, Kathryn Boor, Christine Bruhn, Ellen Pusey, Sally Foulke, Bonnie Tanner, Bettie Collins, Sue Snyder, Chuck Waybeck, and George York. Also thanks to Dot Tringali of the National Broiler Council, to Connie Parvis of the Delmarva Poultry Industry, to Joy Schrage from the Whirlpool Corporation, and Lisa Readie from the Barbecue Industry Association.

PREFACE
Why I Chickened Out

Want to know a high-stress situation? Try being a food writer and cookbook author, and then marry Frank Perdue. You come home from the honeymoon, everything has been wonderful and then . . . *it's time to Cook the First Meal!*

I remember that afternoon so vividly. I knew he'd be coming home around six and that he'd be *hungry.* Now up until that day, I had always felt fairly confident in the kitchen. After all, I love cooking. Trying new recipes is a favorite pastime. But cooking chicken for Frank Perdue? I began to get stage fright. As I was trying to find where the pots and pans were in his kitchen, I realized there are probably few people in the world who've eaten chicken more times than my husband. "He's been eating chicken almost daily for his entire life," I thought. "My cooking is about to be judged by a world-class expert."

As I rummaged around looking for the right herbs and spices—and couldn't find the ones I liked—my stage fright grew worse. "This man must be one of the world's greatest experts on cooked chicken," I thought to myself. "He's attended dozens and dozens of chicken cooking contests, he's been part of hundreds and hundreds of taste testings for Perdue products. Everywhere he goes, people know he likes chicken and the best chefs and hostesses in the world have served it to him." In my mind I ran through some of the times when we'd driven an hour out of the way to go to a restaurant that cooked chicken particularly well, and how he always seemed to have lists of the restaurants he wanted to visit.

Help! The thirty-year-old oven didn't seem to be heating right, but I couldn't be sure because there wasn't any oven thermometer. The "elbow test," which our grandmothers used to use before the days of thermometers (you stick your elbow in the oven and feel how hot it is), told me that things weren't right, but I didn't know how far off the oven was to compensate. As I rubbed my elbow with my other hand, I thought of Frank's reputation for being demanding. If you've seen the ad that we call "Boot Camp," you know what I mean. (He plays the part of a drill sergeant in this ad and teaches the new Perdue recruits the fifty-seven quality points they have to inspect—and then he's all over one recruit for missing what seems like an invisibly small hair.)

It's a funny thing, but when you start losing your confidence, you start asking some basic questions about what you're doing. Part of me was saying that cooking chicken is pretty simple; after all, I'd been doing it for most of my life. But another part of me realized that I knew very little of the basics of cooking chicken. Like, for example, what makes a chicken tender? How do you *really* know when it's done—and not over done? How do you get the best flavor? Should you salt before or after cooking?

In desperation, I made a two-part deal with myself. First, I'd let myself take the easy way out that first meal, and not even try to cook the chicken myself. Instead, dinner would be a never-fail salad, pasta (Frank loves pasta), plus store-bought fully cooked Perdue Tenders. In return for letting myself off so easily, I'd make it my business from then on to learn how to make the best chicken every time. That meant asking Frank every question that popped into my head; checking with the food technologists who work for Perdue; getting tips from the farmers who grew the Perdue chickens; and systematically going through the thousands of recipes that Frank has in his files, trying a different one each night.

Dinner that night wasn't the showpiece I would have liked to create, but it was good enough. Frank happens to love his own Tenders. In the time since, I've tried to live up to the second part of my deal, the one about learning how to serve the best chicken every time.

In this book, I'd like to share with you the most useful cooking tips and the most appealing, most successful recipes developed by Perdue Farms over the last twenty years. The first chapter contains the kinds of information I wished I'd known from the beginning. You don't *need* to read this chapter, because chicken isn't that hard to cook; but there are tips in it that can save you time and money, and enable you to cook with greater confidence. This chapter also has the latest tips on food safety.

The remaining chapters are organized by the kind of occasion you're facing. You want to put some spark and variety into everyday meals? You want to make the most of your microwave? Or you're in a hurry today? Maybe you need something that will please kids? Or you're dieting? You've got a bunch of leftovers? You have to cook for a hundred people tomorrow night? I tried to think of the kinds of situations in which you could need recipes and then I organized Frank's recipes around them.

Jean Brillat-Savarin, the famous French gourmet, once said, "A chicken to a cook is like a canvas to a painter." Enjoy the recipes and tips that follow, and may they help you to feel the creativity and confidence that make cooking *fun* and eating a *joy!*

YOU DON'T HAVE TO WING IT! LET FRANK TAKE YOU UNDER HIS.
Everything You Wanted or Needed to Know about Cooking Chicken

Frank gets roughly 40,000 consumer letters a year. Half of these are requests for pamphlets, but many of the others are requests for information on selecting, storing, serving, or cooking his products.

These letters are tremendously important to Frank. Often when he has a few extra minutes, such as waiting for an airplane, he'll dash to a pay phone to answer one of the letters with a phone call. He also likes to attend store openings or conventions or other public places because he genuinely wants to hear what people are thinking. One of the marketing men once told me that he was embarrassed about a day he had planned for Frank because it included meetings with people who owned just a few stores. When I passed this on to Frank, he answered that these were some of the best meetings because the owners of the smaller stores were so close to their customers. He went on to say that the reason he likes to visit butchers (and in New York, he's called on as many as thirty in two days) is that these men are close to the needs and wants of their customers and he can learn things from them that he'd learn in no other way.

I've heard there's almost no other head of a Fortune 500–size company who would spend as much time with the people who buy his products. People are often surprised that a man with his responsibilities would take the time for this much face-to-face contact. But the fact is, learning what people care about is almost a religion to him.

Here are some of the questions that people either write to Frank or ask him in person. In answering the questions, I've either used the information I've heard Frank give, or else I've checked with the Perdue food scientists or home economists.

WHAT SHOULD I LOOK FOR WHEN I SHOP FOR CHICKEN?

Whatever city we're in, whether it's on the East Coast, or Puerto Rico, or even London or Moscow or Tokyo, Frank visits supermarkets the way other people visit museums or monuments. He notices the following kinds of things himself and would recommend that you do also when selecting chicken.

- Give the package a little squeeze. Are there signs of ice along wings, backs, or edges? Some chicken producers blast their birds with air as cold as −40°F, but Perdue never does. Freezing causes a breakdown in protein, loss of natural juices, and could reduce tenderness. Also, when you cook a frozen bird, the bones and nearby meat may turn an unappetizing dark color.
- Look at the thickness of the meat in proportion to the bone. If, for example, the breast looks scrawny, you're paying a lot for bone rather than meat.
- Read the labels so you know what you are getting. Many different parts and combinations are available, and some look surprisingly alike even to Frank's trained eye. The label tells exactly what is inside.
- Ask questions. If any meat or poultry product doesn't look, feel, or smell just right, check with the professionals behind the counter.
- Notice the pull date. Most stores are scrupulous about removing chicken before the pull date expires—but sometimes there's a slip-up.
- Was the chicken well-cleaned? Or are there little traces of feathers or hairs? These can look really unattractive when the bird is cooked.
- Is the chicken stored correctly on the chilling shelf, or are the trays of chicken stacked so high that the top ones aren't kept cold? When that happens, the shelf life of the top ones is seriously shortened.
- Is the meat case kept so cold that the fresh chicken is frozen and ends up with ice crystals on the tray? If so, complain to the manager.
- Look at the ends of the bones. Are they pink or are they turning

gray? Generally, the more pink the bone ends are, the fresher the chicken.

HOW SHOULD I STORE CHICKEN AT HOME?

Chicken, like all meat, is perishable. It should be stored in the coldest part of the refrigerator (40°F or below), kept sealed as it comes from the market, and used within two or three days of purchase.

SHOULD I FREEZE CHICKENS?

Frank doesn't recommend freezing poultry. However, if a bird must be held beyond three days, freezing will keep it wholesome.

HOW DO I FREEZE POULTRY?

When freezing is necessary, seal chicken or other poultry in an airtight container, heavy plastic bag, plastic wrap, foil, or freezer paper. Try to have the wrapping tight against the chicken, because any place where it isn't, small ice crystals will form. That means moisture has been drawn from the meat, and where that's happened, the meat will be tough and breading won't stick. Frozen uncooked chicken can be stored up to six months; frozen cooked chicken should be used within three months. Personally I try to avoid freezing chicken since I know that freezing makes the chicken less tender and less juicy. Still, in spite of good intentions, I sometimes end up doing it. I make it a point to have a wax marking pencil and freezer tape handy, so I can label the package with the date and contents. It's unbelievably easy to lose track of how long things have been in there.

Do not stuff poultry before freezing, and freeze cooked birds and stuffing separately.

CAN FROZEN CHICKEN BE THAWED AND FROZEN AGAIN?

Each time you freeze chicken, you sacrifice quality. If carefully handled, however, it is safe to defrost uncooked chicken and to freeze it again after cooking. If frozen *after* cooking, do not thaw and freeze chicken again.

WHY IS CHICKEN SOMETIMES IMPLICATED IN ILLNESS?

In a warm, moist environment, illness-causing bacteria can grow in high-protein, low-acid foods such as meat, fish, poultry, eggs, and milk. But there is no reason to become ill from eating or serving these foods, if they are cooked thoroughly and served or refrigerated immediately. To prevent transferring bacteria from one food to another, use warm water and soap to wash hands, utensils, and work surfaces before and after use.

WHAT MAKES CHICKEN TENDER—OR TOUGH?

Frank does his best to make Perdue chickens as tender as possible, but there's also a lot you can do.

- Don't let chicken dry out in the refrigerator; dry chicken is tough chicken. Keep it wrapped in the package it comes in until you use it.
- Avoid freezing it. When the juices inside the cells freeze, they act like little spears and they'll rupture some of the cell walls. When you defrost the chicken, you'll lose some of the juice and the chicken will be less tender.
- Cook chicken to the proper temperature, using a meat thermometer or pop-up guide. Cook bone-in chicken to 180°F and boneless chicken to 170°F. Undercooked chicken will be tough and rubbery because it takes a fairly high internal temperature to soften the proteins in the muscles and make them tender. But don't overcook chicken either, because moisture will start to steam off, and the more chicken dries out, the tougher it gets.
- Keep the skin on chicken during cooking. The skin helps keep juices in, and tenderness and juiciness go hand in hand. I've tried this both ways, and the difference is significant.
- When microwaving any chicken product, cover it with a loose tent of waxed paper to prevent drying.
- Some authorities feel strongly that you should not salt the

chicken before cooking because salt draws the juices out during cooking and toughens the meat. In my experience, there *is* a detectable difference in tenderness between salting before or after cooking. Still, I would guess that most people, myself included, wouldn't notice a big difference unless they were specifically paying attention to it. The difference doesn't jump out at you as it does with overcooking or freezer burn.

• Fry or roast breast pieces rather than microwaving them if tenderness is a top priority for you. Microwaving is significantly faster, but there's a greater risk of toughness when you microwave breast meat. Breast meat is fairly dry to begin with, and you don't have a whole lot of latitude between overcooking and undercooking.

WHY ARE SOME CHICKENS YELLOW-SKINNED AND SOME WHITE?

A chicken's skin color comes from the diet it is fed. The diet that produces a yellow skin is more expensive than the usual diet, but the people at Perdue Farms feel it's worth it because a yellow skin color is one of the fastest ways Frank's inspectors have of finding and disqualifying an inferior bird. If a bird is sick or off its feed, it doesn't absorb nutrients well and won't develop the rich golden color that is characteristic of Perdue birds. Also, if part of a bird's outer skin is "barked," that is, rubbed off due to rough handling during processing, the Perdue inspectors can detect it more easily than with a white-skinned bird. Detecting and removing chicken with barked skin is important because damaged skin shortens the shelf life and both dries and toughens the meat.

SOMETIMES WHEN I OPEN A PACKAGE OF CHICKEN, THERE'S A PUNGENT ODOR THAT DOESN'T SMELL SPOILED, BUT IT'S DEFINITELY UNPLEASANT. SHOULD I THROW THE CHICKEN OUT?

If the odor lasts only a matter of seconds, your chicken is probably fine. Meat is chemically active, and as it ages, it releases sulfur. When you open a bag that doesn't have air holes, you may notice the accumulated sulfur, but it will quickly disperse into the air. In fact, I've heard of cases where a wife will call her husband over and say, "Smell this, I think it's gone bad." He'll take a deep whiff and find nothing wrong with it. She'll take another sniff and then wonder if it was her imagination. It wasn't. It's just that once the package was opened, the sulfur smell faded into the air like smoke rings.

If the chicken still smells bad after a couple of minutes, that's an entirely different story. The problem is bacterial spoilage or rancidity or both. Return the chicken to the store where you bought it and write to Frank. Rancidity can also occur in frozen chicken if the freezer where the meat was stored wasn't cold enough or if the product was kept there for a very long time (more than six months for uncooked chicken, or more than three months for cooked chicken). I don't like to focus on this unpleasant stuff, but I do want you to get your money's worth when you're buying chicken.

ARE CHICKENS GIVEN HORMONES?

Never. It's against the law to give chickens hormones.

CAN I COOK FROZEN CHICKEN, OR DO I HAVE TO LET IT DEFROST FIRST?

In a pinch, go ahead, but allow extra cooking time. For the best texture and tenderness, however, you're better off starting from refrigerator temperatures; you can be more sure of getting an evenly cooked product.

HOW LONG CAN I KEEP CHICKEN AT ROOM TEMPERATURE?

From the point of view of food safety, you're taking a risk if you leave it outside the refrigerator for more than two hours. Unfortunately, bacteria grow and multiply at temperatures between 40°F and 140°F, and they flourish at room temperature. To avoid food borne illness, all foods of animal origin should be kept either hotter than 140°F or colder than 40°F.

If you know you won't be returning home directly after shopping, bring along an insulated bag or box to keep cold foods cold until you can get them into the refrigerator.

DO I NEED TO RINSE CHICKEN BEFORE COOKING?

Advice on this has varied over the years, including the advice Frank gives. The latest research shows that from a health point of view, washing is not necessary. Any microbes that you'd wash off will be entirely destroyed by heat when you cook the meat. It's actually far more important to wash your hands, your cutting board, and your utensils since they won't be sterilized by cooking.

HOW DO I GET THE BEST FLAVOR?

That depends on whether you're after a mild and delicate flavor, or a strong and robust flavor. The younger the bird, the milder the flavor. A *game hen,* which is five weeks old, will have the mildest flavor of all. A *broiler,* at seven weeks, will still have a quite mild and delicate flavor; a *roaster,* on the other hand, is usually about five weeks older than a broiler and it will have a much more pronounced "chickeny" flavor. Frank and I enjoy chicken at all ages, but if we had to choose on flavor alone, we'd most often go for the roasters. For a really strong, chickeny flavor, see if you can find *fowl* or spent hens or stewing hens. These birds are around eighteen months old, which means they're going to be quite tough, but if you use them in soups or stews, they'll add an excellent flavor.

I'VE HAD CHICKEN IN THE FREEZER FOR A YEAR. IS IT STILL EDIBLE?

From a health point of view it would be okay, but the flavor and texture will have deteriorated and it just won't be particularly tasty. I stored chicken in the freezer for a year once as an experiment. It wasn't awful, but it was kind of flat and tasteless.

WHY ARE BONES SOMETIMES DARK?

Darkened bones occur when the product has been frozen. Freezing causes the blood cells in the bone marrow to rupture. When the chicken is thawed, these ruptured cells leak out and cause visible reddish splotches on the bones. When cooked, these discolorations will turn from red to almost black.

IS IT BETTER TO COOK A CHICKEN QUICKLY AT A HIGH TEMPERATURE—OR SLOWLY AT A LOW TEMPERATURE?

Both work, but with high temperatures, you run a greater risk of uneven cooking, with the wings and legs becoming overcooked before the rest of the bird is done. Usually we recommend a moderate temperature of 350°F for whole birds and 350–375°F for parts. If you are in a hurry and want to use a higher temperature, shield the wings and legs by wrapping them with aluminum foil when they start to become too brown.

HOW MUCH SHOULD I ALLOW FOR SHRINKAGE WHEN COOKING CHICKEN?

For each 3-ounce serving of cooked poultry, buy an extra ounce to allow for shrinkage and an extra 2 ounces to allow for bone.

IF I WANT TO USE DIFFERENT PARTS OF THE CHICKEN FROM WHAT THE RECIPE CALLS FOR, HOW DO I GO ABOUT MAKING SUBSTITUTIONS?

This table should help:

Chicken Part	Approximate Number of Parts That Will Equal One Whole Chicken
Whole breasts	3
Half breasts	6

Chicken Part	Approximate Number of Parts That Will Equal One Whole Chicken
Whole leg (thigh and drumstick)	6
Thigh	12
Drumsticks	14
Wing	14
Drumette (upper part of wing)	24

When using cooked chicken, allow one pound of whole uncooked chicken for each cup of cooked, edible chicken meat.

SOME OF YOUR RECIPES CALL FOR ROASTERS. I DON'T LIVE IN AN AREA WHERE PERDUE CHICKEN IS SOLD, AND I HAVEN'T BEEN ABLE TO FIND ROASTERS IN THE STORES. WHAT EXACTLY IS A ROASTER, AND CAN I SUBSTITUTE A BROILER?

A Perdue Oven Stuffer Roaster is a twelve-week-old bird especially developed for a broad breast. Roasters have a more favorable meat-to-bone ratio than broilers. Because they are older birds, they also have a much deeper, richer flavor. You can use broilers in roaster recipes, but plan on the chicken being done sooner and having a noticeably milder flavor.

Frank, by the way, is the man responsible for creating the roaster market. Back in the early 1970s, when few people had ever heard of a roaster, he worked hard to breed these broad-breasted birds and put effort into advertising so people would learn about the new product. One of the men who worked with Frank told me that he was amazed that Frank, who will hang on to an old pair of shoes to save $50, was willing to spend millions to let people know about the product, and further, he did it without a qualm, because he had such belief in it. If you haven't tried an Oven Stuffer Roaster and you're visiting the East Coast, try one, and you'll see why Frank believed in it so much.

TRUSSING

1. Place the chicken on its back, breast up and legs pointed toward you. Center a string, 3 to 4 feet long, under tail and tie it around legs. Cross the string and place between legs and breast.
2. Turn chicken over on its breast; loop string ends around wings and fold wings back. Tie string in center between wings. Cut off excess string.

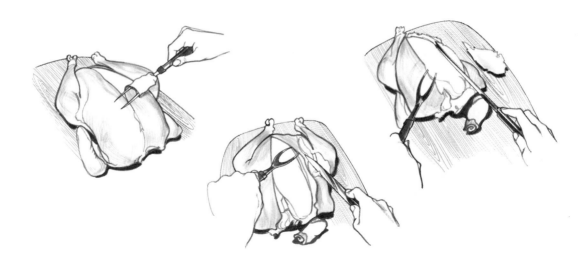

CARVING AN OVEN STUFFER FOR COMPANY

To add a flourish to carving that also assures crisp skin for all, first "unwrap" the breast.

1. Use a well-sharpened knife and fork. Carve and serve one side at a time. From neck, cut just through skin down middle of breast and around side. Hook fork on skin at tail and roll skin back to neck.
2. Holding bird with fork, remove leg by severing hip joint. Separate drum from thigh and serve.
3. Cut thin slices of breast at slight angle and add a small piece of skin to each serving. Repeat all steps for other side of bird. Remove wings last.

1

CHICKEN FOR EVERY DAY

Napoleon's cook once bet his employer that he could cook chicken a different way every day of the year. It was an easy bet to win, and I can see why, having looked at the recipes in Frank's files. Perdue Farms home economists have been developing chicken recipes since the early 1970s and as a result, Frank has more than two thousand chicken recipes. If only I could get someone like Napoleon to bet with me!

In this chapter, you'll find some of Frank's and my favorites for everyday cooking. I've divided the chapter into three sections that represent three different kinds of everyday cooking.

The first section, *Fast-Food Chicken from Your Refrigerator,* is for when you're in a hurry and want dinner on the table in the shortest possible time. None of these recipes takes more than fifteen minutes, and many are ready in five. However, you will find special tricks to make the food more interesting than just heat and serve.

The second section, *Perdue Plus Five,* is for when you don't mind if dinner isn't ready for another hour or so, but you want your part of the preparation to be as brief as possible. The recipes in this section use only five ingredients in addition to chicken, salt, and pepper. All of the recipes are simple to prepare but may take a while to cook.

The third section, *Family Favorites,* is for when you don't mind spending some time putting together something your family will really like.

FAST-FOOD CHICKEN FROM YOUR REFRIGERATOR

Frank loves to tell people how they can pick up delicious, fast-food chicken. "When you're hungry and in a hurry," he says, "you don't need to rush across town for great chicken. You can just walk (slowly) to your refrigerator and pick up my *Perdue Done It!*® chicken."

Although fried foods are notoriously high in fat—particularly fast food ones—*Perdue Done It!*® is an exception. Frank flash-fries the *Perdue Done It!*® products. They are in oil for only seconds. Further, to assure the chicken is as low in saturated fat as possible, Perdue uses only polyunsaturated soybean oil.

In the recipes that follow, I've used generic nuggets, cutlets, tenders, and other fully cooked products. However, try for the *Perdue Done It!*® if you live in the Perdue marketing area, which is the East Coast and some of the Midwestern states. The Perdue nuggets, cutlets, and tenders come from white meat fillets. Some of the other brands are pressed and formed from dark meat chicken and don't have the best texture or flavor.

TENDERS AND NUGGETS

Chick on a Biscuit: Split hot baked biscuits. Fill each with a heated breaded chicken nugget and a thin slice of ham; top with mustard.

Chicken Mexicali: Top heated cutlets or tenders with prepared salsa and avocado slices.

Chicken Parmesan: Top partially heated cutlets with spaghetti sauce and sliced mozzarella cheese; broil briefly to melt cheese.

Super Caesar Salad: Quarter heated nuggets and toss with croutons, Romaine lettuce, and Caesar salad dressing.

Holiday Crepe: Heat breast tenders and place on a warm crepe. Top with cranberry sauce and roll up; serve with sour cream.

Japanese Meal-in-a-Bowl: Prepare Japanese-style noodle soup (ramen) as directed. Add heated chicken breast nuggets or tenders, sliced scallions, and a dash of soy sauce. (I often put this in a thermos and bring it to Frank at his office when he's working late.)

Nugget Sticks: On metal skewers, alternately thread 4 to 5 chicken breast nuggets with 2-inch pieces of bacon. Heat in oven as directed on nugget package. Dip into prepared chutney or sweet-sour sauce.

Golden Nugget Salad: Heat 1 package of chicken breast nuggets. Combine with Romaine lettuce, halved cherry tomatoes and diced avocado. Toss with your favorite dressing.

Nuggets or Tenders with Dip: Following package directions, warm nuggets or tenders in a conventional oven or, using package tray, heat in a microwave oven. Serve with ketchup or your favorite mustards.

Substantial Sub: Split a loaf of Italian bread lengthwise. Pile on heated breaded chicken cutlets or tenders, provolone cheese, sliced tomato, sweet onion, pimentos and shredded lettuce. Douse with bottled salad dressing and dig in.

Tenders Under Wraps: Brush Boston lettuce leaves with prepared hoisin sauce or Chinese-style duck sauce. Place a heated tender or 2 nuggets and a piece of scallion on top. Roll up lettuce around tender, securing with a toothpick.

PRECOOKED HOT & SPICY WINGS

Chicken Antipasto: Arrange hot & spicy wings on platter with slices of provolone cheese, sliced tomatoes, marinated artichoke hearts, and olives.

Out-of-Buffalo Wings: Warm hot & spicy wings and arrange with celery sticks around a blue cheese dip. For the dip, combine ¾ cup mayonnaise, ⅓ cup crumbled blue cheese and 1 minced scallion in a small bowl.

Speedy Arroz Con Pollo: Prepare a box of Spanish rice mix as package directs. During last 10 minutes of cooking time, add 1 package hot & spicy wings, 1 package thawed frozen peas and ½ cup sliced olives. Cover and heat through.

PRECOOKED BARBECUED WINGS

Tostados Platter: Arrange heated wings on platter with wedges of avocado and tomato, chunks of cheddar cheese, crisp taco chips and a bowl of prepared taco sauce for dipping.

ROASTED CHICKEN AND CORNISH HENS

Aloha Salad: Halve a fresh pineapple and cut fruit into chunks. Toss with chunks of roasted chicken, toasted almonds, and chopped scallions. Blend in mayonnaise flavored with curry powder and spoon back into pineapple shell to serve.

Cheesy Chick: Prepare packaged stuffing mix as directed, adding 1 cup shredded Jarlsberg or Swiss cheese. Stuff whole roasted chicken or Cornish hens with mixture; heat in a 350°F oven until warmed through.

Chicken Frittata: Shred roasted chicken or cut breaded chicken into cubes. Add to beaten eggs, along with mushrooms, onions, and any leftover vegetables. In a skillet, cook mixture quickly, forming into an open-faced omelet or frittata.

Chicken Normandy: Arrange cut-up roasted chicken or Cornish hen meat in a shallow baking dish and scatter thinly sliced apples around pieces. Cover and heat in a 350°F oven until hot and apples are tender. Stir in a little light or heavy cream and warm to serve.

Chicken Reuben: Thinly slice roasted chicken. Pile on sliced rye that's been spread with Russian dressing. Top with prepared sauerkraut, a slice of Swiss cheese, and another slice of rye. Grill or pan-fry sandwiches until cheese melts.

Chicken Sesame: Brush roasted chicken or Cornish hens with bottled salad dressing; sprinkle surface with sesame seeds and heat as directed.

Fabulous Fajitas: Slice roasted chicken into strips. Saute in oil, adding lime juice, garlic, and ground cumin to taste. Roll up in warm flour tortillas and top with chunks of avocado, chopped scallion, and cherry tomatoes.

Pasta Pizazz: Sauté pieces of roasted or breaded chicken with sliced zucchini, chopped onion, sliced mushrooms, and garlic. Add a dash of heavy cream and toss with hot cooked spaghetti or noodles.

Power Pita: Slice roasted chicken and stuff into a whole wheat pita bread. Top with shredded carrots, alfalfa sprouts, red pepper strips and a dressing made of plain yogurt seasoned with lemon juice, curry powder, and salt and pepper to taste.

Stir-Fried Chicken: Dice roasted chicken into a wok or skillet and stir-fry with scallions, celery, mushrooms, and peas. Add cooked rice and soy sauce to taste; toss well.

Super Spud: Halve a microwaved or leftover baked potato and top with shredded roasted chicken mixed with a little mayonnaise. Pile on shredded Swiss cheese, bacon bits, and chopped chives; bake or microwave until cheese melts.

Taco Perdue: Cube roasted chicken and serve in taco shells, topped with shredded lettuce, chopped tomatoes, onion, shredded cheese, and taco sauce.

PERDUE PLUS FIVE

When was the last time you baked a pie from scratch?

I'm asking you this question because I'm guessing that you're like many other people who've told me that today they'd never have time to bake a pie from scratch.

In the last few years I've asked this question dozens and dozens of times and almost always, I get the same answer: that people who once had had the time to do a lot of cooking now seldom do. They want to eat well, they enjoy cooking, but they just can't find the time.

Well, I haven't found time to bake a pie from scratch in years either. Frank keeps me so busy that sometimes I think that I'm married to a whirlwind. People joke that he's the only man you'll ever meet who can enter a revolving door in the compartment behind you and come out ahead of you.

Quick recipes have become more important to me than ever, and this section contains a selection of the best. The heating and cooking time may take an hour or so, but your part in the kitchen should be no more

- To reduce baking time, select boneless chicken breasts. Cooking time is only 20–30 minutes at 350°F. A bone-in breast takes 30–40 minutes.
- Stir-fry chicken can be done in as little as 4 minutes.
- Cook double batches and freeze the extras in serving size packages. On days when time is short, pop a package into the microwave for "fast food."
- Take advantage of your supermarket's time-saving convenience items. If you're in a hurry, don't bother to slice and chop your fresh ingredients. The salad bar has probably done it for you. You can also find time-savers such as shredded cheese and frozen chopped onion. The supermarket industry has watched restaurants and fast food stores take more and more of your food dollars away each year. They're now doing everything they can think of to reverse this trend and make supermarket shopping so attractive, quick, convenient and economical that you'll want to cook at home.
- Learn to cook chicken in the microwave. A pound of broiler parts that would take 40 minutes in a 350° oven takes only 6–10 minutes in the microwave. See Chapter 2, Chicken for the Microwave.

than fifteen minutes. The recipes are uncomplicated with few steps, and none have more than five ingredients in addition to chicken, salt, pepper and water.

If, like me, you also are looking for ways to prepare meals that taste good, look good, and give you more satisfaction than microwaving a store bought frozen dinner, but don't require a long time in the kitchen, this section is for you.

BAKED ONION CHICKEN

1 chicken, cut in serving
   pieces
Dehydrated onion soup mix

*R*ecipes don't get much easier on the cook than this. Anne Nesbit developed it for Perdue Farms. One of her jobs as a Perdue home economist was to translate some of the world's most successful recipes into ones that were both easy to assemble and quick to prepare. "I'm an admirer of simple recipes," says Anne. "My heart was in this work because I believed in it. People want food that looks good and tastes good, but they don't have time to put a lot of work into getting there." The recipe isn't fancy, and it may be old-fashioned, but it's a treasure when you're in a hurry.

◆ ◆ ◆

Preheat oven to 350°F. Roll chicken lightly in dry soup mix. Place chicken in a single layer, skin side up, on baking sheet. Bake, uncovered, until fork tender. Allow 25–35 minutes for wings, 30–40 minutes for breasts, 35–45 minutes for drumsticks, and 40–50 minutes for thighs.

BASIC FRIED CHICKEN

⅓ cup flour
1 teaspoon salt or to taste
¼ teaspoon ground pepper or
   to taste
1 chicken cut in serving
   pieces
½ cup vegetable shortening

*T*his is fried chicken in its simplest form. It's good enough so that the last time I made it, the grandchildren were making off with pieces almost as fast as I could cook them. Frank's daughter Anne Oliviero particularly recommends basic fried chicken served cold the next day for picnics.

◆ ◆ ◆

In a large plastic bag combine flour with salt and pepper. Shake chicken in bag with mixture. In a large, deep skillet over medium heat, melt shortening. Cook chicken uncovered, until fork tender. Allow 7–12 minutes on each side for breasts and wings, 12–17 minutes on each side for thighs and drumsticks.

OVEN-FRIED CHICKEN, SOUTHWESTERN STYLE

1 chicken, cut in serving
  pieces
¾ teaspoon Tabasco, optional
1 cup buttermilk
Vegetable oil for frying
½ cup flour
½ cup corn meal
1 teaspoon salt
¾ teaspoon chili powder
¼ teaspoon ground pepper

Any basic fried chicken recipe may be adapted for oven frying. It is a useful technique when cooking larger quantities of chicken and is less messy than stovetop frying (especially if you have a self-cleaning oven). Simply follow the basic cooking instructions as given in the Southwestern version below.

♦ ♦ ♦

Place chicken in a large bowl. Sprinkle with Tabasco. Pour buttermilk over all and allow to marinate for 10–15 minutes. Preheat oven to 375°F. Place ½ inch of oil in the bottom of a heavy baking pan large enough to hold chicken without crowding. Place pan in oven to heat for 10 minutes. In a plastic bag combine remaining ingredients. Shake chicken in seasoned flour. Remove pieces one at a time and quickly slip into hot oil. Place in oven and bake for 15 minutes. Turn and cook for another 10–25 minutes, until fork tender. The wings and breasts will be done first and the drumsticks and thighs will take longer. Drain chicken on crumpled paper towels.

BASIC ROAST CHICKEN

SERVES 4

1 whole chicken
1 teaspoon salt or to taste
1 package (7½ ounces)
  stuffing mix, prepared as
  directed on package

Sometimes there is nothing else that will fill the bill like roasted chicken. Here's the easiest way to do it. You can brush the surface with melted butter, margarine or oil, but it isn't really necessary.

♦ ♦ ♦

Preheat oven to 350°F. Sprinkle cavity of chicken with salt, and stuff with favorite prepared stuffing. Skip the stuffing if you're really in a hurry. Place chicken in baking pan (no rack needed).

ROAST WHOLE CHICKEN

Kind	Unstuffed	Additional Time If Stuffed	Amount of Stuffing
Broiler (350°F—2½ to 4 pounds)	1–1½ hours	15–20 minutes	1½–2 cups
Roaster (5–7 pounds)	1¾–2½ hours	20–25 minutes	3–3½ cups
Cornish Game Hen (18–24 ounces)	55–65 minutes	15–20 minutes	½–¾ cup

There's considerable variation in oven thermostats so these are approximate cooking times. Chicken is done when you can insert a fork in the breast easily or when a meat thermometer inserted in the thickest part of the meat registers 180°F.

BIRD OF PARADISE

SERVES 4

1 chicken, cut in serving pieces
Salt and ground pepper to taste
1 egg, beaten
¼ cup milk
⅓ cup grated Parmesan cheese
½ cup butter or margarine
1 cup sherry

The recipe calls for a chicken cut in serving pieces, but naturally you can substitute any parts that you particularly like, such as breasts or thighs. Three breasts or 6 thighs with the drumsticks attached would come out to about the same amount as the 1 chicken called for in this recipe.

♦ ♦ ♦

Season chicken with salt and pepper. In a shallow bowl combine egg and milk. Place cheese in a shallow baking bowl. Dip chicken in egg mixture; then roll in cheese. In a large, deep skillet, over medium heat, melt butter. Add chicken and brown for 5–6 minutes on each side. Add sherry. Cover and cook at medium-low heat for 35–45 minutes or until cooked through.

CORN-CRISPED CHICKEN

1 cup cornflake crumbs
1 teaspoon salt or to taste
¼ teaspoon ground pepper
½ cup evaporated milk,
    undiluted
1 chicken, cut in serving
    pieces

I grew up on this recipe. It's not new, but it's good and the preparation time is minimal. If you don't have cornflakes, you can substitute almost any breakfast flakes as long as they don't have raisins in them. (The raisins can scorch in the oven.) For variations, you can add a teaspoon of dried italian seasonings or chili powder or curry powder to the cornflake crumbs.

◆ ◆ ◆

Preheat oven to 350°F. On a sheet of wax paper combine cornflake crumbs, salt and pepper. Place evaporated milk in a shallow bowl. Dip chicken in milk; then roll in seasoned crumbs. Place chicken, skin side up, in a baking pan. Bake, uncovered, until fork tender. Allow 25–35 minutes for wings, 30–40 minutes for breasts, 35–45 minutes for drumsticks, and 40–50 minutes for thighs.

CUTLET PAILLARDS WITH BASIL BUTTER

4 skinless, boneless chicken
    breast halves or 1 thin
    sliced boneless roaster
    breast
1 tablespoon olive or
    vegetable oil
6 tablespoons butter or
    margarine
3 tablespoons minced fresh
    basil, or 1 tablespoon
    dried
1 small clove garlic, minced
1 teaspoon lemon juice
Salt and ground pepper to
    taste
Lemon slices, for garnish

When I made this recipe, I happened to be in a hurry, and didn't have time to get fresh basil, so I used dried basil instead. Frank liked it and had seconds. The name "Paillard" comes from a European restaurant famous at the end of the nineteenth century.

◆ ◆ ◆

Place chicken between sheets of plastic wrap and pound to ½ inch thickness. If using thin sliced boneless roaster breast, omit placing in plastic wrap and pounding. Brush cutlets lightly with oil. Grill over hot coals 2–4 minutes per side, rotating to form crosshatch marks characteristic of paillards, or broil 2–4 minutes per side or until cooked through. Place butter, basil, garlic, and lemon juice in a small pan and melt on top of the stove or on the side of the grill. Spoon butter over paillards and season with salt and pepper. Garnish with lemon slices.

EASY OVEN CHICKEN

1 chicken, cut in serving
  pieces
¼ cup olive or vegetable oil
1 teaspoon salt or to taste
¼ teaspoon ground pepper
1 small clove garlic, minced

This recipe has been one of my favorites since college days. The true chicken flavor comes out with just a touch of garlic.

♦ ♦ ♦

Preheat oven to 350°F. In a shallow baking pan arrange chicken in a single layer, skin side up. Pour oil over chicken. Sprinkle with salt, pepper and garlic. Bake, uncovered until fork tender. Allow 25–35 minutes for wings, 30–40 minutes for breasts, 35–45 minutes for drumsticks, and 40–50 minutes for thighs.

HONEY LEMON CHICKEN

1 chicken, cut in serving
  pieces
½ cup honey
¼ cup lemon juice
1 teaspoon salt or to taste

This recipe was originally designed for broiling, but this version requires less attention.

♦ ♦ ♦

Preheat oven to 350°F. In a shallow baking pan arrange chicken in a single layer, skin side down. In a small bowl combine honey, lemon juice and salt. Pour half of this sauce over chicken. Bake, uncovered, until fork tender. Allow 25–35 minutes for wings, 30–40 minutes for breasts, 35–45 minutes for drumsticks, and 40–50 minutes for thighs.

HONEY-MUSTARD BAKED BREAST

1 whole boneless roaster
  breast
Salt and ground pepper to
  taste
4 tablespoons melted butter
  or margarine
½ cup honey
¼ cup Dijon mustard
¼ teaspoon curry powder

Have you ever been concerned about whether the honey you have in your cupboard is fresh or whether it should be thrown out? Not to worry! Honey is itself a natural preservative and samples of honey have been found in the tombs of Ancient Egypt that were still edible. If it's crystallized, just heat it gently until it reliquifies.

◆ ◆ ◆

Preheat oven to 350°F. Season breast with salt and pepper. Combine butter, honey, mustard and curry powder. Spoon half of sauce into a shallow baking dish. Add breast and turn to coat well. Bake, uncovered, for 30–40 minutes or until cooked through. Turn and baste with remaining sauce once during cooking time.

IT'S-A-DILLY CHICKEN

1 chicken, cut in serving
  pieces
1 teaspoon salt or to taste
¼ teaspoon ground pepper
1 can (4 ounces) whole small
  mushrooms (with liquid)
½ teaspoon dill seed

When I read this recipe in the files, I noticed several hand-scrawled notes saying that it was really good. One note described it as "a dilly of a recipe." But the recipe didn't sound as special as the notes indicated, especially since the ingredients include canned mushrooms rather than fresh. I was curious enough that I went to the kitchen and made the recipe, expecting that this would be one of the recipes that I wouldn't include in this book. But to my surprise, I discovered that yes, dill seed and canned mushrooms, along with the juice from the mushrooms, really do something terrific for chicken.

◆ ◆ ◆

Preheat oven to 350°F. In a shallow baking pan arrange chicken, skin side up, in a single layer. Add salt, pepper, mushrooms (with liquid from can) and dill. Bake, uncovered, until fork tender. Allow 25–35 minutes for wings, 30–40 minutes for breasts, 35–45 minutes for drumsticks, and 40–50 minutes for thighs.

KIWI-GLAZED CORNISH HENS

SERVES 2

2 fresh Cornish game hens
Salt and ground pepper to taste
3 tablespoons butter or margarine
1 tablespoon sugar
1 ripe kiwifruit, peeled and mashed

Kiwifruit is only sweet and mild when it's fully ripe. A kiwifruit grower told me that kiwifruits are ripe when they're "soft as a baby's bottom." When they're underripe, they taste like something between a lemon and a crabapple. If your kiwifruit is hard when you bring it home, give it a couple of days to ripen on your kitchen counter.

♦ ♦ ♦

Preheat oven to 350°F. Remove giblets. Season hens inside and out with salt and pepper. Tie legs together, fold wings back and arrange in baking pan. In a small saucepan over medium-low heat, melt butter. Brush hens with 2 tablespoons butter, reserving remainder. Put hens in oven, and while they are cooking, prepare kiwi glaze. Add sugar to remaining butter in pan and heat over medium-low until sugar dissolves. Add mashed kiwi and cook one minute. Remove from heat. After 45 minutes of cooking time, brush hens generously with kiwi glaze. Continue baking for 10–15 minutes or until juices run clear with no hint of pink when thigh is pierced.

FAMILY FAVORITES

In contrast to the preceding recipes, these recipes have more ingredients and require more preparation time, but if you've got the time, they're worth it.

SOUPS

Wherever there are people and chickens, there are chicken soups. Virtually every immigrant group arriving in America brought along favorite chicken soup recipes and often the treasured family soup pot, too.

If you grew up on canned, frozen, and dried soups, you may not realize how easy it is to make truly wonderful soups at home. Why not try it for yourself, perhaps with these American classics. All the soups are based on a key ingredient: rich, homemade chicken stock, made from either whole birds or from parts, in about three hours. Stock needs little tending—just slow easy cooking to bring out all the flavor and wholesome goodness. With the help of your freezer, you can enjoy the results many times in the coming months.

- Older, larger birds, such as the 5- to 7-pound oven stuffer roasters, make the best soups. An older bird will have developed more of the rich, intense chickeny flavor than the younger, milder-flavored broilers or Cornish hens.

- Use roaster parts if you want to save time. They cook faster and are excellent when you need only a small amount of broth. The richest flavor comes from the muscles that are exercised most, which happen to be the dark meat muscles. All parts will make satisfactory soup, but the legs, thighs, and necks provide the fullest flavor.

- For clear, golden broth, do not add liver. It turns stock cloudy. And avoid a greenish cast by using only parsley stems and the white parts of leeks or scallions.

- As the stock cooks down, foam will float to the top. Skim it off, or strain it out through double cheesecloth when the stock is complete. Tie herbs and greens in cheesecloth as a "bouquet garni," so you won't inadvertently remove them during the skimming.

- Always simmer stock over low to medium heat. Boiling the stock at too high a heat makes the broth cloudy.

- Most soups develop better flavor if you'll store them, covered, in the refrigerator for a day or two. To seal in the flavor while you're storing the soup, don't remove the fat that's on top. When you're ready to serve the soup you can lift the congealed fat off as a sheet. To remove the last particles of fat, place unscented paper towel on the surface. Draw towel to one side and remove.

- When freezing stock, allow ½ to 1 inch head room in containers so soup can expand. Freeze some in quart-size or larger containers for use in soups. Ladle the rest into ice cube trays or muffin cups for adding to vegetables, sauces, or gravies. Freeze and then transfer frozen stock cubes to a plastic bag or freezer container and keep frozen until ready to use.

- Leftover vegetables and those past their prime are good pureed in cream soups. When thickening such recipes with egg, prevent curdling by stirring a cup of hot soup first into the egg, then back into the soup. Be careful to keep the soup from boiling once you've added the egg.

- Soup may be stored in the refrigerator 2 or 3 days or frozen for 3 to 4 months. When reheating, make sure to bring the broth to a boil. Soups enriched with eggs are, unfortunately, not good candidates for reheating; they're apt to curdle.

BASIC CHICKEN STOCK

1 roaster (5–7 pounds)
Chicken giblets, except liver
1 large bay leaf
2 whole cloves
1 teaspoon white peppercorns
1½ teaspoons fresh thyme or
 ½ teaspoon dried
4 quarts water or enough to
 cover chicken generously
1 cup dry white wine,
 optional
2 medium onions, quartered
2 large carrots, sliced
2 ribs celery, sliced
1 leek, white part only,
 cleaned and sliced,
 optional
1 bunch fresh parsley, stems
 only
1 teaspoon salt or to taste

If you need to, you can make the following substitutions for the roaster: 1 stewing hen or spent fowl (5–7 pounds); 2 fresh young chickens (2–4 pounds); or 6 pounds fresh chicken parts, preferably dark meat portions. (As I mentioned earlier, young chickens will not provide as rich a flavor as the older birds but the taste will still be good.) Cooking times for meat will vary from 3 hours for stewing hens or spent fowl, to 1½ hours for 2 smaller birds to slightly less time for parts. In each case, time it from the beginning of the simmer. Return the bones to the stock for an additional ½ hour after you've removed the meat.

Chicken stock is delicious served as a simple broth with herbs, shredded or julienne vegetables, slivers of meat, or rice. It also is the base from which countless other soups are made.

♦ ♦ ♦

Remove giblets from roaster and discard bird-watcher thermometer, if it has one. Place roaster along with giblets in a large stockpot (8 to 10 quarts) or other large sauce pot. Wrap bay leaf, cloves, peppercorns, and thyme in cheesecloth as bouquet garni; tie closed with string. Add to stockpot along with remaining ingredients. Cover pot and simmer over medium-low heat for 2½ hours or until meat is tender. Carefully skim stock from time to time with a ladle or spoon to remove fat particles and foam.

To check roaster for doneness, pull back a leg or cut into meat close to bone; it is cooked when no pink color remains in meat. Remove pieces with a slotted spoon. Cut away meat from bones and return bones to stock; simmer 30 minutes longer. (See Chapter 10, Chicken for Planovers, for uses for the cooked meat.)

Strain stock through a fine sieve. If you want, prepare in advance to this point and refrigerate or freeze. Skim off top fat before using. To make a soup, bring as much stock as needed to a simmer. Then follow the soup recipe, adding chicken, vegetables, thickeners, seasonings, and garnishes.

CHICKEN-IN-EVERY-POT SOUP

1 cup potatoes, cut in ½-inch cubes
4 cups chicken broth
¼ cup dry sherry
1 teaspoon salt or to taste
⅛ teaspoon ground pepper
1 cup onions, halved and thinly sliced
1 cup carrots, in ¼-inch by 2-inch sticks
1 cup celery, in ¼-inch by 2-inch sticks
1 cup fresh or frozen green beans, in 2-inch pieces
2 cups cooked chicken, in ¼-inch by 2-inch julienne strips
1 cup zucchini, in ¼-inch by 2-inch sticks

For the best flavor, use fresh vegetables, varying them according to the season. Speaking of fresh vegetables, do you know how to tell a good carrot? Look at the "crown," (that's the stem end). If the crown is turning brown or black or has regrowth visible where the stem was, you've got a carrot that's been around awhile. If the crown and shoulders are a bright orange, you've got a nice, fresh carrot.

◆ ◆ ◆

Place potatoes in a saucepan with enough salted water to cover. Bring to a boil over medium-high heat. Cook potatoes 5 minutes; drain, rinse under cold water and set aside. In large saucepan over medium-high heat, bring broth and sherry to a boil. Season with salt and pepper. Add onions, carrots, and celery and simmer 5 minutes. Stir in green beans and chicken and heat soup to boiling. Add zucchini and potatoes and simmer 1 minute longer or until vegetables are as tender as you like them.

VARIATION: **Chicken Minestrone**
Add 1 cup chopped stewed tomatoes in their juice and 2 cups cooked, drained fusilli or other pasta and ½ cup cooked kidney beans when adding zucchini and potatoes. Stir in ½ cup grated Parmesan cheese just before serving. Other fresh vegetables may be added according to their cooking times. Minestrone happens to be one of Frank's favorites, although he skips the cheese because of its cholesterol.

NEW ENGLAND CHICKEN 'N' CORN CHOWDER

¼ pound bacon or salt pork, diced
1 cup chopped onion
½ cup chopped celery
4 cups chicken broth
2 cups peeled potatoes, cut in ½-inch cubes
1 package (10 ounces) frozen corn or kernels from 2 ears of corn
1 teaspoon salt or to taste
⅛ teaspoon ground pepper
2 cups cooked, diced chicken
1 cup (½ pint) heavy cream
Oyster crackers, for garnish

Chowders are thick soups which take their name from the large French pot used in soup-making called a "chaudiere." You can use fresh corn in this recipe, but frozen corn can actually taste sweeter and fresher than the fresh corn you buy at the supermarket. Corn loses 50 percent of its sweetness in just 24 hours at room temperature, and it can take days for corn to get from the fields to the supermarket to your house. Frozen corn is rushed from the fields to the freezer in just a few hours, and once frozen, it stops losing its sweetness.

♦ ♦ ♦

In large saucepan over medium-high heat, sauté bacon for 3 minutes until its fat has been rendered. Add onions and celery and cook 3 minutes longer. Stir in broth and bring to a boil, whisking constantly. Add potatoes and corn, season with salt and pepper and cook 5–10 minutes or until tender. Stir in chicken and cream, simmer 3 minutes and serve with oyster crackers.

VARIATION: **Shellfish Chowder**
Add 1 cup chopped green pepper and 1 cup cooked crab or shrimp to soup when adding chicken.

HEARTY LANCASTER CHICKEN, VEGETABLE AND DUMPLING SOUP

6 cups chicken broth
2 cups cooked, diced chicken
1 teaspoon salt or to taste
1/8 teaspoon ground pepper
1/2 cup parboiled potatoes, cut in 1/2-inch cubes
1/2 cup parboiled carrots, cut in 1/2-inch pieces
1/2 cup shredded green cabbage
1 cup thinly sliced leek, white and tender green parts only, or 1 medium onion, thinly sliced
1 package (10-ounces) frozen corn or kernels from 2 ears of corn

Knepp:
1 egg
3/4 cup flour
1/3 cup water
1/4 teaspoon salt or to taste
1/8 teaspoon baking powder
Pinch ground nutmeg
1 teaspoon minced, fresh parsley, optional garnish

This is a famous Pennsylvania summer soup made with extra vegetables for hearty winter eating. You can substitute noodles for the dumplings, or add crackers, or pretzels—some people have told me that even popcorn works. I'm skeptical about the popcorn, but if you're feeling adventurous, give it a try.

♦ ♦ ♦

In large saucepan over high heat, bring broth to a boil. Add other ingredients and reduce heat to low. Simmer for 3 minutes while making dumplings.

Knepp (Little Dumplings):
In small bowl, beat egg; stir in flour, water, salt, baking powder, and nutmeg. Drop batter by half teaspoons into the simmering soup. When dumplings rise to top, stir in parsley and serve.

VARIATION: **Chicken Spinach Straciatella**
Omit dumplings. Clean and stem 1/2 pound fresh spinach; stack and cut into 1/2-inch strips. Whisk together 2 eggs with 1/2 cup grated Parmesan cheese. Stir in spinach with chicken and vegetables, then heat soup just to boiling. Immediately pour in the egg mixture in a thin stream, while stirring. The goal is to end up with thread-like strands of cooked egg. Cook until soup simmers again; stir gently just before serving.

RECIPES WITH CHICKEN BREASTS

The recipes that follow will refer to "breasts" and "breast halves." A breast half usually serves one. A cutlet is a breast half (or thigh) that is both skinless and boneless and sometimes has been pounded flat. A scaloppine is a cutlet sliced almost in half lengthwise and then opened, like the wings of a butterfly or a thin slice from a large roaster breast. To save time, look for chicken scaloppine which have already been made for you: the Perdue thin-sliced Oven Stuffer Roaster Breasts are ready-made scaloppine.

The recipes will also specify whether to use a chicken breast or a roaster breast. You can interchange them, but the results will be different. A roaster has a more intense flavor and is juicier. It's also bigger, and requires longer cooking. When a recipe calls for a roaster breast, it means with the bone in unless specified otherwise.

BAKED BREASTS WITH CHEESE

SERVES 4

3 tablespoons butter or margarine, divided
1 roaster boneless breast
Salt and ground pepper to taste
2 scallions, thinly sliced
1 tablespoon fresh chopped parsley
1½ teaspoons fresh thyme or ½ teaspoon dried
½ cup chicken broth
3 tablespoons dry white wine
¾ cup grated Swiss cheese
2 tablespoons grated Parmesan cheese
2 tablespoons bread crumbs

When the Perdue Oven Stuffer Roasters and Roaster Parts first came out, Frank used to have recipe cards put in each one because it was a new product and most people didn't know how they should be cooked. The practice was discontinued once Roasters become well-known. The woman in charge of distributing recipes told me that sometimes the recipes became family favorites, and often when a person lost a card, he or she would actually take the trouble to write to Frank for a replacement. I learned that over the years, Frank has received thousands of letters requesting replacement cards. This is one of the recipes that people have asked for over and over again.

♦ ♦ ♦

Preheat oven to 375°F. Lightly butter a shallow baking dish. Place chicken in baking dish and sprinkle with salt, pepper, scallions, parsley, and thyme. In a measuring cup combine broth and wine and pour over chicken. Cover and bake 20 minutes. In a small bowl combine cheeses and bread crumbs. Remove chicken from oven and sprinkle with cheese mixture. Dot with remaining butter and place under broiler until cheese is melted and golden.

BERLINER SCHNITZEL BREAST

SERVES 4

1 roaster boneless breast or 1 package of thin sliced boneless roaster breast
2 eggs
¾ teaspoon salt or to taste
Ground pepper to taste
⅓ cup flour
1 cup dry breadcrumbs
Vegetable oil
6 tablespoons butter or margarine
2 tablespoons fresh lemon juice
3 tablespoons capers, drained
1 hard-cooked egg, finely chopped
2 tablespoons minced fresh parsley

You'll notice that I call for a "hard-cooked" egg in this recipe, not "hard-boiled." It's better never to boil an egg, but rather to cook it in water that's just below boiling. Boiled eggs end up with an unattractive greenish color where the yolk meets the white. Cooked at lower temperatures, the yolk will be more tender and won't discolor.

♦ ♦ ♦

Separate fillets from breast halves and put away for another use. Then cut breast halves in half, lengthwise. Place breast pieces between sheets of plastic wrap. Pound chicken to a ¼-inch thickness to form scaloppine. If using thin sliced breast skip this step. In a shallow bowl beat eggs with salt and pepper. Place flour and bread crumbs on sheets of wax paper. Dredge chicken in flour then dip in egg and coat with breadcrumbs. Heat ¼ inch oil in a large skillet over medium-high heat. Add chicken and sauté for 3–4 minutes per side or until lightly browned and cooked through. Remove to serving platter. Pour oil from skillet and wipe clean. Add butter to skillet and melt over medium heat. Add lemon juice and capers carefully to avoid spatters; pour over schnitzels. In a small bowl toss together hard-cooked egg and parsley and sprinkle over top. Serve with buttered noodles.

BONELESS BREAST PARMESAN

1 roaster boneless breast or 1
  package thin sliced
  boneless roaster breast
1¼ teaspoons salt, divided
Ground pepper to taste
2 eggs, beaten
¾ cup plain bread crumbs
¾ cup grated Parmesan
  cheese
⅓ cup flour
1 pound fresh ripe tomatoes,
  chopped
1 small clove garlic, minced
¾ cup olive oil, divided
2 tablespoons minced fresh
  basil or 2 teaspoons dried

To get the best flavor from the tomatoes, make sure your supermarket doesn't store them on the chilling shelf and don't refrigerate them when you bring them home. Store them at room temperature and use them soon after you buy them.

◆ ◆ ◆

Separate fillets from breast halves and put away for another use. Then cut breast halves in half, lengthwise. Place breast pieces between sheets of plastic wrap and pound to ¼-inch thickness to form scaloppine. If using thin sliced breast, skip the previous step. In a shallow bowl beat eggs with ¾ teaspoon salt and pepper. Place flour on a sheet of wax paper. On another sheet of wax paper combine bread crumbs and Parmesan cheese. Dredge cutlets in flour, dip in egg and roll in bread crumb mixture. Refrigerate while making sauce. In a small serving bowl combine tomatoes, garlic, ¼ cup olive oil, basil and salt and pepper. In a large skillet over medium-high heat, heat remaining oil. Add chicken and sauté for 3–4 minutes per side or until lightly browned and cooked through. Transfer to a warmed serving dish. Pass sauce separately.

BREAST COQ AU VIN

2 tablespoons butter or margarine
1 roaster breast, bone in
1 cup dry red wine
Salt and ground pepper to taste
1 sprig each of fresh thyme and rosemary or ¼ teaspoon each, dried
1 clove garlic, minced
16 pearl onions, if available, otherwise 8 small white onions, peeled and quartered, or 1 large onion, chopped.
¼ pound fresh mushrooms, quartered
1 tablespoon cornstarch
¼ cup water
2 slices bacon, cooked and crumbled
1 tablespoon fresh minced parsley.

The famous food writer, Malcolm R. Herbert, tells a story that I've always loved about coq au vin (chicken in wine). According to Herbert, a lady lavished praise on Alexander Dumaine, one of France's outstanding chefs, for his version of chicken in wine.

"Madam, I'm not satisfied," Dumaine replied.

"But you have been making coq au vin for thirty years," the woman protested. "How can you not be satisfied?"

"That, madam, was practice."

Dumaine's version of coq au vin uses red wine, white wine, and brandy, and it takes a good twenty-four hours to prepare. This version is a lot simpler, but still very good. The day I made it, I couldn't find pearl onions or small onions in my local supermarket, so I used a large white onion, chopped. The pearl onions would have been prettier, but the taste was fine.

♦ ♦ ♦

In a Dutch oven over medium-high heat, melt butter. Add breast and brown on all sides, 12–15 minutes. Add wine, seasonings, garlic and onions. Cover and simmer until tender—40–60 minutes. Add mushrooms and simmer 10–15 minutes longer or until breast is cooked through. Drain juices into a small saucepan; blend cornstarch and water; stir into pan juices and cook, over medium heat, stirring constantly, one minute or until sauce thickens and clears. Carve breast and serve with wine sauce. Garnish with crumbled bacon and parsley.

BREAST WITH APPLE-PECAN STUFFING

SERVES 4

1 roaster breast, bone in
Salt and ground pepper to
taste
2 cups seasoned
breadcrumbs
6 tablespoons butter or
margarine, divided
¼ cup hot chicken broth or
water
2 apples, peeled, cored and
chopped
½ cup chopped pecans

Make sure that the pecans you use are fresh. In the shell, they'll last in a cool dry place for six months. Shelled pecans should be kept in the refrigerator, in an air tight container. If you plan to keep them for longer than half a year, freeze them.

◆ ◆ ◆

Preheat oven to 375°F. Season breast inside and out with salt and pepper. In a bowl, combine breadcrumbs, 4 tablespoons butter, broth, apples and pecans. Stuff breast cavity and cover exposed stuffing with aluminum foil. Carefully place breast, skin side up in roasting pan. Rub remaining butter over breast and bake about 1 hour or until juices run clear with no hint of pink when pierced.

BUTTERMILK PECAN CHICKEN

SERVES 4

1 egg
½ cup buttermilk
¾ cup pecan halves, divided
½ cup flour
½ cup ground pecans
2 teaspoons paprika
1 teaspoon salt or to taste
¼ teaspoon pepper
2 tablespoons sesame seed
4 chicken breast halves
¼ cup oil

The pecan halves are more appetizing-looking when you put them on top of the chicken during the last 10 minutes of baking; the nuts get a delicious-looking brown. I come back to this recipe when I want something that's never-fail.

◆ ◆ ◆

In a mixing bowl beat egg with buttermilk. Chop ½ cup of pecans coarsely, reserving remaining halves for garnish. On a sheet of wax paper mix together chopped pecans, flour, paprika, salt, pepper and sesame seed. Dip chicken pieces in buttermilk mixture; then pecan mixture. Pour oil in shallow baking pan. Place chicken breasts, skin side down, in pan and turn to coat with oil, finishing with skin side up. Bake, uncovered, at 350°F, until fork tender. Allow 25–35 minutes for wings, 30–40 minutes for breasts, 35–45 minutes for drumsticks, and 40–50 minutes for thighs. During last 10 minutes of baking, place reserved pecan halves on top of chicken.

CHICKEN AVOCADO MELT

4 skinless, boneless chicken breast halves or 1 package thin sliced boneless roaster breast
2 tablespoons cornstarch
1 teaspoon ground cumin
1 clove garlic, minced
½ teaspoon salt
1 egg, slightly beaten
1 tablespoon water
⅓ cup cornmeal
3 tablespoons cooking oil
1 ripe avocado, peeled, sliced
1½ cups shredded Monterey Jack cheese
½ cup sour cream, divided
¼ cup sliced scallion greens
¼ cup chopped sweet red pepper
Cherry tomatoes
Parsley sprigs

For years I made it a kind of hobby to ask cookbook authors and recipe contest winners how they came up with their recipes. The people who create the real winners seem to me as mysterious and impressive as someone who composes a hit song or writes a best selling novel.

Marge Fortier, who won the $10,000 Grand Prize at the National Chicken Cooking Contest, didn't do any tinkering, tasting, and adjusting the way most of us would. Her recipe for Chicken Avocado Melt came to her seemingly out of nowhere. "I was vacuuming the living room," she told me, "when all of a sudden, I don't know how, it just came to me." She grabbed a pencil, jotted down the recipe on a notepad— and won $10,000. Her recipe calls for chicken breast halves, but you can simplify things a little if you use thin-sliced boneless roaster breast pieces instead.

♦ ♦ ♦

Preheat oven to 350°F. Pound the chicken to ¼-inch thickness. If using thin sliced breast, skip the previous step. In a shallow bowl, mix the cornstarch, cumin, garlic, and salt. In another bowl mix egg and water. Place cornmeal in a third small bowl. Coat chicken first with the cornstarch mixture, then with the egg, and finally with the cornmeal.

In a large skillet over medium-high heat, heat oil. Add chicken and sauté for two minutes on each side "to firm up the crust," then remove pieces to a shallow baking pan. Before putting cutlets in oven, top them with avocado slices and sprinkle with cheese. Bake for 15 minutes or until cooked through. Top each chicken breast with sour cream and a sprinkling of scallions and red pepper. Garnish with cherry tomato halves and parsley.

CHICKEN IN MUSTARD SAUCE

SERVES 4

1 roaster boneless breast or 1 package thin sliced boneless breast
3 tablespoons vegetable oil, divided
½ pound mushrooms, sliced (2 cups)
2 tablespoons minced, fresh parsley
1 tablespoon minced shallot or scallion
⅛ teaspoon ground pepper
½ cup chicken broth
¼ cup dry white wine
1 tablespoon Dijon mustard

Home economist Michelle Scicolone developed this recipe for Perdue, and she has the ultimate compliment for it: "It's what I make all the time when I'm cooking at home." You get crunchiness and crispness but it's not fried. It comes out just fine with any mustard that you have on hand or with other chicken parts.

♦ ♦ ♦

Slice breast thinly if using whole breast. In large skillet, over medium-high heat, heat 2 tablespoons oil. Add breast slices a few at a time, placing them so that pieces do not touch. Sauté about 2 minutes per side, until chicken is lightly browned and cooked through. Remove from skillet; keep warm. Heat remaining oil. Add mushrooms, parsley, shallot, and pepper. Stirring frequently, cook 2 minutes. Stir in broth and wine; bring to a boil and cook until liquid is reduced by half (about ⅓ cup). Reduce heat to low; stir in mustard until well blended. Spoon over chicken.

LEMON-PARSLEY BREAST

SERVES 4

1 roaster boneless breast
salt and ground pepper to taste
4 tablespoons melted butter or margarine, divided
¼ cup bread crumbs
2 tablespoons minced, fresh parsley
2 tablespoons minced shallots or scallions
1 clove garlic, minced
1 lemon, thinly sliced

A friend of mine who grows garlic in California and is a member of the Society of the Lovers of the Stinking Rose says, "The most common misconception about garlic is that garlic breath is bad breath." In fact, the society's slogan is, "Get rid of mouthwash breath; eat garlic!" This recipe won't give you garlic breath, however, since cooked garlic is quite mild in its effects.

♦ ♦ ♦

Preheat oven to 375°F. Season breast with salt and pepper. Pour 3 tablespoons melted butter into a baking dish. Add chicken to dish and turn to coat with butter. In a small bowl combine bread crumbs, parsley, shallots and garlic and spoon over chicken. Drizzle with remaining 1 tablespoon butter. Top with lemon slices. Bake 25–30 minutes or until chicken is cooked through.

HOT PINEAPPLE BREAST

1 roaster boneless breast cut into ¼-inch by 2-inch strips
4 tablespoons butter or margarine
1 green pepper, cut into strips
1 cup celery, sliced diagonally
1 20-ounce can pineapple chunks, with liquid
¾ cup chicken broth
¼ cup chopped onion
1 tablespoon fresh tarragon or 1 teaspoon dried
1 tablespoon cornstarch
1 4-ounce can pimento, drained and cut into strips
½ teaspoon salt or to taste

My teenage son Carlos says he likes this better cold the next day with a small handful of slivered almonds tossed over it. Myself, I like it hot, served over rice. If you have leftover chicken broth (as you probably will if you're using canned broth), use it as part of the liquid you use to cook the rice. Also, if you like peppers to stay a bright green and don't mind if there's still some crunch to them, add them at the same time that you add the cornstarch rather than earlier in the recipe. They are a pretty accent to the bright red of the pimentos.

♦ ♦ ♦

In a large skillet or wok over medium-high heat, melt butter. Add chicken and sauté for 5 minutes until lightly browned. Add green pepper and celery and cook 3 minutes, stirring. Drain pineapple, reserving liquid. Add drained pineapple, ½ cup of pineapple juice, broth, onion and tarragon. Bring mixture to a boil; reduce heat to medium-low and simmer 5 minutes. Blend cornstarch with 2 tablespoons water to make a smooth paste. (If you like the sauce quite thick, use an extra teaspoon of cornstarch.) Add to skillet and continue to cook, stirring, until thickened. Add pimento and serve immediately.

LAYERED CHICKEN
(Hawaiian)

8 skinless, boneless chicken breast halves
1½ cups quick-cooking rice, uncooked
1 can (3½ ounces) shredded coconut
1 can (20 ounces) pineapple chunks, drained . . . reserve juice
¾ cup water
2 teaspoons fresh lemon juice
4 tablespoons orange marmalade
4 tablespoons butter or margarine, melted
4 tablespoons soy sauce
2½ teaspoons ground ginger

If you have a sweet tooth, this recipe could end up one of your favorites. Frank likes it a lot. Once I happened to have leftovers of both chicken and rice, so I substituted them for the first two ingredients in this recipe. I also omitted the water and pineapple juice. If you make this substitution in the recipe, you won't need to bake it. Just keep it in the oven long enough to heat it through. It's not quite as delicious as the original, but it's still very good. The layered arrangement of this dish is typically Hawaiian; don't stir or mix the ingredients.

◆ ◆ ◆

Preheat oven to 350°F. Cut chicken into 1-inch cubes. Place half of chicken in bottom of large shallow baking dish. Layer rice on top of chicken, then arrange remaining chicken on rice. Add a layer of coconut; then a layer of pineapple chunks. Dot marmalade in spaces between chunks of pineapple. Mix water, lemon juice and pineapple juice; pour over layers. Pour melted butter or margarine and soy sauce over all. Sprinkle ginger on top. Bake, covered, for 30–40 minutes or until chicken and rice are done. Remove cover during last 5 minutes of baking for browning.

MARYLAND BREAST
OF CHICKEN

¾ cup butter or margarine, divided
¼ pound fresh crab meat (or frozen, thawed)
¼ cup thinly sliced scallions
1 tablespoon prepared horseradish
1 teaspoon tomato paste

This recipe calls for scallions. If you have trouble finding scallions, ask for green onions; they're the same thing.

◆ ◆ ◆

Preheat oven to 375°F. Melt 2 tablespoons of butter and toss in a mixing bowl with crab meat, scallions, horseradish, tomato paste, lemon juice, breadcrumbs and salt and pep-

1 tablespoon fresh lemon
   juice
2 tablespoons fresh
   breadcrumbs
Salt and ground pepper to
   taste
½ cup dry white wine
1 roaster breast, bone in
1 tablespoon vinegar

per. With your forefinger carefully loosen skin from the neck end of the chicken breast to form a pocket, taking care not to detach sides or bottom. Stuff crab mixture between breast and skin. Rub breast with 1 tablespoon butter; sprinkle with salt and pepper and place in roasting pan. Bake approximately one hour, until skin is brown and meat is tender. Remove to serving platter and keep warm. Skim off any fat from drippings; add wine and vinegar and bring to a boil. Reduce pan juices to about ¼ cup and remove from heat. Whisk in remaining butter, strain into a sauceboat and serve separately.

QUICK SWEET AND SOUR BREAST

SERVES 4

1 roaster boneless breast
Salt and ground pepper to
   taste
Flour
5 tablespoons butter or
   margarine
1 medium onion, chopped
1 garlic clove, minced
1 medium green pepper,
   chopped
1 cup canned chopped
   tomatoes (with liquid)
1 can (8¼ ounces) cubed
   pineapple (plus 2
   tablespoons pineapple
   juice from can)
3 tablespoons ketchup
2 tablespoons vinegar
1 tablespoon cornstarch
   dissolved in 3 tablespoons
   water

In most cases, I prefer fresh produce to canned. Tomatoes are, at times, an exception. If you're buying out-of-season tomatoes, and if you don't know the source, there's a good chance that they were picked green and artificially ripened. One tomato grower told me she'd rather eat cotton than an out-of-season tomato because the taste was so disappointing. There is some good news on the subject, though. Tomatoes retain their flavor during canning exceptionally well, and canned tomatoes are picked vine ripe. If you want the next best thing to a vine-ripened tomato, and it's winter, try canned tomatoes, as suggested in this recipe.

♦ ♦ ♦

Cut roaster breast into 1-inch pieces. Season with salt and pepper; coat with flour and set aside. In saucepan, over medium heat, melt 2 tablespoons butter and cook onions, garlic and green pepper for 5 minutes stirring often. Add tomatoes, pineapple and juice, ketchup and vinegar. Stir and simmer over low heat. Meanwhile, in a large skillet, over medium-high heat, melt remaining 3 tablespoons butter. Sauté chicken, half at a time, until golden and cooked through, about 5–7 minutes per batch. Drain and place on serving dish. To sauce in pan, add dissolved cornstarch; cook, stirring, over high heat until sauce thickens. Pour over chicken pieces.

STUFFED BREAST PARMENTIER

3 medium-size potatoes,
   boiled, peeled and cut into
   ½-inch cubes
1 roaster breast, bone in
Salt and ground pepper to
   taste
¼ pound bacon, cooked and
   crumbled
½ cup chopped red onion
½ cup chopped celery
2 tablespoons dry bread
   crumbs
½ cup sour cream
2 tablespoons butter or
   margarine, softened

Two hundred years ago, Parmentier, a French food writer, popularized the use of potatoes, which many people feared were poisonous. Today, when the name "Parmentier" occurs in a recipe, it's a signal that there will be potatoes in it.

◆ ◆ ◆

Boil potatoes in salted water to cover until just tender, 30–45 minutes. Drain, cool slightly, peel and cut into ½-inch cubes. Preheat oven to 375°F. Season breast inside and out with salt and pepper to taste. Toss potatoes with bacon, onion, celery, bread crumbs, sour cream and salt and pepper to taste. Stuff breast and neck cavities with potato mixture, covering exposed stuffing with foil. Place chicken breast-side-up in roasting pan. Rub skin with butter. Bake approximately an hour, or until tender. Transfer to serving dish; remove foil and serve.

RECIPES WITH CORNISH HENS

A Cornish game hen is a very young bird, usually about five weeks old, as opposed to a broiler, which is seven weeks, or a roaster, which is twelve weeks. Typically, they're tenderer and lower in fat than older birds.

All Cornish game hens are very young chickens, but the Perdue Cornish game hens have been bred to produce the broadest breasted Cornish hens in the industry.

BUFFALO-STYLE CORNISH PIECES

**Creamy Blue Cheese
  Dressing:**
½ cup mayonnaise
¼ cup sour cream
2 tablespoons crumbled blue
  cheese
2 tablespoons minced fresh
  parsley
1 tablespoon fresh lemon
  juice
1 scallion, thinly sliced
1 small clove garlic, minced

2 fresh Cornish game hens
Salt and ground pepper to
  taste
Oil for deep frying
2 tablespoons butter or
  margarine, melted
2 tablespoons Tabasco

You can re-use the frying oil called for in this recipe, or any deep frying recipe, for that matter. As long as you never heat the oil to the smoking point and as long as you strain it through cheesecloth to remove any particles of food, you can use it over and over again. The oil is good as long as it retains its golden color. When it has turned a dark brown, it's time to replace it. If you don't have cheesecloth handy for straining, laundered nylon stockings make a good substitute.

♦ ♦ ♦

In a small serving bowl prepare dressing by blending mayonnaise and sour cream. Stir in blue cheese, parsley, lemon juice, scallion, and garlic. Chill. Quarter hens and remove backbones. Pat pieces dry with paper towels and season with salt and pepper. Heat oil to 375°F or until a small cube of bread sizzles when placed in oil. Deep-fry hens 10 minutes, turning once. Drain well. In a small bowl blend melted butter and hot sauce; brush on chicken pieces. Serve warm with Creamy Blue Cheese Dressing.

CORNISH SAUTÉ WITH SUMMER SQUASH

2 fresh Cornish game hens
Salt and ground pepper to
  taste
2 tablespoons olive oil
1 medium onion, sliced
1 clove garlic, minced
1 medium zucchini, sliced
1 medium yellow squash,
  sliced
½ cup chicken broth
2 tablespoons minced fresh
  parsley
1 tablespoon fresh lemon
  juice

To keep the olive oil called for in this recipe in its best condition, store it in an airtight container in a cool cupboard away from the light. It's not necessary to refrigerate it—cold temperatures will make it cloudy and difficult to pour.

♦ ♦ ♦

Halve hens and remove backbones. Season with salt and pepper. In a large skillet, over medium-high heat, heat oil. Add hen halves and brown on all sides, 10–12 minutes. Add onion and garlic; sauté 3–4 minutes. Add squash, broth, parsley, and lemon juice. Cover, reduce heat to medium-low, and cook 15–20 minutes or until hens are cooked through.

GRECIAN HEN SAUTÉ

2 fresh Cornish game hens
2 tablespoons olive oil
1 clove garlic, minced
1 bay leaf
1½ teaspoons minced, fresh
    oregano or ½ teaspoon
    dried
Salt and ground pepper to
    taste
½ cup white wine
2 ripe tomatoes, peeled and
    quartered
¼ pound feta cheese, cut into
    ½-inch cubes
2 tablespoons ripe olives,
    sliced

The easiest way to peel fresh tomatoes is to place them in boiling water for 20–40 seconds. You'll find that the skin slips off quite easily. The riper the tomato, the quicker the skin loosens in boiling water.

♦ ♦ ♦

Cut hens into quarters and remove backbones. In a large skillet over medium-high heat, heat oil. Add chicken and brown 5–6 minutes per side. Add garlic, bay leaf, oregano, salt, pepper, and wine. Cover and simmer over medium-low heat for 15 minutes. Add tomatoes and cook 10 minutes. Stir in cheese and olives. Cook 5 minutes longer or until hens are cooked through. Remove bay leaf before serving.

HENS NORMANDY WITH APPLES

2 fresh Cornish game hens
Salt and ground pepper to
    taste
1 tablespoon minced, fresh
    sage or 1 teaspoon dried
3 tablespoons butter or
    margarine, melted
⅔ cup apple juice
2 Golden Delicious apples,
    peeled
⅓ cup chicken broth or white
    wine
½ cup heavy cream
1 tablespoon minced fresh
    parsley

Apples age five times faster at room temperature than they do in the refrigerator so they'll keep fresher longer if you store them in the refrigerator instead of in a fruit bowl.

♦ ♦ ♦

Preheat oven to 350°F. Season hens inside and out with salt and pepper. Put half of sage in each cavity. Tie legs together and fold wings back. Place hens in a flame proof baking pan just large enough to hold them comfortably. Brush with melted butter. Add apple juice to baking pan. Bake for 30 minutes, basting several times. Core and quarter apples; add to pan and baste. Bake 30 minutes, until hens and apples are tender, basting several times. Remove hens and apples to serving platter; keep warm. On top of stove, bring pan drippings to a boil; add broth or wine and cook until reduced by half. Stir in cream; cook 2–3 minutes until slightly thickened. Pour sauce over hens and apples. Sprinkle with parsley and serve.

WINE-COUNTRY CORNISH

4 fresh Cornish game hens
Salt and ground pepper to
   taste
3 tablespoons olive oil
1 large onion, thinly sliced
2 cloves garlic, minced
1 tablespoon flour
½ cup dry white wine or
   vermouth
½ cup chicken broth
2 tomatoes, peeled and
   chopped
2 tablespoons tomato paste
1½ teaspoons minced, fresh
   oregano or ½ teaspoon
   dried

*F*resh tomatoes should be stored at room temperature. Refrigerator temperatures destroy a tomato's flavor and texture. Try to use ripe tomatoes soon after you buy them.

◆ ◆ ◆

Season hens inside and out with salt and pepper. Fold wings back and tie legs together. In a Dutch oven large enough to hold all 4 Cornish, over medium-high heat, heat oil. Brown hens on breast sides. If you don't have a pan big enough to do four at a time, brown one or two at a time. Remove hens and reserve. Add onion and garlic and sauté for 5 minutes. Stir in flour. Add remaining ingredients and season to taste with salt and pepper. Stir. Return hens to Dutch oven, breast side up, and bring liquid to a boil. Reduce heat to medium-low, cover and simmer for 45 minutes. Cornish are done when juices run clear with no hint of pink when thigh is pierced.

RECIPES WITH CHICKEN PIECES

In the early 1970s, 75 percent of the chicken sold was whole chicken. Today it's less than 25 percent. If you want to substitute all legs or all breasts or some other combination, see pages xxii–xxiii for a chart showing equivalent amounts.

BATTER-FRIED CHICKEN

SERVES 4

1⅓ cups flour
1 teaspoon salt or to taste
¼ teaspoon ground pepper
2 teaspoons baking powder
1 cup milk
1 egg, beaten
1 chicken cut in serving
   pieces
Oil for deep frying

I bet you can make this in less time than it takes to drive to the local fast food place, wait in line for service and drive back again. It should cost a lot less too. Remember, you can re-use the frying oil many times. Just don't let it get so hot that it smokes, and be sure to strain it after you've finished with the frying.

♦ ♦ ♦

In a deep fryer heat oil to 350°F. In a mixing bowl combine dry ingredients; add milk and egg gradually to make batter. Dip chicken in batter. Deep fry the chicken parts in small batches, adding the pieces a few at a time so that the oil doesn't cool down. Remove when golden brown. Wings should take 10–15 minutes, drumsticks 15–20 minutes, split breasts and thighs 20–25 minutes.

BEER-AND-PRETZELS CHICKEN

⅓ cup flour
1 teaspoon paprika
1 teaspoon salt or to taste
¼ teaspoon ginger
¼ teaspoon ground pepper
½ cup beer
1 egg
½ cup finely crushed pretzels
¼ cup grated Parmesan
  cheese
2 slices bacon, cooked crisp,
  crumbled
3 tablespoons minced, fresh
  parsley
1 chicken cut in serving
  pieces

This dish is at its best when the bacon and pretzels are finely chopped. Use your blender or food processor to make the job easy.

♦ ♦ ♦

Preheat oven to 350°F. In a mixing bowl combine flour, paprika, salt, ginger, and pepper. Add beer and egg; beat with a hand beater to make smooth batter. Mix crushed pretzels, Parmesan cheese, bacon, and parsley in a large plastic bag. Dip chicken pieces one at a time in batter; then place in bag with pretzel mix and shake to coat. Place coated chicken pieces in shallow baking pan, skin side up. Bake, uncovered, until fork tender. Allow 25–35 minutes for wings, 30–40 minutes for breasts, 35–45 minutes for drumsticks, and 40–50 minutes for thighs.

CAPITAL CHICKEN

1 chicken, cut in serving
  pieces
2 teaspoons ground ginger
½ teaspoon dried oregano
2 tablespoons brown sugar
1 tablespoon flour
2 cloves garlic, sliced
½ cup rosé wine
½ cup soy sauce
½ cup oil
¼ cup water

This is a rather highly seasoned dish. Your family might prefer it with a little less ginger—but mine loves it this strong.

♦ ♦ ♦

Preheat oven to 350°F. Place chicken in single layer, skin side up, in shallow baking pan. In a mixing bowl combine remaining ingredients and pour over chicken. Bake, uncovered, until fork tender. Allow 25–35 minutes for wings, 30–40 minutes for breasts, 35–45 minutes for drumsticks, and 40–50 minutes for thighs. Baste occasionally.

CHICKEN ORANGE-ANO

SERVES 4

⅓ cup flour
1 teaspoon salt or to taste
⅛ teaspoon ground pepper
1 chicken, cut in serving
   pieces
¼ cup butter or margarine
1 can (6 ounces) frozen
   orange juice concentrate
1 can (6 ounces) water
2 tablespoons dark brown
   sugar
¼ teaspoon dried oregano
½ teaspoon nutmeg

What if you find that your brown sugar has hardened into a brick and you can't measure it anymore? I used to take a hammer and wallop it and then use the pieces. But then a sugar cane producer told me to heat the sugar at 250°F in the oven until it softens. The advantage of this is that it works. The disadvantage is that whatever's left is twice as hard once it cools. You can re-heat it again, but it gets more bricklike with each heating.

♦ ♦ ♦

In a large plastic bag, combine flour, salt, and pepper. Add chicken pieces and shake to coat. In a large, deep skillet over medium-high heat, melt butter or margarine. Add chicken and brown on each side. Allow 7–12 minutes on each side for breasts and wings, 12–17 minutes on each side for thighs and drumsticks. Remove chicken and reserve. Pour off and discard butter or margarine. Add remaining ingredients and stir to combine. Return chicken to skillet. Cover and cook over low heat until heated through and fork tender.

FRUIT AND NUT CHICKEN

SERVES 4

2 tablespoons oil
1 chicken cut in serving
   pieces
1½ cups orange juice
1 teaspoon salt or to taste
¼ teaspoon cinnamon
Ground pepper to taste
½ cup golden raisins
½ cup slivered almonds

Inflation hits all of us, but in this recipe, you'll find one ingredient has come down in price over the years. In Roman times, raisins weren't just expensive, they were money. You could buy a young slave for 2 amphora (jars) of raisins.

♦ ♦ ♦

In a large skillet over medium heat, heat oil. Add chicken and brown 12–15 minutes per side. Pour orange juice over chicken. Sprinkle salt, cinnamon, pepper, raisins, and almonds on top. Cover and simmer for approximately 30 minutes or until cooked through.

OVEN-BARBECUED CHICKEN

1 chicken, cut in serving
  pieces

Barbecue Sauce:
1 teaspoon salt or to taste
¼ cup water
¼ cup chili sauce
¼ cup vinegar
2 tablespoons Worcestershire
  sauce
¼ cup brown sugar
2 tablespoons oil

This isn't new or unique, but it's good. Of course, you can always use your favorite prepared barbecue sauce if you prefer.

♦ ♦ ♦

Preheat oven to 350°F. Place chicken in single layer, skin side up, in shallow baking pan. In a mixing bowl combine remaining ingredients and pour over chicken. Bake, uncovered, until fork tender. Allow 25–35 minutes for wings, 30–40 minutes for breasts, 35–45 minutes for drumsticks, and 40–50 minutes for thighs.

RECIPES WITH GROUND CHICKEN

Ground Chicken is a perfect substitute for ground beef in dishes such as spaghetti, chili, meatloaf, lasagna, or even plain burgers. The fat content will vary according to the individual manufacturer's formulation, but it will almost invariably be less than the approximately 30 percent fat content of regular ground beef. Perdue ground chicken is 10 percent fat. As of this writing, this is as low as any you'll find on the market.

If I weren't connected with the industry, I would have thought that to get ground chicken, you just put it in a grinder the way you do to get hamburger, and that would be it. Ah, but it's not so! The fibers of chicken meat are shorter and more delicate than beef. To get the right texture took a full year of experimentation and fine tuning at Perdue. The food scientists working on the project had to discover which parts of the bird tasted best in hamburger, what size holes the meat should be forced through in the grinding machine, what temperature would be best, and so on. A difference of a mere 2°F in the meat's temperature meant the difference between a desirable texture and one that was merely passable.

I remember the first time Frank and I tried ground chicken outside of the laboratory. We were at a barbecue at his son's and daughter-in-law's house. Jim and Jan had chicken hamburgers and beef hamburgers grilling side by side, and Frank beamed like a kid with a new toy when he saw how the chicken burgers stayed plump and didn't shrink. Meanwhile the hamburgers were dwindling into hockey pucks.

CHICKEN STROMBOLI

SERVES 4

2 tablespoons olive oil
1½ cups thinly sliced onion
1 large green pepper, thinly sliced
1 package (about 1 pound) fresh ground chicken
¼ cup tomato paste
1 clove garlic, minced
1 teaspoon dried oregano
1 teaspoon salt
1 prepared recipe pie crust mix
2 tablespoons butter or margarine, melted

I've had this at a restaurant, made with bread dough, but I liked it better using pie crust dough. The day I made it, I was late (as usual), and took a shortcut: I used prepared pie crusts, the kind that come frozen and already shaped in aluminum pie pans.

♦ ♦ ♦

In a large skillet over medium-high heat, heat oil. Add onion and pepper and sauté 3–5 minutes. Add chicken, tomato paste and seasonings and cook 8–10 minutes until chicken is cooked through. Preheat oven to 375°F. Roll out prepared pie crust into a round ⅛ inch thick. Cut circle in quarters to form four wedge-shaped pieces. Place ¼ of filling on the wide rounded end of each wedge; fold in sides and roll up. Place stromboli seam-side down on baking sheet, brush with butter and bake 30 minutes or until pastry is lightly browned.

POJARSKI-STYLE CHICKEN

SERVES 4

1 package fresh ground chicken (about 1 pound)
½ cup sour cream, divided
⅛ teaspoon nutmeg
Salt and ground pepper to taste
½ cup flour
2 tablespoons butter or margarine

Pojarski-style dishes use ground meat. They are typically made from beef, veal, salmon, or chicken. One of the most famous Pojarski dishes is salmon shaped to look like a pork chop. Doing the same thing with chicken tastes and looks delicious and costs a lot less.

♦ ♦ ♦

Mix ground chicken with ¼ cup sour cream, nutmeg, and salt and pepper to taste. Cover and refrigerate 15 minutes. Form mixture into four "chop"-shaped cutlets and coat each

1 cup sliced fresh
   mushrooms (4 ounces)
2 tablespoons minced fresh
   dill or parsley

lightly with flour. In a large skillet over medium heat, melt butter. Add cutlets and sauté 7–8 minutes on each side until lightly browned and cooked through. Remove to a serving dish and keep warm. Add mushrooms to skillet and sauté 2–3 minutes. Add remaining sour cream and mix well. Spoon sauce over cutlets. Sprinkle with fresh dill.

BASIC COOKING GUIDE FOR CHICKEN BURGERS

Whether you sauté, broil, or grill it, be sure to cook ground chicken all the way through. Unlike hamburgers, which can be cooked rare, ground chicken should be well done with no pink inside.

Sauté: Shape one package fresh ground chicken into patties. Sauté in a small amount of oil over high heat, 1–2 minutes on each side to brown. Reduce heat to medium and continue to cook 5–6 minutes on each side until meat is thoroughly cooked and springs back to the touch.

Broil: Shape one package fresh ground chicken into patties. Broil on a rack 4 inches from heat 5–6 minutes on each side until meat is thoroughly cooked and springs back to the touch.

Grill: Shape one package fresh ground chicken into patties. Place burgers on hottest area of lightly oiled grill 1–2 minutes on each side to brown. Move burgers toward the outside of the grill and continue to cook 5–6 minutes on each side until meat is thoroughly cooked and springs back to the touch.

CHICKEN BURGERS BORDELAISE

1 package (about 1 pound)
  fresh ground chicken
1 to 1½ teaspoons coarsely
  ground black pepper
1 tablespoon vegetable oil
  (optional)
1¼ cups red wine
¼ cup minced shallots or
  scallions
1 tablespoon sugar
2–3 teaspoons Dijon mustard
¼ teaspoon dried thyme
1 to 2 tablespoons butter or
  margarine
1 tablespoon minced fresh
  parsley

These are good just as they are, but I've also found that they're wonderful made into cocktail-size meatballs to pass during parties. At one of my parties, I tried to determine whether it was better to use the maximum or the minimum amount of pepper and mustard in this recipe. Some guests liked the meatballs highly seasoned and others preferred them mild, so I guess one isn't better than the other; it's just what your family or guests like.

◆ ◆ ◆

Form chicken into 4 burgers. Press pepper into both sides. In a large, non-stick skillet, over medium-high heat, heat oil. Add burgers and brown for 2 minutes on each side. Salt burgers lightly and reduce heat to medium-low. Continue cooking 5–6 minutes per side until thoroughly cooked through. While burgers are cooking, combine wine, shallots, sugar, mustard, and thyme in a saucepan. Cook over high heat 5–6 minutes until liquid is reduced to ¾ cup. Remove burgers from skillet and keep warm. Add wine mixture to skillet and stir over medium heat to combine with pan juices. Whisk in butter and parsley. Spoon sauce over burgers and serve.

RECIPES WITH THIGHS AND DRUMSTICKS

If you haven't liked dark meat up until now, try these recipes with an open mind. Thigh meat, drumsticks, or the meat from any well-exercised muscle, has more flavor and is apt to be juicier.

I was present at a taste testing at Perdue when Teri Benson, a food technician, asked the dozen or so participants to rate the flavor of various parts of a chicken. The chicken was ground and fried in patties so none of us could identify which parts we were eating. The test was replicated with many different groups, but the results were fairly uniform: people prefer the flavor and juiciness of thigh meat. Try a few of these recipes; you may discover some new family favorites.

DRUMSTICKS ZINGARA

5 roaster drumsticks
¾ cup (3 ounces) minced
  fresh mushrooms
¾ cup (¼ pound) minced
  ham
½ cup minced shallots or
  scallions
3 tablespoons Madeira or
  brandy, divided
1½ teaspoons minced, fresh
  tarragon, or ½ teaspoon
  dried
4 tablespoons butter or
  margarine, softened,
  divided
Salt and ground pepper to
  taste

The word zingara *is from a French sauce with mushrooms, ham, and truffles. In this version, I've skipped the truffles.*

◆ ◆ ◆

Preheat oven to 375°F. Pull back the skin of each drumstick and cut lengthwise slits in the meat in four places. Pull skin back into place. In a mixing bowl, combine mushrooms, ham, shallots, 1 tablespoon Madeira, tarragon, 3 tablespoons butter, and salt and pepper. Stuff mixture under the skin of each drumstick and secure with toothpicks. Melt remaining butter and baste drumsticks. Bake 60–75 minutes or until tender and cooked through. Remove to a serving platter and remove toothpicks. To drippings in pan, add 2 tablespoons Madeira and bring to a boil, stirring. Pour sauce over drumsticks.

CHILI THIGHS RELLENOS

4 roaster boneless thigh
  cutlets
1 can (4 ounces) whole, mild
  green chilies, seeded
1 egg, beaten
Salt and ground pepper to
  taste
½ cup seasoned bread
  crumbs
1 tablespoon butter or
  margarine
1 tablespoon olive oil
1 can (8 ounces) tomato
  sauce
½ cup shredded Monterey
  Jack Cheese

Even if you're not sure how old the eggs you have in your refrigerator are, the chances are that they're still good. As long as they're clean, dry, have no cracks, and have been kept cold and uncooked, they'll last for months in your refrigerator. Eggs that are several months old won't have the quality of a perfectly fresh egg, and I wouldn't use them for frying, but they're still suitable for cooking in dishes like this.

◆ ◆ ◆

Open thighs and lay flat. Divide chilies in four equal amounts and place in the center of each thigh. Roll up and secure with toothpicks. In a shallow bowl, combine egg and salt and pepper to taste. Dip thighs in egg and roll in bread crumbs. Refrigerate 15 minutes. In a large skillet, over medium heat, melt butter with oil. Add thighs and cook, turning, 10–12 minutes or until brown on all sides. Spoon tomato sauce over thighs. Reduce heat to medium-low and cover. Cook for 20 minutes or until thighs are cooked through. Sprinkle with cheese; cover and cook 2 minutes longer.

DRUMSTICKS WITH HERB SAUCE

SERVES 2

5 roaster drumsticks
Salt and ground pepper to
taste
1 clove garlic, minced
2 tablespoons olive oil

Sauce:
¼ cup minced fresh basil, or
1 tablespoon dried
¼ cup minced, fresh parsley
¼ cup thinly sliced scallions
2 tablespoons white vinegar
1 tablespoon minced fresh
tarragon, or 1 teaspoon
dried
1 tablespoon capers
¼ cup olive oil

When serving this recipe, take a tip from Bev Cox, a woman who not only is responsible for many of my favorite Perdue recipes over the years, but who is also one of the best food stylists around. She likes to have the garnishes mirror the seasonings of the dish. For example, she'd be apt to garnish this chicken recipe with fresh basil. She also believes that garnishes should be edible. These chicken drumsticks served with boiled new potatoes and whole sautéed green beans would be a simple dinner, but sprinkle the new potatoes with chopped chives, and stick a red pepper ring around the green beans and you have something that looks special as well as tastes special.

♦ ♦ ♦

Preheat oven to 375°F. Place drumsticks in a baking pan and season with salt and pepper. In a small bowl combine garlic and olive oil and baste drumsticks generously. Bake drumsticks 60–75 minutes until tender and cooked through, turning and basting once. Meanwhile, in a bowl make sauce by whisking together remaining ingredients. Serve drumsticks, passing sauce separately.

INDONESIAN STIR-FRY THIGHS

SERVES 4

4 roaster boneless thigh
cutlets
2 tablespoons peanut or
vegetable oil
⅓ cup soy sauce, divided
3 tablespoons molasses
3 tablespoons white distilled
vinegar
2 teaspoons minced, fresh
ginger or to taste

This recipe originally called for much more ginger, but I like a milder flavor, so I reduced it. You may want to increase the amount suggested here if you like highly seasoned food. To store fresh ginger, keep it in the refrigerator in a plastic bag along with a dampened paper towel to keep it from drying out.

♦ ♦ ♦

Cut thighs into ⅛-inch strips. In a wok or large skillet over medium-high heat, heat oil. Add chicken and stir-fry 2

1 clove garlic, minced
¼ teaspoon salt or to taste
¼ teaspoon red pepper flakes
   or ground pepper
Pinch ground cloves
⅛ teaspoon nutmeg
1 teaspoon cornstarch
1 cup carrots, cut in matchstick strips
1 cup peeled cucumber,
   halved, seeded and cut
   into matchstick strips
½ cup thinly sliced scallions

minutes. Add 4 tablespoons soy sauce, molasses, vinegar, ginger, garlic, and seasonings; bring to a boil. Cover, reduce heat to medium-low and steam chicken 5 minutes, stirring once, until tender. In a small bowl dissolve cornstarch in remaining soy sauce and reserve. Add carrots and steam, covered, 2 minutes. Stir in cucumber, scallions, and cornstarch mixture and stir until liquid comes to a boil. Serve over hot fluffy rice.

STIR-FRIED THIGHS WITH BEANSPROUTS

SERVES 4

4 roaster boneless thigh
   cutlets
1 tablespoon cornstarch
1 egg white, slightly beaten
Salt to taste
2–3 tablespoons peanut oil,
   as needed
1 or 2 cloves garlic, minced
1 red, sweet, bell pepper, cut
   into thin strips
½ cup thinly sliced scallions
¼ pound (2 cups) snow peas,
   sliced diagonally
½ pound (4 cups)
   beansprouts, washed and
   drained
¼ cup soy sauce
Few drops Tabasco, to taste

Stir-frying isn't more difficult than regular frying, but one big difference is that the pan is kept hotter than would be usual for American-style frying. To tell if it's hot enough, place your frying pan—or wok if you have one—over high heat. The pan or wok is hot enough if a drop of water dropped onto it sizzles and then evaporates. Add the oil, and let the oil heat until it's almost at the smoking point. When adding the ingredients, stir them constantly until done.

♦ ♦ ♦

Cut thighs into ¼-inch strips. In a shallow bowl, combine cornstarch, egg white, and salt. Add chicken, turning to coat well. Cover and refrigerate 1 hour. In a wok or large skillet over high heat, heat 1 tablespoon oil. Add thighs and garlic and stir-fry 3 minutes. Remove chicken and set aside. Add additional oil to wok, if necessary. Add pepper strips and stir-fry 1 minute. Remove and set aside. Add scallions and snow peas and stir-fry 1 minute. Add beansprouts and cook, tossing, 2 minutes. Return chicken and pepper to wok and toss. Add soy sauce and Tabasco. Heat thoroughly. Serve over hot cooked rice.

ISLAND THIGHS

SERVES 4

4 roaster boneless thigh
    cutlets
3 tablespoons cornstarch
2 tablespoons vegetable oil
1 cup sliced fresh
    mushrooms (4 ounces)
1 cup thinly sliced scallions
1 cup chicken broth
1½ cups fresh snow peas or
    1 package (6 ounces)
    frozen snow peas, thawed
¾ cup seedless, green grapes,
    halved
2 teaspoons slivered lemon
    peel
1 teaspoon minced, fresh
    ginger, or ¼ teaspoon
    ground

One of the best money-saving tips I know for buying food is one you can use in this recipe. A Pennsylvania mushroom grower told me that if you're using mushrooms for cooking, buy slightly browned mushrooms on sale. They're often a fraction of the price of the cosmetically perfect mushrooms. The mushroom flavor will be more intense since the mushrooms are older and they'll have dried slightly so you won't be paying for as much water.

♦ ♦ ♦

Cut thigh cutlets into ¼-inch by 2-inch strips. Toss with cornstarch to coat well. In a wok or large skillet, over medium-high heat, heat oil. Add chicken and sauté until browned on all sides, 3–4 minutes. Add mushrooms and scallions. Sauté, stirring until mushrooms are golden, about 1 minute. Stir in remaining ingredients. Cook, stirring, until sauce is thickened and smooth. Reduce heat and simmer 1–2 minutes. Serve over rice.

WALDORF SALAD

SERVES 4

1 quart chicken broth
4 roaster boneless thigh
    cutlets
¼ cup fresh lemon juice
1 teaspoon Dijon mustard
¼ cup vegetable oil
2 tablespoons minced, fresh
    parsley
Salt and ground pepper to
    taste
½ cup celery, thinly sliced
1 to 2 McIntosh apples,
    unpeeled in ½-inch cubes
    (about 1 cup)
½ cup walnut halves
1 head Bibb or Boston lettuce

You could use other apples in this recipe, such as Red Delicious or Granny Smith, but the McIntosh with its characteristic crispness, juiciness, and mildly tart flavor works particularly well. You can tell a McIntosh by its two-toned red and green skin.

♦ ♦ ♦

In a 2-quart saucepan over medium heat, bring chicken broth to a boil. Add chicken and simmer over low heat for 30 minutes, uncovered. Drain thighs and cut into bite-size pieces. Reserve broth for other use. In a mixing bowl blend together lemon, mustard, oil, parsley, and salt and pepper. Toss warm chicken with sauce and allow to cool. Toss with celery, apples, and walnuts and serve on beds of Bibb or Boston lettuce.

SWEET AND SOUR THIGHS

4 roaster boneless thigh
    cutlets
2 tablespoons peanut oil
1½ cups sliced green pepper
⅔ cup sliced celery
½ cup sliced scallions, stems
    included
1 can (8½ ounces) sliced
    water chestnuts, drained
6 ounces fresh or frozen
    (thawed) snow peas
1 can (8¾ ounces) pineapple
    chunks in syrup
½ cup chicken broth
1 tablespoon cornstarch
2 tablespoons sugar
1½ teaspoons minced fresh
    ginger or ½ teaspoon
    ground
2 tablespoons vinegar
2 tablespoons soy sauce

Cornstarch yields a more transparent sauce, and has roughly twice the thickening power of flour. The transparency makes it appropriate for oriental recipes like this.

♦ ♦ ♦

Cut thighs into bite-size pieces. In a wok or large skillet, over medium-high heat, heat oil. Add thigh pieces and stir-fry 5 minutes. Add green pepper, celery, scallions, and water chestnuts. Stir-fry 2 minutes. Add snow peas, pineapple and syrup, and chicken broth. Reduce heat to medium and cook 2 minutes, stirring often. In a small bowl, blend together cornstarch, sugar, ginger, vinegar, and soy sauce. Add to wok and cook until sauce is slightly thickened, about 2 minutes. Serve over hot cooked rice.

SZECHUAN STIR-FRY THIGHS

4 roaster boneless thigh
    cutlets
4 tablespoons peanut or
    vegetable oil
1 cup carrots, cut into
    matchstick strips
½ cup cashews
1 teaspoon hot chili pepper,
    finely chopped, or to taste
1 clove garlic, minced
2 teaspoons minced fresh
    ginger
¼ cup soy sauce
¼ cup dry sherry
1 tablespoon cornstarch

The woman in charge of supervising the entire Perdue recipe program, says that this is her personal favorite.

♦ ♦ ♦

Cut boneless thighs into strips (about ¼-inch by 2-inch). In a wok or large skillet over high heat, heat 2 tablespoons oil. Add chicken and stir-fry 2–3 minutes. Remove chicken and reserve. Add remaining 2 tablespoons oil to wok and add carrots, cashews, chili pepper, garlic, and ginger. Stir-fry 3 minutes until carrots just begin to soften. Return chicken to wok. In a small bowl blend together soy sauce, sherry, and cornstarch. Add to wok and cook, stirring constantly, until sauce boils and thickens. Serve over hot cooked rice.

THIGH CHILI

4 roaster boneless thigh
  cutlets
2 tablespoons vegetable oil
½ cup chopped onion
1 large garlic clove, minced
1 green pepper, seeded and
  chopped
1 can (16 ounces) tomatoes,
  chopped, with liquid
1 can (16 ounces) kidney
  beans, drained
1 tablespoon chili powder
Salt and ground pepper to
  taste
Tabasco, to taste

This is a healthy, low-cholesterol chili.

♦ ♦ ♦

Cut chicken into bite-size pieces. In a Dutch oven over medium-high heat, heat oil. Add chicken, onion, garlic, and green pepper. Cook, stirring until chicken loses its pink color. Add remaining ingredients and stir. Simmer, covered, over medium-low heat 30 minutes or until chicken is tender. Adjust seasonings according to taste.

THIGH FLAUTAS

4 roaster boneless thigh
  cutlets
1 quart chicken broth
½ pound Monterey Jack or
  Cheddar cheese, coarsely
  grated (about 2 cups)
¼ cup red or green chili salsa
Salt to taste
8 flour tortillas
Vegetable oil, for frying
⅓ cup sour cream, optional

Guacamole:
1 large ripe avocado
1 tablespoon fresh lemon or
  lime juice
½ cup chopped tomato
¼ cup chopped onion
1 tablespoon red or green
  chili salsa

You can tell if an avocado is ripe if it yields to gentle pressure when you hold it between your palms. If it feels hard, like a baseball, it's not ripe. Wait a few days, and it will have a richer, creamier texture and flavor. You can speed the ripening by keeping the avocado in a paper bag, at room temperature, along with a banana or pear or apple.

♦ ♦ ♦

In a large saucepan over medium-high heat bring chicken broth to a boil. Add boneless thighs, reduce heat to medium-low and simmer, uncovered, 30 minutes. Remove thighs, reserving broth for other use. Shred meat and place in a mixing bowl. Toss with 1½ cups cheese, salsa, and salt to taste. Divide mixture among tortillas and roll up, securing with a toothpick, if necessary. In a large, heavy skillet over medium-high heat, heat ½ inch oil. Fry flautas in hot oil, turning to brown lightly on all sides. Transfer to serving dish and keep warm. To make guacamole, scoop out avocado flesh, chop and toss with lemon juice. Combine lightly with remaining ingredients. Serve flautas topped with guacamole, remaining cheese, and sour cream, if desired.

2

CHICKEN FOR THE MICROWAVE

When I was organizing this chapter, I was tempted to include all of these microwave recipes in the Chicken for Every Day chapter. After all, the microwave is certainly becoming part of our everyday life.

The reason I didn't is—well, there are two reasons. First, if I put all the microwave recipes in one chapter, you won't have to waste time hunting for them. Second, there are a number of tips on using the microwave successfully, and I thought you might like to have them all in one place.

The microwave is a wonderful convenience, but I used to use it for reheating foods or for boiling water and not much else. Are you the same? Ah, but there's so much more to it than that! Having spent time with the Perdue food technologists and home economists, and especially after studying the techniques and recipes from Rita Marie Schneider, the home economist who developed the majority of the Perdue microwave recipes, I've come to appreciate the versatility of the microwave as well as the speed.

There's a reason I happen to have spent time with the Perdue experts. Once when Frank was microwaving nuggets for himself at HIGH, he found that by the time all of them were heated, one of them was badly overcooked and, therefore, dried out and—*tough*. Frank didn't know that the microwave was the problem and instead assumed it was his product that was at fault.

How can I even tell you about the crisis that one tough "tender" caused? Frank seemed more upset than he'd been when a whole processing plant burned down the year before. Because of that one tough tender, he called the plant manager, the quality control people, the packaging people, the man who wrote the cooking directions, the food technologists, the woman who runs the tasting lab, and probably a half-dozen other people as well. He kept repeating disconsolately, "I have no right to sell a product like this."

Eventually, one of the Perdue food technicians came out to our house and checked the microwave and suggested that we'd get more even cooking if we used MEDIUM HIGH. At this setting, the microwaves reach an equilibrium so heating is much more even. And when there are no hot spots and no cold spots, the chicken gets uniformly warm with no dried-out tough parts.

She had a number of other tips for me as well, and as I talked with other Perdue people, I collected still more. By now, knowing a few little tricks about the microwave, I know how to make much better use of it. Because of the time it saves in cooking, and the time it saves in clean-up (no baked-on bits of food to scrub), I use the microwave about as often as my oven.

- The best microwave tip I know is: learn about the "cold spots" in your microwave so you don't end up with unevenly cooked chicken. To do this, line the bottom of your microwave oven with wax paper and then spread an eighth-inch layer of pancake batter over it. Turn the oven on HIGH, and then check it at 30-second intervals. At some point, (in my case after a minute and a half), you'll see that in places the batter is dried out and hard, while in others, it's still soupy, as if the heat hadn't touched it. As you will see, microwaves don't necessarily cook evenly, so be sure to compensate by stirring or turning foods as directed in microwave recipes.

- Do not use utensils with metal trim (including the gold trim on fine china), handle clamps, or fastening screws. Metal trim can cause arcing (sparking). Aluminum foil in small amounts, on the other hand, won't cause arcing in most microwave ovens as long as it doesn't touch the sides of the oven.

- The coverings used in microwave cooking have definite purposes: use plastic wrap to steam and tenderize; use wax paper to hold in heat without steaming; use paper towels to absorb moisture, yet hold in heat.

- To obtain a crisp, crunchy crumb-coated chicken, first cook covered with wax paper, then switch to a paper towel covering and, finally, complete cooking with chicken uncovered.

- If the bony parts of your chicken are overcooking before the meatier parts are done, shield the bony parts by placing strips of thin aluminum foil over them.

- If you're microwaving chicken livers, prick each one to allow steam to escape. I had them explode in the oven before I knew this tip.

- Microwave recipes usually call for smaller amounts of seasonings than conventionally cooked dishes. Microwaving tends to intensify flavors, so you don't need as much seasoning.

- Don't ignore the standing time called for in some of these recipes. In microwave cookery, standing time allows for further cooking after the food is removed from the microwave oven. Covering the food holds heat in and speeds this final, important step. When I've cheated on this step, I've found the chicken hard to carve and undercooked.

- When possible, arrange food in a circular or doughnut shape; without corners, food cooks more evenly from all sides. For example, if you're cooking drumsticks, arrange them like a wagon wheel with the meatier portions at the outer edge, and the drumstick end in the center.

- Thin foods cook faster than thick foods because microwaves lose power after they penetrate food.
- Ingredients also affect cooking time. Foods higher in sugar or fat heat faster and to higher temperatures than do those with lower sugar or fat content.
- When the recipe says "70 percent power," or MEDIUM HIGH, don't be tempted to get things done faster by going for 100 percent power. At 70 percent power, the microwaves cook the product more slowly but also more evenly, so there's less worry about cold spots.

ROASTED CHICKEN WITH ALMOND SAUCE

SERVES 4

1 roasted chicken
1 tablespoon cornstarch
1 cup chicken broth
2 tablespoons Amaretto or other almond liqueur
1½ teaspoons fresh lemon juice
¼ cup sliced toasted almonds

Of course you can serve a pre-cooked chicken just as it comes from the store. I've done this many times with our Perdue Done It!® roasted chicken when I've been in a hurry. But this recipe only takes a few extra minutes and you'll have a showpiece at the end. Let's be grateful we're not making this recipe in the year 1911. A typical recipe in a December issue of The Wisconsin Farmer *assumes that you've already plucked the bird and removed its head and feet. It directs you "to singe the bird over a burning newspaper on a hot stove." The stove would probably have been a wood-burning one, and in all probability, it would have been up to you to get the wood for the stove. When I think of then and I think of now, I'm glad "We've come a long way, baby."*

♦ ♦ ♦

Heat pre-cooked roasted chicken in its own microwave tray following package directions.

In 2-cup glass container, combine cornstarch, broth, liqueur, and lemon juice. Cover with plastic wrap and microwave at HIGH (100 percent power) 3–4 minutes until bubbly and thick; stir twice during cooking. Add almonds. Slice chicken onto a platter and top with sauce.

CHICKEN POCKET SANDWICHES

1 roaster boneless breast
¼ cup olive oil
2 tablespoons fresh lemon juice
2 tablespoons finely chopped onion
1 clove garlic, minced
½ teaspoon salt or to taste
½ teaspoon dried oregano
⅛ teaspoon Cayenne pepper
4 pita breads
Lettuce leaves
1 container (8 ounces) plain yogurt
3 tablespoons finely chopped green onion

You could use regular chicken breasts for this, but the roaster breast has a richer, more chickeny flavor. (Chickeny is a word, by the way. Frank uses it all the time, and he ought to know.)

♦ ♦ ♦

Cut chicken into 1-inch chunks. In 3-quart microwave-safe utensil, combine olive oil, lemon juice, onion, garlic, salt, oregano, and Cayenne pepper; add chicken chunks and stir. Cover with wax paper; microwave at HIGH (100 percent power) 10 minutes or until chicken has turned white. Stir mixture three or four times during cooking. Let stand, covered, 5 minutes. Cut each pita bread into two pockets, line with lettuce and spoon in chicken. In small bowl, combine yogurt and green onion; serve over chicken.

CHICKEN À LA MONTMORENCY

1 roaster breast, bone in
1 can (16 ounces) pitted dark sweet cherries
¼ cup dry red wine
Water
5 teaspoons cornstarch
2 tablespoons red currant jelly (optional)
1 tablespoon butter or margarine
Salt and ground pepper to taste

Any recipe with the word Montmorency is apt to have cherries in it. The sauce for this one is particularly good and Frank liked it enough to spread the leftovers on toast the next day at breakfast. If you don't want to microwave the roaster breast, just cook it in your oven, following the package directions. When I'm in a hurry, I use this microwave recipe, even though breasts are the hardest part of the chicken to keep tender in a microwave. They're fairly dry to begin with, and, if you overcook them, they'll get tough.

♦ ♦ ♦

Place breast, skin side down, on microwave-safe roasting utensil. Cover with wax paper; microwave at HIGH (100 percent power) 5 minutes. Reduce power to MEDIUM HIGH (70 percent power) and cook 12 minutes per pound.

Halfway through cooking time, turn breast, skin side up; brush with drippings in utensil. Re-cover with wax paper; complete cooking. Let stand, covered, 15 minutes. Test for doneness after standing; juices should run clear with no hint of pink when breast is cut near bone.

Drain cherries, reserving syrup in a 4-cup glass container. Place cherries and red wine in small bowl. Add enough water to cherry syrup to measure 1 cup. Stir in cornstarch, mixing until well blended. Microwave at HIGH 3 minutes, stirring twice. Stir cherries with wine into thickened syrup. Continue cooking at HIGH 1–2 minutes or until mixture thickens and boils for 1 minute. Add jelly, if desired, and butter; stir until smooth.

To serve, slice chicken and place on warm platter. Spoon some of cherry sauce over chicken slices; pass remaining sauce.

CHICKEN À LA NANCY

SERVES 4

4 skinless, boneless chicken breast halves or 1 package thin sliced boneless roaster breast
1 tablespoon vegetable oil
1 clove garlic, minced
½ lemon with peel, very thinly sliced
½ pound fresh mushrooms, sliced
¼ cup dry white wine
1 tablespoon flour
½ teaspoon salt or to taste
¼ teaspoon ground pepper
¼ teaspoon dried oregano
1 can (14 ounces) water-packed whole artichoke hearts, drained and quartered

Unlike me, Frank does not enjoy puttering around in the kitchen. He loves the results, but cooking is not his favorite way to spend his free time. (He'd be more apt to watch a game on TV or visit with friends.) When he does cook, I can almost guarantee that it will be something quick and carefree. But there is one exception, and it's this recipe. I've never dared ask just who Nancy is, but Frank once won a cooking contest using her recipe, so he's been fond of it ever since.

He says to point out that the cooked lemon with rind does remain as a part of the food. It adds an unusual taste and texture. If you don't like a strong lemony flavor, you might start by using half the lemon that the recipe calls for. That's what I do when I make this recipe.

♦ ♦ ♦

Place chicken breasts between sheets of plastic wrap. Pound to ¼-inch thickness and cut into 2-inch squares. If using thin sliced boneless Roaster breast, skip the pounding and simply cut into 2-inch squares.

Microwave Method:

In 3-quart microwave-safe round dish, combine oil, garlic, lemon slices, and mushrooms; cover with plastic wrap. Microwave at HIGH (100 percent power) 3 minutes, stirring once. In a 1-cup glass measuring cup, combine wine and flour; stir into mushroom mixture.

Arrange chicken pieces on top of mushroom mixture and cover with wax paper. Microwave at MEDIUM-HIGH (70 percent power) 6 minutes per pound, stirring mixture three times. Sprinkle with salt, pepper, and oregano. Stir in artichoke quarters; re-cover and microwave at HIGH 2 minutes. Let stand, covered, 5 minutes.

CHICKEN THIGHS PARMESAN

SERVES 3–4

6 chicken thighs
½ cup seasoned bread crumbs
¼ cup grated Parmesan cheese
¼ cup melted butter or margarine
1 tablespoon Dijon mustard
1½ teaspoons Worcestershire sauce

The Dijon mustard called for in this recipe is quite sharp before it's cooked. After heating in the microwave, you'll find that it loses much of its sharpness and leaves behind a subtle spicy flavor. Yellow mustard won't produce the same effect.

♦ ♦ ♦

Remove skin from thighs. On wax paper, combine bread crumbs and Parmesan cheese. In shallow dish, combine butter, mustard, and Worcestershire sauce. Brush thighs with butter mixture and then roll in crumbs to lightly coat both sides. Reserve remaining butter mixture and crumbs.

Arrange thighs in circular pattern on microwave-safe roasting utensil; cover with wax paper. Microwave at MEDIUM-HIGH (70 percent power) 10 minutes per pound. Halfway through cooking time, turn thighs over; spoon on remaining butter mixture and sprinkle with remaining crumb mixture. Cover with a double thickness of paper towels. Complete cooking; remove paper towels during last 2 minutes cooking time. Let stand, uncovered, 2 minutes before serving.

CHICKEN WITH MANGO SAUCE

1 roaster breast, bone in
1 tablespoon butter or
    margarine
1 tablespoon cornstarch
2 tablespoons brown sugar
½ cup fresh orange juice
2 ripe mangos, peeled and cut
    into chunks
2 tablespoons cherry- or
    orange-flavored liqueur
Salt and pepper to taste

Mangos, which are rich in vitamins A and C, make a delicious, colorful, and unusual sauce for a roaster breast. When mangos aren't available, try fresh or canned peaches.

♦ ♦ ♦

Place skin side down on microwave-safe roasting utensil. Cover with wax paper; microwave at HIGH (100 percent power) 5 minutes. Reduce power to MEDIUM-HIGH (70 percent power) and cook 12 minutes per pound. Halfway through cooking time, turn breast skin side up; brush with drippings in utensil. Re-cover with wax paper and complete cooking. Let stand, covered, 15 minutes. Test for doneness after standing; juices should run clear with no hint of pink when breast is cut near the bone.

In a 4-cup glass container, place butter. Microwave at HIGH 30 seconds or until melted. Stir in cornstarch until blended; stir in brown sugar and orange juice. In blender or food processor fitted with steel blade, puree mango chunks. Stir pureed mangos into orange juice mixture. Microwave at HIGH 4 minutes, stirring twice. Add liqueur; microwave 1 minute longer. To serve, slice chicken and place on warm platter. Spoon some of mango sauce over slices, then pass remaining sauce.

CURRY-GLAZED BREAST

1 whole roaster breast, bone
    in
2 tablespoons butter or
    margarine
¼ cup honey
2 tablespoons Dijon mustard
2 teaspoons curry powder
¼ teaspoon salt or to taste

Curry powder is actually a blend of many spices. Indian Curry Powder is mild and Madras Curry Powder is quite hot.

♦ ♦ ♦

Place breast bone side down on a microwave-safe roasting utensil.

Place butter in a 2-cup glass container; microwave at HIGH (100 percent power) 45 seconds. Stir in honey, mustard, curry powder, and salt; brush mixture all over breast. Cover with wax paper; microwave at MEDIUM-HIGH (70 percent power) 12 minutes per pound. Baste breast and rotate utensil three or four times during cooking. Let stand, covered with wax paper, 15 minutes. Test for doneness after standing; juices should run clear with no hint of pink when breast is cut near bone.

HAM AND CHICKEN ROLL-UPS

SERVES 4

4 skinless, boneless chicken breast halves or 1 package thin sliced boneless roaster breast
1 tablespoon olive oil
1 teaspoon dried rosemary, crumbled
Salt and ground pepper to taste
4 thin slices prosciutto

If you can't find the prosciutto called for in this recipe, substitute any thinly sliced ham, such as the pre-sliced ham you find in the deli section of your supermarket. Or try thin slices of smoked turkey ham.

If you slice the cooked Roll-Ups crosswise, they make wonderful hors d'oeuvres or appetizers.

◆ ◆ ◆

Place chicken breast halves between 2 sheets of plastic wrap and pound to ½-inch thickness. Skip the previous step if you are using thin sliced boneless roaster breast. Brush breasts with olive oil to help seal in moisture; sprinkle with rosemary, salt, and pepper. Roll up each breast half, starting from narrow end. Wrap a slice of prosciutto around each roll.

In 8-inch square microwave-safe baking dish, place chicken rolls seam side down. Cover with wax paper. Microwave at HIGH (100 percent power) 8 minutes, rotating dish two or three times during cooking. Let stand 5 minutes. Check for doneness after standing; juices should be clear with no hint of pink when chicken is cut near center.

HEAVENLY CHICKEN

4 chicken breast halves
12 fresh or frozen asparagus
    spears
¼ cup water
¼ cup butter or margarine
4 tablespoons flour
⅛ teaspoon ground ginger
1½ cups chicken broth
½ cup dry white wine
Salt and freshly ground
    pepper to taste
¼ cup chopped pecans
¼ cup crushed crackers

If you're using fresh asparagus spears for this, here's how to tell the tender part from the tough part. Take the bud end of an asparagus spear in one hand and the butt end in the other and then bend the spear until it breaks. The part on the bud side is tender enough to use. The spears will break at just that point. But don't throw away the tough end. If you peel it with a potato peeler, you can use the tender, edible part underneath. Cook the leftover parts until tender and use them in soups or omelettes.

♦ ♦ ♦

On microwave-safe roasting pan, arrange breasts, bone side up, in a circular pattern. Cover loosely with plastic wrap; microwave at MEDIUM-HIGH (70 percent power) 8 minutes per pound. Halfway through cooking time turn breasts over; re-cover with plastic wrap and complete cooking. Let stand, covered, 10 minutes.

Rinse asparagus and remove tough ends. On microwave-safe rack, arrange asparagus with stem ends toward outside. Place rack in microwave-safe utensil. Add water; cover with plastic wrap. Microwave at HIGH (100 percent power) 5–7 minutes or until tender-crisp. Let stand, covered, 3–5 minutes.

In 4-cup glass container, place butter; microwave at HIGH 1 minute. Blend flour and ginger into melted butter. Gradually add chicken broth, wine, salt, and pepper, stirring constantly. Microwave at HIGH 5 minutes or until thick and smooth, stirring 3 times.

In 12×8-inch microwave-safe dish, arrange cooked asparagus, with stem ends toward outside; pour half of wine sauce over asparagus. Arrange chicken breasts on top with meatier portions toward outside; spoon remaining sauce over breasts. Sprinkle pecans and cracker crumbs on top; cover with a double thickness of paper towels. Microwave at MEDIUM-HIGH 5 minutes or until heated through.

MICROWAVE MARMALADE DRUMSTICKS

SERVES 4

5 roaster drumsticks
2 tablespoons butter or
    margarine
¾ cup finely chopped onion
½ cup orange marmalade
    (You can also use currant
    jelly.)
½ teaspoon curry powder

To tell for sure if your utensil is suitable for the microwave place the utensil and a cup of water in a glass measure side by side in the microwave oven. Turn the oven to the HIGH setting for 1 minute. If the dish is hot, then it is absorbing microwave energy. Do not use it in the microwave oven. If the dish is warm, use it only for warming food. If it remains at room temperature it is microwave safe.

♦ ♦ ♦

In 9-inch microwave-safe utensil, combine butter and onion. Cover; microwave at HIGH (100 percent power) 5 minutes. Blend in marmalade and curry powder; turn drumsticks in mixture. Place drumsticks with meatier portions toward outer edge of utensil; cover with wax paper. Microwave at MEDIUM-HIGH (70 percent power) 12 minutes per pound. Halfway through cooking time, turn chicken over, re-cover with wax paper and microwave remaining time.

Let stand, covered, 15 minutes.

SAUCY MICROWAVE CHICKEN WINGS

SERVES 4

½ cup honey
¼ cup soy sauce
2 tablespoons ketchup
1 small clove garlic, minced
16 chicken wings

To make an attractive presentation, try tucking the tip of each wing under to form a triangle.

♦ ♦ ♦

In 12 × 8-inch microwave-safe utensil, combine all ingredients except wings; turn wings in mixture. Cover with wax paper. Microwave at MEDIUM-HIGH (70 percent power) 8 minutes per pound, turning wings over three to four times during cooking.

Let stand, covered, 10 minutes.

TEX-MEX DRUMSTICKS

SERVES 4

6 chicken drumsticks
¼ cup finely chopped pecans
¼ cup fine, dry bread crumbs
1 tablespoon minced fresh
    parsley
1 teaspoon chili powder
¼ cup taco-flavored or other
    pourable salad dressing

Removing skin from chicken is an easy way to reduce calories, and because moisture doesn't evaporate readily in microwave cooking, the chicken will remain juicy and flavorful.

◆ ◆ ◆

Remove skin from drumsticks. On wax paper, combine pecans, bread crumbs, parsley, and chili powder. Brush drumsticks with taco dressing, then roll in crumb mixture to coat all sides. Reserve crumbs and dressing.

On microwave-safe roasting pan, arrange drumsticks in circular pattern, with meatier portions toward outside. Cover with wax paper; microwave at MEDIUM-HIGH (70 percent power) 10 minutes per pound. Halfway through cooking time, turn drumsticks over, spoon on remaining dressing, and sprinkle with reserved crumb mixture. Cover with a double thickness of paper towels. Complete cooking, removing paper towels during last 2 minutes. Let stand, uncovered, 5 minutes before serving.

MICROWAVE CHICKEN BREASTS PAPRIKASH

SERVES 4

2 tablespoons vegetable oil
2 green peppers, thinly sliced
1 large onion, thinly sliced
1 can (8 ounces) tomato
    sauce
1 tablespoon sweet paprika
½ teaspoon dried marjoram
½ teaspoon salt or to taste
Ground pepper to taste
4 chicken breast halves
1 container (8 ounces)
    commercial sour cream
1 tablespoon flour

One way of avoiding having your eyes tear when slicing the onion in this recipe is to do the cutting under running tap water. The vapors that hurt your eyes won't have a chance to get into the air, but instead will just wash down the drain.

◆ ◆ ◆

In a 12 × 8-inch microwave-safe utensil, combine oil, peppers, and onion. Cover with plastic wrap; microwave at HIGH (100 percent power) 5 minutes. Stir in tomato sauce, paprika, marjoram, salt, and pepper. On top of tomato mixture, place breasts bone side up with meatier portions toward outside. Cover with wax paper; microwave at HIGH 5 minutes; reduce power to MEDIUM-HIGH (70 percent power) and cook 10 minutes per pound. Halfway through cooking time, turn breasts over and stir mixture. Re-cover with wax paper and microwave remaining time. Let stand 5 minutes.

Remove chicken breasts. Stir sour cream and flour into tomato mixture. Cover; microwave at HIGH 1 minute. Stir and let stand 2 minutes. Pour over chicken breasts.

CORNISH HENS WITH LEMON TARRAGON SAUCE

2 fresh Cornish game hens
¼ cup flour
1½ teaspoons fresh tarragon, divided, or ½ teaspoon dried
1 cup chicken broth
Juice of one lemon (about ¼ cup)
Salt and ground pepper to taste
½ pound fresh asparagus, or substitute green beans
2 teaspoons water

You can get more juice from a lemon if you roll it around on a flat surface first while pressing your palm against it fairly hard. This ruptures the little juice sacks. You'll also get more juice if the lemon is at room temperature.

♦ ♦ ♦

With sharp knife or poultry shears, cut hens in half, lengthwise. Remove and discard backbone and skin. Coat hen pieces lightly with flour and sprinkle with half of tarragon. Place hens bone side up, with legs to inside, on a microwave-safe roasting utensil.

In a 4-cup glass container, combine chicken broth, lemon juice, remaining tarragon, and pepper. Microwave at HIGH (100 percent power) 3–4 minutes, or until boiling. Baste hens with half of hot broth. Cover with wax paper; microwave at MEDIUM-HIGH (70 percent power) 10 minutes per pound combined weight of hens. Halfway through cooking time, turn hens bone side down and baste with remaining broth mixture. Re-cover and complete cooking. Let stand, covered, 10 minutes.

Slice asparagus diagonally into 1-inch pieces and place in a 2-quart microwave-safe utensil with water. Cover; microwave at HIGH 3–4 minutes. Let stand 2 minutes; drain and set aside. When ready to serve, add asparagus to lemon sauce and pour over hens.

MICROWAVE HENS JUBILEE

2 fresh Cornish game hens
1 can (16 ounces) dark sweet
  cherries in syrup
¼ cup dry sherry
2 tablespoons cornstarch
½ cup chili sauce
1 clove garlic, minced
Salt and freshly ground
  pepper to taste

This is a close cousin of Chicken à la Montmorency, but it's spicier and less sweet. Serve over hot rice.

♦ ♦ ♦

With poultry shears or sharp knife, split hens lengthwise, removing backbone, if desired. In 12 × 8-inch microwave-safe utensil, arrange hens, bone side up with meatier portions to outside.

In 2-quart microwave-safe utensil, drain liquid from cherries; blend in sherry and cornstarch. Add cherries, chili sauce, garlic, salt, and pepper. Microwave at HIGH (100 percent power) 3–4 minutes, stirring once, until mixture begins to boil and thicken. Pour sauce over hens. Cover loosely with wax paper. Microwave at MEDIUM-HIGH (70 percent power) 8 minutes per pound, turning the hens over halfway through cooking time. Re-cover with wax paper and microwave remaining time. Let stand, covered, 10 minutes.

PINEAPPLE BAKED CORNISH HENS

2 fresh Cornish game hens
1 green pepper, cored, finely
  chopped
1 medium onion, finely
  chopped
2 teaspoons vegetable oil
1 can (8 ounces) crushed
  pineapple in natural juices
2 tablespoons soy sauce
2 teaspoons dry mustard
½ teaspoon ground ginger

Green peppers and most other fresh vegetables are ideal for microwaving. They retain their clear color and stay crunchy and fresh tasting. For extra color, substitute ½ sweet red pepper and ½ green pepper for the single whole green pepper.

♦ ♦ ♦

With poultry shears or sharp knife, split hens lengthwise and remove and discard skin. Place hens bone side up on a microwave-safe 12 × 8-inch utensil, arranging with legs to inside.

In a 2-quart microwave-safe utensil, place green pepper, onion, and oil. Microwave at HIGH (100 percent power)

2–3 minutes or until pepper is tender. Add pineapple, soy sauce, mustard, and ginger; microwave at HIGH 1–2 minutes.

Baste hen halves with half of pineapple mixture. Cover with wax paper. Microwave at MEDIUM-HIGH (70 percent power) 10 minutes per pound combined weight of hens. Halfway through cooking time, turn hens bone side down and baste with remaining pineapple mixture. Re-cover and complete cooking. Let stand, covered, 10 minutes. Serve with pineapple sauce.

ROSEMARY HENS WITH LIGHT WINE GRAVY

SERVES 4

2 Cornish game hens
6 sprigs fresh parsley
1 small onion, halved
1 clove garlic, halved
3 small carrots, peeled, cut in ½-inch slices (1 cup)
2 medium tomatoes, peeled and cut in wedges, or 6 cherry tomatoes, halved
1 medium zucchini, cut in ¾-inch slices (1 cup)
¼ pound mushrooms, quartered (about 1 cup)
½ cup chicken broth
¼ cup dry white wine
1½ teaspoons minced, fresh rosemary or ½ teaspoon dried
Salt and freshly ground pepper to taste
2 tablespoons cold water
2 teaspoons cornstarch

Game hens are sold both fresh and frozen. If you've selected a frozen one, follow your microwave manufacturer's directions for defrosting and turn and rearrange the birds frequently for even defrosting. I've tried game hens both fresh and frozen, and I found that there's enough of a difference in flavor and tenderness to make me strongly prefer fresh.

◆◆◆

Into each hen cavity, place 3 sprigs parsley, ½ onion, and ½ garlic clove. Place carrots, tomatoes, zucchini, and mushrooms in a microwave-safe baking dish. Combine chicken broth, wine, and ¼ teaspoon rosemary; pour over vegetables. Cover with plastic wrap and microwave at HIGH (100 percent power) 5 minutes. Arrange hens, breast side down, on top. Sprinkle with remaining rosemary and pepper. Cover with wax paper. Microwave at MEDIUM-HIGH (70 percent power) 11 minutes per pound combined weight of hens. Halfway through cooking time, stir vegetables; turn hens breast side up and rotate dish. Re-cover with wax paper.

Remove hens to serving platter, reserving juices for gravy. Using slotted spoon, arrange vegetables around hens and cover with foil; allow to stand 10 minutes. Cut hens in half to serve.

To prepare gravy, in a 4-cup glass container, combine

water and cornstarch. Slowly add reserved cooking juices (about ¾ cup) from hens; stir to blend. Microwave at HIGH 2 minutes or until thickened, stirring twice. Serve with Cornish hens.

HONEY MUSTARD ROASTER

1 whole roaster (about 6 pounds)
4 tablespoons butter or margarine
½ cup honey
¼ cup Dijon mustard
¼ teaspoon curry powder
1 teaspoon salt or to taste
⅛ teaspoon ground pepper

In a conventional oven a sweet honey-mustard basting sauce could overbrown. Instead, in the microwave it dries as the roaster skin cooks and forms an attractive golden glaze on the bird.

♦ ♦ ♦

Remove giblets from roaster. With rounded wooden picks, fasten skin across cavity and neck openings. Place roaster, breast side down, on microwave-safe roasting pan.

Melt butter in a 1-cup glass measuring cup by microwaving at HIGH (100 percent power) 1 minute. Stir in honey and remaining ingredients; brush roaster with mixture and cover with wax paper. Microwave at HIGH 5 minutes. Reduce power to MEDIUM-HIGH (70% power) and cook 12 minutes per pound, brushing frequently with honey mixture. Halfway through cooking time, turn roaster breast side up; complete cooking. Let stand, covered, 20 minutes. Test for doneness after standing; juices should run clear with no hint of pink when thigh is pierced. Pour drippings from utensil into remaining sauce mixture in measuring cup; microwave at HIGH 2 minutes or until heated through. Serve sauce with roaster.

MEXICAN MICROWAVE CHICKEN CASSEROLE

SERVES 4

2 tablespoons butter or
    margarine
1 large onion, chopped (1
    cup)
1 large green pepper, chopped
    (1 cup)
1 clove garlic, minced
1 can (14.5 ounces) tomato
    sauce
2 tablespoons flour
1 teaspoon salt or to taste
½ teaspoon ground cumin
½ teaspoon dried oregano
¼ teaspoon ground pepper
1 chicken cut in serving
    pieces
1 can (17 ounces) corn,
    drained

Leftover Mexican Chicken Casserole makes a fast and delicious taco filling. Shred chicken, reheat in sauce and serve with shredded lettuce and shredded cheese and a dollop of sour cream.

♦ ♦ ♦

In 3- to 5-quart microwave-safe utensil, combine butter, onion, pepper, and garlic. Cover with plastic wrap; microwave at HIGH (100 percent power) 3–5 minutes or until onion and pepper are tender. Stir in tomato sauce, flour, salt, cumin, oregano, and pepper.

Place chicken pieces, bone side up with meatier portions toward outside of utensil, on top of mixture. Cover with wax paper; microwave at HIGH 5 minutes. Reduce power to MEDIUM-HIGH (70 percent power) and cook 10 minutes per pound. Halfway through cooking time, turn chicken pieces over; re-cover with wax paper and microwave remaining time. Let stand, covered, 10 minutes. Remove chicken pieces to serving dish; cover. Add corn to sauce in utensil; cover with plastic wrap. Microwave at HIGH 2 minutes. To serve, pour sauce over chicken.

PLUM-SPICED CHICKEN

SERVES 4

1 chicken, cut in half
    lengthwise
1 cup plum jelly or preserves
½ cup chicken broth
¼ cup chopped onion
3 tablespoons red wine
    vinegar
1½ teaspoons soy sauce
½ teaspoon ground ginger
½ teaspoon Chinese five-
    spice powder (optional)

The plum sauce is a low-fat way to make the chicken develop an attractive color as it cooks in the microwave.

♦ ♦ ♦

Place chicken halves, skin side down, on microwave-safe roasting utensil, set aside.

In a 4-cup glass container, combine jelly and remaining ingredients. Microwave at HIGH (100 percent power) 4 minutes, stirring three times. Brush chicken halves with sauce; cover with wax paper.

Microwave at MEDIUM-HIGH (70 percent power) 10–12 minutes per pound, brushing chicken frequently with sauce. Halfway through cooking time, turn chicken halves over; brush with sauce. Re-cover with wax paper; complete cooking. Let stand, covered, 15 minutes.

STUFFED CHICKEN CHARLESTON STYLE

SERVES 4

1 whole chicken
4 strips uncooked bacon, diced
¼ cup chopped onion
¼ cup chopped celery
1½ cups packaged cornbread stuffing
¼ cup coarsely chopped pecans
5 tablespoons butter or margarine, melted, divided
½ cup plus 2 tablespoons dry sherry, divided
2 tablespoons water
2 tablespoons minced fresh parsley
1 teaspoon salt or to taste
Ground pepper to taste

The microwave oven makes it possible to make this succulent roast chicken and all the trimmings in less than an hour. To complete the meal with "baked" potatoes, you can microwave them during the chicken's standing time.

♦ ♦ ♦

Remove giblets. In 1½-quart microwave-safe utensil, place diced bacon; cover with paper towel. Microwave at HIGH (100 percent power) 3 minutes or until crisp, stirring twice. With slotted spoon, remove bacon to paper towel to drain; set aside. Reserve drippings. In same 1½-quart microwave-safe utensil, combine onion and celery; cover with plastic wrap. Microwave at HIGH 2 minutes.

In a mixing bowl, combine onions and celery with stuffing, pecans, and cooked bacon. In cup, blend 2 tablespoons butter, 3 tablespoons sherry and water; toss with stuffing. Spoon stuffing loosely into cavity and neck openings of chicken. With rounded wooden picks, fasten skin across cavity and neck openings.

Combine 1 tablespoon butter with 1 teaspoon sherry; brush on chicken. Place chicken, breast side down, on microwave-safe roasting utensil; cover with wax paper. Microwave at MEDIUM-HIGH (70 percent power) 10 minutes per pound, brushing chicken frequently with butter-sherry mixture and drippings. Halfway through cooking time, turn chicken breast side up; re-cover with wax paper. Complete cooking. Let stand, covered, 15 minutes. Test for doneness after standing; juices should run clear with no hint of pink when thigh is pierced.

Pour pan drippings into a 2-cup glass container. Add ½

cup sherry to roasting utensil to loosen pan juices; pour into container with drippings. Microwave at HIGH 3 minutes; stir in remaining 2 tablespoons butter and parsley. Serve chicken, sliced, with stuffing and enriched pan juices.

CHEESY MICROWAVE THIGHS

6 chicken thighs
4 tablespoons butter or
    margarine, divided
1 cup finely chopped onion
2 tablespoons flour
½ teaspoon salt or to taste
1 cup milk
½ cup grated Swiss cheese
¼ cup grated Parmesan
    cheese
2 tablespoons white wine
Pinch freshly grated or
    ground nutmeg
Minced, fresh parsley
    (optional)

Chicken thighs and drumsticks are fairly uniform in size, making them an ideal choice for quick cooking in the microwave.

♦ ♦ ♦

Remove and discard skin from thighs. In a 12×8-inch microwave-safe utensil, combine 2 tablespoons butter and onion. Microwave at HIGH (100 percent power) 5 minutes. Arrange thighs in a circular pattern on top of onions. Cover with wax paper; microwave at MEDIUM-HIGH (70 percent power) 10 minutes per pound. Halfway through cooking time, turn thighs over; re-cover with wax paper and microwave remaining time. Let stand, covered, 10 minutes.

Place remaining butter in 4-cup glass container; microwave at HIGH 30–50 seconds. Blend in flour and salt; gradually stir in milk, mixing well. Microwave at HIGH 3–5 minutes, stirring frequently, until mixture boils and thickens. Add cheeses, wine, and nutmeg; stir until cheese is melted. Pour sauce over chicken thighs; cover with wax paper. Microwave at MEDIUM-HIGH 2–3 minutes or until heated through. Garnish with parsley if desired.

CHICKEN MARENGO

6 chicken thighs
2 teaspoons olive oil
2 cups coarsely chopped
    fresh plum tomatoes
½ cup chopped green pepper
¼ cup finely chopped onion
2 cloves garlic, minced
2 tablespoons minced, fresh
    parsley
½ teaspoon dried oregano
¼ teaspoon ground pepper
½ teaspoon salt or to taste

Frank admires Napoleon not only because he was such an effective leader and motivator of men but also because the famous French general liked chicken so much that during his campaigns, he ate it almost every night. In 1800 when Napoleon was fighting in Italy, the supply wagons were late and his chef had to scour the countryside for whatever food he could find. The result was a chicken dish made with olive oil, mushrooms, tomato, garlic, and other ingredients available from the nearby farms. Napoleon liked the dish so much that he named it "Chicken Marengo," in honor of the battlefield where he had just been fighting, and from then on ordered it served to him after every battle.

◆ ◆ ◆

Remove and discard skin from thighs. In 3-quart microwave-safe utensil, combine remaining ingredients; cover with plastic wrap. Microwave at HIGH (100 percent power) 5 minutes, stirring twice. Arrange thighs in circular pattern on top of tomato mixture; spoon mixture over thighs. Cover with wax paper; microwave at MEDIUM-HIGH (70 percent power) 10 minutes per pound. Halfway through cooking time, turn thighs over; re-cover and complete cooking. Let stand, covered, 10 minutes before serving.

CHINESE CHICKEN

4 chicken drumsticks
4 chicken thighs
4 tablespoons butter, melted
2 tablespoons soy sauce
¼ teaspoon ground pepper
⅛ teaspoon minced, fresh
    ginger
1 can (3 ounces) chow mein
    noodles
¼ cup sliced almonds
Salt to taste

The shape of foods affects microwave cooking results. Thin areas cook faster than thicker ones, so meatier portions should always be placed toward the outer edge of the utensil, where microwave energy is greater.

◆ ◆ ◆

Remove and discard skin from drumsticks and thighs. In small bowl, mix butter, soy sauce, pepper, and ginger. In blender or food processor fitted with steel blade, finely chop chow mein noodles, almonds, and salt; transfer to wax paper. Brush chicken with soy mixture, then roll in noodle mixture to coat all sides. Arrange on microwave-safe roasting pan, with meatier portions toward outside; cover with wax paper. Reserve remaining soy mixture and noodle mixture. Microwave at MEDIUM-HIGH (70 percent power) 10 minutes per pound. Halfway through cooking time turn legs and thighs over; spoon on remaining soy mixture and sprinkle with remaining noodle mixture. Cover with a double thickness of paper towels. Complete cooking, removing paper towels during last 2 minutes. Let stand, uncovered, 5 minutes before serving.

DRUMSTICKS LITTLE ITALY STYLE

1 cup chopped, canned tomatoes
¾ cup long grain rice
1 cup chicken broth
½ cup dry white wine
1 medium onion, chopped
1 large clove garlic, crushed
½ teaspoon dried thyme
5 roaster drumsticks
Salt and ground pepper to taste
2 tablespoons or more minced, fresh parsley

The aim of cooking perfect rice is to have all the little starch granules inside each grain swell with water but not burst. You can tell that rice is undercooked if you pinch a grain and feel a hard or gritty core. You can tell that it's overcooked if you look at a grain closely and find that the edges are split and ragged. A perfectly cooked grain is the same smooth shape as the uncooked grain, only puffed, swollen, and soft.

♦ ♦ ♦

In a 3-quart microwave-safe utensil, combine tomatoes and rice. Stir in broth and wine; add onion, garlic, thyme, and mix well. Cover with plastic wrap; microwave at HIGH (100 percent power) 5 minutes. Arrange drumsticks over top of mixture, with meatiest portions to the outer edge of utensil. Re-cover with plastic wrap; microwave at HIGH (100 percent power) 5 minutes then at MEDIUM-HIGH (70 percent power) 12 minutes per pound. Halfway through cooking time stir and turn drumsticks over. Re-cover and complete the cooking. Let stand, covered, 10 minutes before serving. Test for doneness after standing; juices should run clear with no hint of pink when drumstick is pierced. Season with salt and pepper. Add parsley to rice mixture for garnish.

OLIVE MICROWAVED CHICKEN

6 chicken drumsticks
1 cup slivered onion strips
½ cup slivered green pepper strips
½ cup thawed lemonade concentrate
½ cup ketchup
¼ cup sliced pimento-stuffed olives
¼ cup sliced pitted ripe olives
2 teaspoons Worcestershire sauce
1 clove garlic, minced

When you saw the title of this recipe, did you hesitate because you were concerned that the calories in olives could wreck your diet? Not to worry! Olives are actually a fairly low-calorie food, with the average one having only 4–5 calories. The largest jumbo olive has only 12 calories.

♦ ♦ ♦

Remove and discard skin from drumsticks. In a 12 × 8-inch microwave-safe utensil, combine remaining ingredients; cover with plastic wrap. Microwave HIGH (100 percent power) 5 minutes, stirring once.

Turn drumsticks in sauce to coat. Arrange drumsticks in circular pattern in sauce with meatier portions toward outside of utensil. Cover with wax paper; microwave at MEDIUM-HIGH (70 percent power) 10 minutes per pound. Halfway through cooking time, turn drumsticks and spoon sauce on top. Re-cover with wax paper; complete cooking. Let stand, covered, 10 minutes before serving.

PENNSYLVANIA DUTCH– COUNTRY DRUMSTICKS

6 tablespoons butter or margarine, divided
¼ cup apple juice
1½ teaspoons soy sauce
⅛ cup brown sugar, firmly packed
Salt and ground pepper to taste
5 roaster drumsticks
2 Red Delicious apples, peeled, cored and cut into 8 wedges each
2 tablespoons sugar

You can tell Red Delicious apples by looking at their base. A Red Delicious always has five knobs or points at the base.

♦ ♦ ♦

Place 2 tablespoons of butter in a 9-inch microwave-safe utensil. Microwave at HIGH (100 percent power) 40 seconds. Combine apple juice, soy sauce, brown sugar, and salt and pepper to taste with melted butter. Place drumsticks in apple juice mixture and turn to coat well. Arrange drumsticks with meatiest portions toward outer edge of utensil. Cover with wax paper. Microwave at MEDIUM-HIGH (70 percent power) 12 minutes per pound. Halfway through cooking time turn drumsticks and spoon sauce over each. Re-cover and complete cooking. Let stand, covered, 5–10 minutes.

Place 2 tablespoons butter in a 2-quart microwave-safe utensil. Microwave at HIGH 40 seconds. Sprinkle butter with sugar; stir. Place apple wedges in sugar mixture; toss gently to coat. Microwave at HIGH 3 minutes, stir. Microwave an additional 3 minutes or until apples are tender. Transfer chicken to serving dish and top with apple wedges. Spoon sauce over top.

ROASTER THIGHS IN WINE

SERVES 4

4 roaster boneless thigh cutlets
4 strips uncooked bacon, diced
1 cup Burgundy or other dry, red wine
2 tablespoons cognac or brandy
16 small whole onions, peeled
8 ounces sliced, fresh mushrooms, 2 cups
3 tablespoons flour
2 teaspoons minced fresh parsley
1 bay leaf
1½ teaspoons minced, fresh thyme or ½ teaspoon dried

For the longest shelf life and the best flavor, don't wash mushrooms until just before using them. And don't soak them, just lightly mist them or wipe them with a damp paper towel. Mushrooms become waterlogged easily and lose some of their flavor.

♦ ♦ ♦

Cut thigh cutlets in half. In 3-quart microwave-safe utensil, place bacon; microwave at HIGH (100 percent power) until crisp, 3–4 minutes. Combine wine and Cognac and add to utensil with bacon and remaining ingredients; stir well. Arrange thighs, with thicker portions toward outer edge, on top of vegetables. Cover with wax paper; microwave at HIGH 5 minutes.

Reduce power to MEDIUM-HIGH (70 percent power) and cook 12 minutes per pound. Halfway through cooking time, stir vegetable mixture and turn cutlets over. Let stand, covered, 15 minutes before serving.

SPICY AFRICAN DRUMSTICKS

6 chicken drumsticks
2 tablespoons vegetable oil
1 cup chopped onion
1 garlic clove, minced
1 can (16 ounces) tomato
    puree
½ teaspoon salt or to taste
⅛ teaspoon crushed red
    pepper
¼ cup peanut butter
¼ cup chopped peanuts

If you eliminate the crushed pepper in this recipe, it could be a dish children would love.

Be sure the peanuts you use are fresh. Once a package has been opened, keep it in the refrigerator since peanuts rapidly go rancid. For peanuts that aren't as fresh as you might wish, try this tip I got from a peanut farmer in Georgia: Put the peanuts in a sieve and pour boiling water over them. The hot water will wash away some of the oils that are responsible for the off-flavor.

◆ ◆ ◆

Remove and discard skin from drumsticks. In a 12 × 8-inch microwave-safe utensil, combine oil, onion, and garlic. Cover with plastic wrap; microwave at HIGH (100 percent power) 5 minutes or until onions are tender. Stir in tomato puree, salt, and red pepper.

Arrange drumsticks in utensil with meatier portion toward outside; spoon tomato sauce over top. Cover with wax paper; microwave at MEDIUM-HIGH (70 percent power) 10 minutes per pound. Halfway through cooking time, turn drumsticks over; re-cover with wax paper and microwave remaining time. Remove drumsticks to serving platter; cover with foil and let stand 10 minutes. Stir peanut butter and peanuts into tomato sauce. Cover with plastic wrap; microwave at HIGH 2 minutes. To serve, spoon sauce over drumsticks.

CORNUCOPIA STUFFED ROASTER

1 whole roaster (about 6 pounds)
¼ cup hot water
¼ cup butter or margarine
1 cup frozen peas and carrots
1½ cups cooked rice
2 tablespoons minced fresh parsley
½ teaspoon dried thyme
1 teaspoon salt or to taste
Browning spray (optional)

A roaster stuffed with vegetables and rice is a tasty meal in one dish. The stuffing doesn't increase the cooking time, which is about 1 hour less in a microwave than required for conventional roasting.

♦ ♦ ♦

Remove giblets. In a 1-cup glass measuring cup, place water and butter; microwave at HIGH (100 percent power) 1 minute.

In 1-quart microwave-safe utensil, place peas and carrots; cover. Microwave at HIGH 4 minutes, stirring once; drain. In a small bowl, combine rice, melted butter mixture, peas and carrots, parsley, thyme, and salt. Place in cavity of roaster; with rounded wooden picks, fasten skin across cavity opening and at neck. Place roaster, breast side down, on microwave-safe roasting pan. Spray with browning spray or brush roaster with melted butter if desired; cover with wax paper.

Microwave at HIGH 5 minutes. Reduce power to MEDIUM-HIGH (70 percent power). Cook 12 minutes per pound, brushing with drippings several times during cooking. Halfway through cooking time, turn roaster over, using paper towels to protect hands. Pour off drippings and reserve, if desired. Baste roaster with drippings or use browning spray; cover with wax paper and complete cooking.

Let stand, covered with aluminum foil, 20 minutes. Test for doneness after standing; juice should run clear with no hint of pink when thigh is pierced. To serve, spoon stuffing into serving bowl and slice roaster.

CHICKEN WING PAELLA

10 chicken wings
1 pound sweet Italian sausage
   links
1 teaspoon browning sauce
1 large onion, chopped
1 sweet red pepper, cut into
   thin strips
1 medium-sized zucchini,
   chopped
1 can (16 ounces) tomatoes,
   undrained
½ cup hot water
1 teaspoon salt or to taste
1 teaspoon dried oregano
½ teaspoon paprika
½ teaspoon ground turmeric
½ teaspoon Tabasco
2 cups hot cooked rice
1 cup frozen peas, thawed

Paella is a Spanish dish with a mixture of rice, vegetables, meat, and sometimes shellfish. I lived in Spain for a couple of years and came to the conclusion that there must be almost as many versions of Paella as there are Spanish cooks—which means that you have a lot of latitude to vary the ingredients according to what you have handy in your refrigerator. I like this better the next day, when the different flavors have had a chance to "marry."

♦ ♦ ♦

Cut wing-tip section from wings. Set tips aside to cook later in soup or stew, if desired. Brush sausages with browning sauce; cut into 1-inch pieces. In 3-quart microwave-safe dish, place sausage pieces; cover with wax paper. Microwave at HIGH (100 percent power) 6–7 minutes, or until sausage loses its pink color, stirring twice. With slotted spoon remove sausage.

To drippings in dish, add onion, red pepper and zucchini; cover with plastic wrap. Microwave at HIGH 5 minutes, stirring twice. Add tomatoes, browned sausages, water, salt, oregano, paprika, turmeric and Tabasco; stir to blend. Arrange chicken wings in circular pattern on top of tomato mixture. Cover with plastic wrap; microwave at HIGH 5 minutes. Reduce power to MEDIUM-HIGH (70 percent power); cook 10 minutes per pound. Halfway through cooking time, turn wings over; re-cover and complete cooking. Stir in hot cooked rice and peas; microwave at HIGH 3 minutes.

To warm for serving, cover with plastic wrap and microwave at HIGH until heated through (3–5 minutes, depending on your microwave). Let stand 5 minutes before serving.

3

CHICKEN FOR DIETERS

Are you concerned about the cholesterol in your diet? Are you watching calories and trying to cut down on fat? Has your doctor suggested that you consume less salt?

Then read on. The wonderful thing about chicken is that the low-cholesterol and the low calorie recipes are the same. And the flavors that add spark to a low calorie recipe are the same ones that can help you get along with little or no salt.

Chicken is the dieter's ray of sunshine. Except for turkey breast, no other popular meat is as low in calories as skinless chicken breast. A 3-ounce portion of skinless broiled chicken breast has only 115 calories. An equivalent size composite portion of cooked lean trimmed beef would average 189 calories, and a composite 3-ounce portion of cooked lean, trimmed pork is 198 calories.

Chicken is also lowest in saturated fat compared with non-poultry meats. The most recently available comparison figures from the USDA and the National Livestock and Meat Board are:

Grams of Saturated Fat

Cooked 3-ounce portion skinless chicken breast:	.4
Composite cooked 3-ounce portion of chicken:	1.1
Composite cooked 3-ounce portion of lean, trimmed beef:	3.2
Composite cooked 3-ounce portion of lean, trimmed pork:	2.8

After a couple of weeks of following a low-salt diet, you'll find that your taste will change and that you'll actually be satisfied with far less salt. You'll even find that the olives and potato chips and peanuts that once tasted just right, now seem too salty. We've found that with salt, the less you eat, the less you feel you need—but be patient because this doesn't happen overnight.

For that matter, a preference for low-fat cooking may not happen overnight either. If you're not used to the low-fat substitutions for rich sauces and gravies, some of the recipes in this chapter may seem down-right spartan to you the first time you try them. But once you're used to them, you may find, as Frank and I have, that with time it's possible not only to get used to lighter cooking, but to actually prefer it.

BARBECUE DRUMSTICKS

SERVES 8

Microwave Recipe
8 roaster drumsticks
1 cup water
½ cup finely chopped onion
⅓ cup tomato paste
1 tablespoon vinegar
2 cloves garlic, minced
1½ teaspoons chili powder
1 teaspoon dry mustard
¼ teaspoon ground pepper

To save additional fat and calories, remove the skin from the drumsticks. I wouldn't recommend this for a conventional oven recipe because the meat would dry out. But microwaving retains moisture, and the sauce adds flavor.

♦ ♦ ♦

Remove skin from drumsticks and discard. In 4-cup glass container, combine water, onion, tomato paste, vinegar, garlic, chili powder, mustard, and pepper until well blended. Cover with plastic wrap; microwave at HIGH (100 percent power) 5 minutes. Stir and microwave, uncovered, 5 minutes longer. Pour half the mixture over bottom of a 12×8-inch microwave-safe utensil.

NUTRITIONAL FIGURES PER SERVING
Calories, 165.
Protein, 25 grams.
Fat, 5 grams.
Carbohydrates, 3 grams.
Sodium, 215 mg.
Cholesterol, 95 mg.

Place drumsticks in sauce with meatier portions toward outer edge of utensil. Pour remaining sauce over drumsticks; cover with wax paper. Microwave at MEDIUM-HIGH (70 percent power) 12 minutes per pound. Halfway through cooking time, turn drumsticks over and move drumsticks to sides of utensil. Re-cover with wax paper; complete cooking. Let stand, covered, 15 minutes before serving.

TIPS FOR AVOIDING BOTH FAT AND CALORIES WHEN COOKING WITH CHICKEN

- Choose breast meat. Although chicken in general is low in fat, the breast is the leanest part.
- Remove the skin. Forty percent of the fat in poultry is attached to the skin and therefore can be easily removed. In other meats the fat is dispersed throughout the meat and not so easily removed. One point, though: If you're broiling or baking or grilling chicken, leave the skin on until you're finished cooking; otherwise the meat will lose too much moisture and become tough.
- Roast, broil, poach, or grill chicken instead of frying it.
- Substitute low-fat dairy products in recipes. Use yogurt or light sour cream instead of sour cream, and non-fat milk instead of regular milk. The taste won't be as rich, but if you're watching calories and cholesterol, these substitutions make a substantial difference. For example, plain low-fat yogurt is 143 calories per cup and light sour cream about 350 calories; the same amount of regular sour cream is 492 calories. Non-fat milk is 86 calories per 8-ounce glass, while whole milk is 149 calories.
- Replace oil or fat in marinades with fresh lemon or lime juice, or with wine or vinegar.
- Broil with wine instead of butter.
- Take advantage of non-caloric pan sprays.
- If you're really counting every single calorie, you may want to choose Cornish hens rather than the older broilers and roasters. Young birds bear the same relationship to the older birds that veal does to beef: the younger the animal, the lower the fat content. For comparison, the white meat of a Cornish is 35 calories per ounce of cooked meat; the white meat of a broiler is 45 calories per cooked ounce.

BURGUNDY CHICKEN

Microwave Recipe
1 chicken, cut in serving
　　pieces
½ cup Burgundy or other dry
　　red wine
½ cup low-sodium chicken
　　broth
1 teaspoon dried thyme leaves
¼ teaspoon ground pepper
1 bay leaf
½ pound pearl onions, peeled
¼ pound small mushrooms,
　　sliced
8 small new poatoes, cut into
　　quarters
2 carrots (about 1 cup),
　　thinly sliced
2 tablespoons water
1½ tablespoons cornstarch

NUTRITIONAL FIGURES PER SERVING
Calories, 364.
Protein, 42 grams.
Fat, 6 grams.
Carbohydrates, 34 grams.
Sodium, 173 mg.
Cholesterol, 124 mg.

The Perdue home economists say that microwave recipes are often more nutritious than their conventional versions because microwaving requires much less liquid, ensuring that vitamins and minerals are not washed away.

♦ ♦ ♦

Remove and discard skin and visible fat from the larger chicken pieces. In a 3-quart microwave-safe utensil, combine wine, chicken broth, thyme, pepper, and bay leaf. Add onions, mushrooms, potatoes, and carrots. Cover and microwave at HIGH (100 percent power) 5 minutes. Arrange chicken on top of vegetables, bone-side up, with meatier portions toward outer edge of utensil. Cover with wax paper; microwave at HIGH 15 minutes. Turn chicken pieces over and rearrange, spooning vegetable mixture over each piece. Re-cover; microwave 5–6 minutes per pound or until chicken and vegetables are fork tender. Remove chicken pieces and vegetables; cover to keep warm. In microwave-safe cup, combine water and cornstarch. Add small amount of hot pan juices to cup and stir to blend; gradually stir cornstarch mixture into remaining juices. Microwave on HIGH 2 minutes; stir and microwave 2 minutes longer or until boiling. Serve sauce over chicken and vegetables.

CHICKEN AU POIVRE

1 roaster boneless breast or 1
　　package thin sliced roaster
　　breast
2 tablespoons flour
2 teaspoons cracked black
　　pepper
1 teaspoon dry mustard
2 tablespoons vegetable oil
1 clove garlic, minced
½ cup dry red wine
1 tablespoon minced, fresh
　　parsley

Pepper's piquant flavor helps disguise the lack of salt.

♦ ♦ ♦

Remove and discard visible fat from boneless breast; slice thin. (You can skip this step if you have the thin-sliced roaster breast.) Place chicken slices between sheets of plastic wrap and pound to ⅛-inch thickness. On wax paper, combine flour, pepper, and mustard. Lightly coat chicken with flour mixture, pressing to make pepper adhere.

　　In large skillet over medium-high heat, heat oil. Add

NUTRITIONAL FIGURES PER SERVING
Calories, 269.
Protein, 39 grams.
Fat, 10 grams.
Carbohydrates, 5 grams.
Sodium, 89 mg.
Cholesterol, 97 mg.

garlic; sauté 30 seconds. Place chicken in skillet so that pieces do not touch. Cook about 4 minutes or until lightly browned, turning once. Remove to serving platter; keep warm. Pour off fat; stir in wine. Cook over high heat, stirring constantly 2–3 minutes or until thickened and liquid is reduced by half. Stir in parsley. Spoon sauce over chicken.

TIPS FOR LOW-SALT DIETS WHEN COOKING WITH CHICKEN

- Avoid prepared sauces such as barbecue sauce or ketchup: usually they are high in salt.
- Season chicken with foods that are naturally high in potassium, such as tomatoes, citrus, raisins, or bananas. When you eat foods high in potassium, you don't miss the sodium so much. Tomato paste, by the way, is very high in potassium, and does not have as much added salt as most prepared or canned foods.
- Season foods with garlic, onion, wine, and a variety of herbs and spices. Again, you'll miss the sodium less.
- Trick your palate by cooking with your own flavored vinegars. Use a cup of whichever fresh herb you can find, such as tarragon or mint or dill, for two cups of plain white vinegar and then add a garlic clove or twist of lemon peel. Store in a screw-top jar for several days—if you want it really strong, leave it for a week. You might taste it along the way to see if it's too strong. Finally, strain it and pour into a sterilized bottle and seal.
- Season chicken with concentrated homemade chicken broth. Make chicken stock (use the recipe on page 16, but omit the salt), boil it down until it's concentrated, and then freeze it in ice cube trays. Use individual cubes to intensify the flavor of casseroles or stir-fry dishes.

CHICKEN PROVENÇALE

Microwave Recipe
4 chicken breast halves
3 cups coarsely chopped
    fresh Italian plum
    tomatoes or a 28-ounce
    can, drained
1½ cups sliced mushrooms
    (12-ounces)
⅓ cup chopped onion
1 clove garlic, minced
½ teaspoon dried basil
¼ teaspoon salt or to taste
¼ teaspoon ground pepper
2 tablespoons dry white wine
1 tablespoon cornstarch
2 tablespoons minced fresh
    parsley

NUTRITIONAL FIGURES PER SERVING
Calories, 191.
Protein, 30 grams.
Fat, 2 grams.
Carbohydrates, 13 grams.
Sodium, 228 mg.
Cholesterol, 68 mg.

Do you know why you brown chicken first in traditional stews and casseroles? It's to seal in the juices. You don't need to in microwave cooking, so you save the calories from the butter or margarine or oil you'd use for browning, and the chicken still ends up moist and tender.

◆ ◆ ◆

Remove and discard skin from chicken breasts. In a 3-quart microwave-safe utensil, combine tomatoes, mushrooms, onion, garlic, basil, salt, and pepper. Cover with wax paper. Microwave at HIGH (100 percent power) 5 minutes. Meanwhile, in cup combine wine and cornstarch, stir into tomato mixture. Place chicken breasts, bone-side up and meatier portions toward outside of utensil, on top of tomato mixture. Cover with wax paper; microwave at HIGH 5 minutes. Reduce power to MEDIUM-HIGH (70 percent power) and cook 10 minutes per pound. Halfway through cooking time, turn chicken breasts over and stir tomato mixture. After cooking, let stand, covered, 10 minutes. Remove chicken to serving platter; stir parsley into tomato mixture and spoon some over breasts; serve remaining sauce on side.

CHICKEN RATATOUILLE

6 chicken drumsticks
2 tablespoons vegetable oil
1 cup coarsely chopped onion
1 clove garlic, minced
½ pound eggplant, peeled and
    cubed
2 medium zucchini (about ½
    pound) cubed
2 medium tomatoes, coarsely
    chopped
1 green pepper, cut in thin
    1-inch strips
1 tablespoon minced, fresh
    basil or 1 teaspoon dried

When ratatouille *appears in a recipe's name, you can be sure it will have eggplant in it and probably tomatoes and peppers as well. These vegetables will be noticeably more delicious if you use them very fresh and unrefrigerated. The flavor of these warm-weather crops deteriorates in the refrigerator. Nature didn't mean for them to be in such chilling temperatures*

◆ ◆ ◆

Remove and discard skin and visible fat from drumsticks. In large skillet, over medium heat, heat oil. Add drumsticks; cook about 15 minutes, turning until browned on all sides. Remove drumsticks; drain on paper towels. Add onion and

¾ teaspoon minced, fresh oregano or ¼ teaspoon dried
¼ teaspoon ground pepper

NUTRITIONAL FIGURES PER DRUMSTICK
Calories, 149.
Protein, 14 grams.
Fat, 7 grams.
Carbohydrates, 8 grams.
Sodium, 61 mg.
Cholesterol, 48 mg.

garlic; cook 1 minute, stirring frequently. Add eggplant, zucchini, tomatoes, green pepper, basil, oregano, and pepper. Cook 5 minutes, stirring occasionally. Place drumsticks in vegetable mixture; cook about 30 minutes longer or until drumsticks are tender, occasionally spooning vegetables over chicken.

CHICKEN IN MUSTARD SAUCE

SERVES 4

1 roaster boneless breast or 1 package thin-sliced roaster breast
3 tablespoons vegetable oil, divided
½ pound mushrooms, sliced (2 cups)
2 tablespoons minced, fresh parsley
1 tablespoon minced shallot or scallion
⅛ teaspoon ground pepper
½ cup low-sodium chicken broth
¼ cup dry white wine
1 tablespoon Dijon mustard

NUTRITIONAL FIGURES PER SERVING
Calories, 301.
Protein, 39 grams.
Fat, 14 grams.
Carbohydrates, 4 grams.
Sodium, 210 mg.
Cholesterol, 97 mg.

If controlling sodium is important to you, use an ordinary table wine for the white wine called for in this recipe. Cooking wines often contain salt and should be avoided by anyone who is watching sodium intake. Likewise, sweet wines and fortified ones such as sherry, Madeira, and Marsala should be used sparingly because they are higher in calories than dry wines. No wines contain alcohol after cooking.

♦ ♦ ♦

Remove and discard visible fat from breast; slice thin. (If using thin-sliced product, skip this step.) In a large skillet over medium-high heat, heat 2 tablespoons oil. Add breast slices a few at a time, placing so that pieces do not touch. Sauté 4 minutes, turning once, until chicken is lightly browned on both sides. Remove from skillet; keep warm.

Heat remaining oil. Add mushrooms, parsley, shallot, and pepper. Stirring frequently, cook 2 minutes. Stir in broth and wine; bring to a boil and cook until liquid is reduced by half (about ⅓ cup). Reduce heat to low; stir in mustard until well blended. Spoon over chicken.

CHICKEN VERONIQUE

SERVES 4

4 skinless, boneless chicken
    breast halves or 1 package
    thin sliced boneless
    roaster breast
½ lemon
Ground pepper
1 tablespoon unsalted
    margarine
1½ teaspoons cornstarch
½ cup low-sodium chicken
    broth
¼ cup dry white wine
1 cup seedless green grapes,
    halved

NUTRITIONAL FIGURES PER SERVING
Calories, 194.
Protein, 28 grams.
Fat, 5 grams.
Carbohydrates, 10 grams.
Sodium, 86 mg.
Cholesterol, 68 mg.

Any recipe with the name Veronique will have grape in it. When buying grapes at the supermarket, you can tell how fresh they are by how green and pliable the stem is. Another way of telling is to give the bunch a quick shake. If it's fresh, none of the individual grapes should fall from the bunch. I should warn you, though, that shaking the bunch will not do anything for your popularity with the store's produce manager.

♦ ♦ ♦

Remove and discard any visible fat. Butterfly breast halves to make scaloppine. Skip the previous step if you are using thin-sliced boneless roaster breasts. Rub with lemon and sprinkle lightly with pepper. In large skillet over medium heat, melt margarine. Add scaloppine, in batches if necessary, so that they do not touch. Sauté 4 minutes, turning once, until chicken is lightly browned on both sides and just cooked through. Remove from skillet; keep warm.

In small bowl, stir together cornstarch, broth, and wine until smooth; add to skillet. Over medium heat, bring to boil; boil 1 minute, stirring constantly. Stir in grapes until heated through. To serve, spoon grapes and sauce over chicken.

CITRUS-MARINATED CHICKEN WINGS

SERVES 3

10 chicken wings
3 tablespoons vegetable oil
Grated peel and juice of 1
    lemon
Grated peel and juice of 1
    orange
2 cloves garlic, minced
6 whole cloves
2 bay leaves

Taste tests show that the parts of the bird that get the most exercise, such as the wings, leg, and neck, have the deepest flavor. The seasonings in this recipe bring out the wonderful flavor of wings. The nutritional analysis below assumes that all the marinade is used. Drain off the marinade when you've finished with it, and the calorie, sodium, and fat content will go down.

♦ ♦ ♦

NUTRITIONAL FIGURES PER SERVING
Calories, 507.
Protein, 30 grams.
Fat, 40 grams.
Carbohydrates, 6 grams.
Sodium, 120 mg.
Cholesterol, 126 mg.

Fold wing tips back to form triangles. Place wings in shallow baking pan. In small saucepan, stir together remaining ingredients and heat over medium heat 5 minutes. Pour mixture over wings. Cover; refrigerate several hours or overnight.

Preheat oven to 400°F. Bake wings 30 minutes or until tender, basting occasionally.

CHICKEN BREASTS WITH VEGETABLES

SERVES 4

4 chicken breast halves
2 tablespoons unsalted margarine
2 large carrots, cut into matchstick strips (1½ cups)
2 ribs celery, cut into matchstick strips (1½ cups)
1 green pepper, cut into matchstick strips (1 cup)
1 small shallot, minced
1 cup low-sodium chicken broth
⅛ teaspoon ground pepper
2 tablespoons water
1 tablespoon cornstarch

Whenever possible, choose crisp, fresh vegetables over their canned or frozen counterparts. Fresh vegetables have better color, flavor, and texture. When using frozen or canned products, be sure to look for those with no salt added. This kind of nutritious, high-vitamin, low-calorie meal that features breast meat is a mainstay for Frank. Frank's grown daughter, Bev Nida, tells me that one of her childhood memories of her father was that if he was late for dinner ("and he always was"), everyone knew to save a chicken breast for him.

♦ ♦ ♦

Remove and discard skin and visible fat from chicken breasts. In large skillet over medium heat, melt margarine. Add chicken, cook 6–8 minutes, turning until browned on all sides. Remove chicken; drain on paper towels.

Add carrot, celery, green pepper, and shallot; cook, stirring constantly, 2 minutes. Remove vegetables; set aside. Stir in broth and pepper; add chicken. Reduce heat to low; cover and simmer 15–25 minutes or until chicken is fork tender.

Remove breasts to serving plate; keep warm. In cup, stir together water and cornstarch until smooth; stir into skillet. Over medium heat, bring to boil; boil 1 minute, stirring constantly. Stir in vegetables; cook until heated through. To serve, spoon vegetables over chicken.

NUTRITIONAL FIGURES PER SERVING
Calories, 226.
Protein, 29 grams.
Fat, 8 grams.
Carbohydrates, 9 grams.
Sodium, 126 mg.
Cholesterol, 68 mg.

CHICKEN STROGANOFF

SERVES 4

4 skinless, boneless chicken
  breast halves or 1 package
  thin sliced boneless
  roaster breast
2 tablespoons vegetable oil,
  divided
2 medium onions, thinly
  sliced
½ pound mushrooms, thinly
  sliced (2 cups)
1 clove garlic, minced
½ cup low-sodium chicken
  broth
⅛ teaspoon ground pepper
2 tablespoons water
1 tablespoon cornstarch
1 container (8 ounces) plain
  low-fat yogurt
Hot cooked noodles, cooked
  without salt

NUTRITIONAL FIGURES PER SERVING
Calories, 266.
Protein, 32 grams.
Fat, 10 grams.
Carbohydrates, 12 grams.
Sodium, 126 mg.
Cholesterol, 72 mg.

This is a 1990s version of a nineteenth-century Russian classic. By substituting plain, lowfat yogurt for sour cream, you spare yourself 332 calories.

♦ ♦ ♦

Remove and discard visible fat from chicken; slice chicken in thin strips. In large skillet over medium heat, heat 1 tablespoon oil. Add onions; cook 2 minutes, stirring frequently. Add mushrooms; cook 3 minutes longer. Remove vegetables from skillet; set aside. Heat remaining oil in skillet. Add chicken and garlic; cook 3 minutes or until chicken turns white, stirring frequently. Return vegetables to skillet; add broth and pepper.

In cup, blend water and cornstarch; stir into skillet. Over medium heat, bring to a boil; boil 1 minute, stirring constantly. Remove from heat; stir in yogurt until well blended. Heat gently over low heat (do not boil). Serve over noodles.

ROASTER BREAST
À L'ORANGE

SERVES 6

1 roaster breast, bone-in
1½ tablespoons cornstarch
1½ tablespoons firmly packed
  brown sugar
Dash ground pepper
⅔ cup orange juice
⅔ cup low-sodium chicken
  broth

If you have a choice when buying the orange for this recipe, buy a Valencia in preference to a Navel. Navel oranges are excellent eating oranges, but they're not good juice oranges and their juice develops an off flavor if not used within half an hour.

♦ ♦ ♦

¼ cup julienne-cut orange
    peel strips
1 tablespoon fresh lemon
    juice

Preheat oven to 350°F. Place breast skin-side up in roasting pan; roast 45 minutes. Meanwhile, in 2-quart saucepan, stir together cornstarch, sugar, and pepper. Gradually stir in orange juice and broth until smooth. Over medium heat, bring to a boil; boil 1 minute, stirring constantly. Remove from heat. Stir in orange peel and lemon juice. Roast chicken, basting frequently with sauce 10–20 minutes longer or until juices run clear with no hint of pink when a cut is made near the bone. Heat remaining sauce and serve with roaster breast.

CURRIED ROASTER DRUMSTICKS

SERVES 4

5 roaster drumsticks
2 tablespoons vegetable oil
2 medium apples (diced, 2
    cups)
¾ cup chopped onion
1 clove garlic, minced
1 tablespoon curry powder
1 teaspoon ground ginger
¼ teaspoon ground pepper
1½ cups low-sodium chicken
    broth
3 tablespoons cold water
1½ tablespoons cornstarch

In this recipe, you'll see vegetable oil instead of butter or margarine or lard. Solid fats contain saturated fat, either because they came from animal sources (butter or lard) or because they have been hydrogenated (shortening or margarine). The nutritional analysis at the end of this recipe is per serving of one drumstick. If you eat two, double the count.

♦ ♦ ♦

Remove and discard skin and visible fat from drumsticks. In large skillet over medium-high heat, heat oil. Add drumsticks; cook about 15 minutes, turning until browned on all sides. Remove; drain on paper towels. Pour off all but 1 tablespoon fat. Add apple, onion, garlic, curry, ginger, and pepper; cook 2–3 minutes, stirring frequently. Stir in broth. Return chicken to skillet; reduce heat to medium low. Simmer, uncovered, stirring occasionally for 40 minutes or until chicken is tender and cooked through. Remove chicken to platter; keep warm.

    In cup, blend water and cornstarch until smooth; stir into skillet. Over medium heat, bring to boil; boil 1 minute, stirring occasionally. Spoon sauce over chicken.

CORNISH HENS WITH MUSHROOMS

SERVES 4

2 fresh Cornish game hens
3 tablespoons vegetable oil
½ pound mushrooms, halved
  or quartered
2 small onions, peeled and
  cut in thin wedges
1 cup low-sodium chicken
  broth
⅛ teaspoon ground pepper
2 bay leaves
1 cup skim milk
1 tablespoon cornstarch

NUTRITIONAL FIGURES PER SERVING
Calories, 417.
Protein, 38 grams.
Fat, 25 grams.
Carbohydrates, 10 grams.
Sodium, 150 mg.
Cholesterol, 111 mg.

Skim milk contains all the calcium and protein of whole milk. Use it to make a prudent version of mushroom "cream" sauce.

♦ ♦ ♦

Remove and discard any fat from cavities of hens. In a 5-quart Dutch oven or large deep skillet, over medium heat, heat oil. Add hens; cook about 20 minutes, turning to brown on all sides. Remove hens from pan and set aside. Pour off all but 2 tablespoons drippings; stir in mushrooms and onion. Cook 3 minutes or until tender, stirring occasionally. Stir in broth, pepper, and bay leaves.

Return hens to pan; reduce heat to medium low. Cover and simmer 45 minutes or until tender. Remove hens to serving platter and cut in half. Discard bay leaves. In cup, blend milk and cornstarch until smooth; stir into liquid in pan. Over medium heat, bring to a boil; boil 1 minute, stirring constantly. Serve sauce with hens.

CORNISH HENS WITH APPLE STUFFING

SERVES 4

Microwave Recipe
2 fresh Cornish game hens
3 tablespoons unsalted
  margarine, divided
1 tart red apple, coarsely
  chopped
¼ cup chopped celery
¼ cup chopped onion
1 cup fresh whole-wheat
  bread cubes (2 slices)
½ teaspoon poultry
  seasoning
⅛ teaspoon ground pepper

No extra cooking time is needed when you stuff fresh Cornish game hens before microwaving.

♦ ♦ ♦

Remove and discard any fat from cavities of hens. Place 2 tablespoons margarine in a 4-cup glass container; microwave at HIGH (100 percent power) 45 seconds. Add apple, celery, and onion; cover with plastic wrap. Microwave at HIGH (100 percent power) 3 minutes, stirring once. Stir in bread cubes, poultry seasoning, pepper, and 1 tablespoon cider. Spoon stuffing mixture lightly into cavities and close openings with toothpicks.

2 tablespoons cider or apple
    juice divided
¼ teaspoon paprika

NUTRITIONAL FIGURES PER SERVING
Calories, 432.
Protein, 36 grams.
Fat, 26 grams.
Carbohydrates, 13 grams.
Sodium, 170 mg.
Cholesterol, 110 mg.

Arrange hens, with legs pointing toward center, on microwave-safe roasting utensil. Place remaining 1 tablespoon margarine in custard cup; microwave at HIGH 25 seconds. Stir in remaining 1 tablespoon cider and paprika; brush mixture on hens. Cover hens with wax paper. Microwave at MEDIUM-HIGH (70 percent power) 10 minutes per pound (combined weight of both hens). Let stand, covered, 10 minutes. To serve, cut hens in half.

GREEK LEMON CHICKEN

SERVES 4

1 chicken (3 pounds),
    quartered
½ cup fresh lemon juice
    (about 2 lemons)
2 tablespoons cold pressed
    (extra virgin) olive oil
1 medium-size onion, sliced
    into thin rings
2 tablespoons minced fresh
    oregano or 2 teaspoons
    dried
2 teaspoons minced fresh
    thyme or ½ teaspoon
    dried
¼ teaspoon ground black
    pepper
Cayenne pepper to taste
    (optional)
Lemon wedges, fresh
    oregano, and thyme leaves
    (optional garnish)

This recipe adapts well to barbecuing.

♦ ♦ ♦

Remove and discard visible fat from chicken. In large, shallow bowl, combine remaining ingredients except garnishes. Add chicken and marinate in refrigerator 30 minutes or longer. Preheat broiler. Drain chicken from marinade; place on rack in broiler pan. Broil chicken quarters, 4 inches from heat, 30–35 minutes or until cooked through, turning and basting with marinade three to four times during cooking. Add onion rings during last 10 minutes of broiling time. Serve chicken with onion slices and garnish with lemon wedges, and sprigs of fresh oregano and thyme, if desired.

NUTRITIONAL FIGURES PER SERVING
Calories, 401.
Protein, 41.
Fat, 24 grams.
Carbohydrates, 3 grams.
Sodium, 124 mg.
Cholesterol, 132 mg.

LEMON DRUMSTICKS AND THIGHS

SERVES 4

4 chicken drumsticks
4 chicken thighs
⅓ cup lemon juice
3 tablespoons water
2 tablespoons vegetable oil
1 tablespoon finely shredded
    lemon peel
1 clove garlic, minced
¼ teaspoon salt (or less)
⅛ teaspoon ground pepper

NUTRITIONAL FIGURES PER SERVING
Calories, 223.
Protein, 26 grams.
Fat, 12 grams.
Carbohydrates, 2 grams.
Sodium, 253 mg.
Cholesterol, 105 mg.

Both the grill and the broiler are good friends to the dieter because any fat that cooks out of your chicken just drops away into the fire or pan below. The juice and rind from lemons help achieve tasty, no-salt basting. The nutritional analysis at the end of this recipe includes all the marinade. Drain the marinade and your calorie, sodium, and fat content will go down.

♦ ♦ ♦

Remove and discard skin and visible fat from drumsticks and thighs. Place in large, shallow dish. In small bowl, stir together lemon juice, water, oil, lemon peel, garlic, salt, and pepper; pour over chicken. Cover; refrigerate several hours or overnight, turning occasionally.

Prepare outdoor grill for cooking or preheat broiler. Remove from marinade. Grill 6 inches from source of heat or broil indoors, cooking 30–40 minutes or until tender and golden brown; turn and baste frequently with marinade.

ORIENTAL CHICKEN AND VEGETABLES

SERVES 4

4 roaster boneless thigh
    cutlets
2 tablespoons cornstarch
Ground pepper to taste
1 cup low-sodium chicken
    broth at room temperature
1 tablespoon reduced-sodium
    soy sauce
2 tablespoons vegetable oil
2 tablespoons sliced scallions
1 clove garlic, minced

Fresh garlic is definitely better than powdered garlic. Look for garlic cloves with plump, firm heads that have a fresh appearance. The paperlike casing should be dry and should completely cover the individual garlic cloves, and there should be no trace of sprouting. Store garlic in a cool, dry place, but don't refrigerate it. Cool temperatures can increase the garlic's tendency to sprout.

♦ ♦ ♦

1 cup diagonally sliced
    carrots (about 2 medium)
1 cup snow peas
1 cup well-drained bean
    sprouts
1 can (8 ounces) sliced water
    chestnuts, drained
Hot cooked rice (cooked
    without salt)

NUTRITIONAL FIGURES PER SERVING
Calories, 310.
Protein, 30 grams.
Fat, 12 grams.
Carbohydrates, 19 grams.
Sodium, 315 mg.
Cholesterol, 102 mg.

Trim visible fat from thighs; cut chicken in thin strips. In small bowl, stir together cornstarch and pepper. Gradually stir in broth and soy sauce until smooth; set aside. In wok or large skillet over medium-high heat, heat oil. Add green onions and garlic; stir-fry 30 seconds. Add chicken and carrots; stir-fry 3–5 minutes or until chicken turns white and carrots are tender crisp. Add snow peas, bean sprouts, and water chestnuts. Stir-fry to heat through. Re-stir cornstarch mixture; add to wok. Over medium heat, bring to a boil; boil 1 minute, stirring constantly. Serve over rice.

TANDOORI CORNISH HENS

2 fresh Cornish game gens
⅓ cup plain yogurt
2 tablespoons vegetable oil
2 tablespoons lime juice
1 tablespoon curry powder
2 cloves garlic, minced
2 teaspoons minced fresh
    gingerroot
1 teaspoon grated lime peel
1 teaspoon chili powder
1 teaspoon paprika

NUTRITIONAL FIGURES PER SERVING:
Calories, 384.
Protein, 35 grams.
Fat, 24 grams.
Carbohydrates, 4 grams.
Sodium, 124 mg.
Cholesterol, 111 mg.

Fresh Cornish game hens contain even less fat and fewer calories than larger poultry and are close in size and flavor to the chickens traditionally used for India's Tandoori Chicken. If you want a barbecue version of this, using chicken breasts, look for Boneless Breasts Tandoori on page 125.

♦ ♦ ♦

With sharp knife or poultry shears, cut hens lengthwise in half. Remove and discard any visible fat from cavities. Place hens in large shallow baking dish. In small bowl, stir together remaining ingredients; brush on all sides of hens. Cover; refrigerate several hours or overnight to marinate.

Preheat oven to 400°F. Place hens on rack in shallow baking pan; brush with marinade. Bake 15 minutes. Reduce oven temperature to 350°F; bake 20–25 minutes longer or until chicken is tender and juices run clear with no hint of pink when thigh is pierced with a fork.

PASTA PRIMAVERA WITH CHICKEN

4 skinless, boneless chicken breast halves or 1 package thin-sliced boneless roaster breast
2 tablespoons vegetable oil, divided
4 scallions, cut in julienne strips (about ½ cup)
2 cloves garlic, minced
1 pound asparagus, peeled, cut in 2-inch pieces or julienne zucchini (about 2 cups)
2 carrots, peeled, cut in julienne strips (about 1 cup)
½ cup low-sodium chicken broth
½ cup dry white wine
¼ cup minced fresh parsley
1½ teaspoons minced, fresh oregano, or ½ teaspoon dried
⅛ teaspoon ground pepper
½ pound spaghetti, cooked, drained
⅓ cup freshly grated Parmesan cheese

Because freshly grated Parmesan cheese has a more intense flavor than pre-grated cheese, you can use less of it, and in the process, you'll be saving on both fat and calories.

When I'm cooking pasta for Frank, I omit both the oil and salt called for in the directions on the pasta package. If we're having guests, though, I use the salt and the oil. People who aren't used to low-fat, low-salt cooking would find it pretty bland otherwise.

♦ ♦ ♦

Slice breast meat into thin strips. In a large skillet, over medium-high heat, heat 1 tablespoon oil. Add scallions and garlic; cook 1 minute, stirring frequently. Add chicken; cook 2–3 minutes or until chicken turns white, stirring constantly. Remove chicken and vegetables; set aside. Heat remaining oil in skillet; add asparagus and carrots and cook 2 minutes, stirring frequently. Stir in broth, wine, parsley, oregano, and pepper; return chicken to pan; simmer 1–2 minutes or until vegetables are tender crisp.

Place spaghetti on large platter; top with chicken mixture. Sprinkle with cheese. Toss and serve.

NUTRITIONAL FIGURES PER SERVING
Calories, 312.
Protein, 27 grams.
Fat, 8 grams.
Carbohydrates, 33 grams.
Sodium, 148 mg.
Cholesterol, 49 mg.

PINEAPPLE-MINTED ROASTER

Microwave Recipe

1 whole roaster (about 6
    pounds)
1 can (20 ounces) pineapple
    chunks in their own juice
About ½ cup pineapple juice,
    orange juice, or water
1½ tablespoons cornstarch
5–6 small sprigs fresh mint
    or 1½ teaspoons dried
    mint leaves
2 tablespoons unsalted
    margarine, melted

*F*at attracts more microwave energy than muscle does. When you microwave chicken, the fat will render out into the drippings where you can easily discard it.

♦ ♦ ♦

Remove and discard any visible fat from roaster cavity. Remove giblets. Place breast side down on microwave-safe roasting utensil. Drain pineapple chunks, reserving juice and chunks. Add additional juice or water to reserved juice to measure 1½ cups. Place cornstarch in 4-cup glass container and gradually stir juice into cornstarch until smooth. Microwave at HIGH (100 percent power) 2 minutes; stir and microwave 2 minutes longer or until mixture boils and thickens. Add mint (if using fresh mint, remove sprigs after five minutes). Remove ½ cup of mixture for glaze; stir pineapple chunks into remaining mixture for sauce and set aside. Brush roaster with melted margarine; cover with wax paper.

Microwave at MEDIUM-HIGH (70 percent power) 10–12 minutes per pound, brushing with glaze several times during cooking. Halfway through cooking time, turn roaster over, using paper towels to protect hands. Pour off drippings and reserve, if desired. Baste bird with glaze and cover again with wax paper; complete cooking. Let stand, covered with aluminum foil, 20 minutes. (Standing time is important even if Bird-Watcher Thermometer has popped.) After standing time, juice should run clear with no hint of pink when thigh is pierced. To reheat sauce, microwave at HIGH 2 minutes. Serve hot sauce with roaster. Remove skin before eating.

NUTRITIONAL FIGURES PER SERVING:
Calories, 344.
Protein, 40 grams.
Fat, 13 grams.
Carbohydrates, 15 grams.
Sodium, 118 mg.
Cholesterol, 117 mg.

ROASTED CORNISH HENS WITH NEW POTATOES

SERVES 4

2 fresh Cornish game hens
Vegetable cooking spray
2 tablespoons unsalted
  margarine, melted
1 teaspoon minced shallot or
  scallion
1½ teaspoons fresh rosemary
  or ½ teaspoon dried
Ground pepper to taste
6 small new potatoes,
  quartered
16 pearl onions, peeled
1 cup low-sodium chicken
  broth
2 tablespoons cold water
1 tablespoon cornstarch

NUTRITIONAL FIGURES PER SERVING
Calories, 475.
Protein, 37 grams.
Fat, 24 grams.
Carbohydrates, 27 grams.
Sodium, 129 mg.
Cholesterol, 110 mg.

When you combine tender-skinned new potatoes with Cornish game hens, you have almost a complete meal in one pan. Add a fresh green vegetable to complete a wholesome menu.

♦ ♦ ♦

Preheat oven to 350°F. With sharp knife or poultry shears, cut hens lengthwise in half. Remove and discard any visible fat from cavity. Spray shallow roasting pan lightly with vegetable cooking spray. Place hens skin-side up in pan. Stir together margarine and shallot; brush on hens and sprinkle with rosemary and pepper. Arrange potatoes and onions around hens. Cover pan with foil. Bake 20 minutes. Uncover and continue baking, basting occasionally, 20–30 minutes or until hens and vegetables are tender. Remove to serving platter. Cover with foil; keep warm.

Pour pan drippings into measuring cup. Allow to stand several minutes until fat drippings separate from hen juices; discard fat. Return hen juices to roasting pan; add broth. Bring to a boil over medium heat, stirring up brown bits from bottom of pan. In cup, blend water and cornstarch until smooth; stir into broth mixture. Bring to a boil; boil 1 minute, stirring constantly. Serve gravy with hens and vegetables.

ROASTER PAPRIKASH

SERVES 8

1 whole roaster (about 6
  pounds)
¼ cup vegetable oil
8 small white onions, peeled
4 carrots, peeled and
  quartered
1¼ cups low-sodium chicken
  broth

This comment has nothing to do with this recipe, but I'm slipping it in here because I thought you might like to know about it. Fitness declines if you exercise two days or less each week. Fitness is maintained if you exercise three days a week. Fitness is improved if you exercise four or more times a week.

♦ ♦ ♦

2 tablespoons paprika,
    divided
¼ teaspoon ground pepper
¼ cup water
2 tablespoons cornstarch
1 cup plain low-fat yogurt

Remove and discard any visible fat from cavity. Remove giblets, tie legs together, and fold wings back. Fasten neck with wooden pick or small skewer. In 8-quart saucepot over medium heat, heat oil. Add roaster. Cook about 30 minutes, turning until browned on all sides. Remove and set aside. Add onions and carrots; cook 3 minutes, stirring frequently. Remove vegetables. Pour off fat and stir in broth, 1 tablespoon paprika, and pepper. Return roaster to saucepot; sprinkle with remaining paprika. Arrange onions and carrots around roaster. Reduce heat to medium low; cover and simmer 1 hour or until roaster juices run clear with no hint of pink when thigh is pierced and vegetables are tender.

Remove roaster and vegetables to serving platter; keep warm. In cup, blend water and cornstarch until smooth; stir into liquid in saucepot. Bring to a boil over medium heat; boil 1 minute, stirring constantly. Remove from heat; add yogurt and stir until well blended and smooth. Heat gently over low heat; do not boil. Serve sauce with roaster and vegetables.

THYME THIGHS

SERVES 4

6 chicken thighs
2 tablespoons flour
⅛ teaspoon ground nutmeg
⅛ teaspoon Cayenne pepper
2 tablespoons vegetable oil
1 tablespoon fresh minced
    thyme, or 1 teaspoon
    dried
½ cup dry white wine

Cooking with wine is a flavor bargain, if you're counting calories. The alcohol calories will evaporate away, but the flavor of the wine remains. The nutritional analysis at the end of this recipe is per serving of one thigh.

♦ ♦ ♦

Remove skin from thighs and trim visible fat. On wax paper, combine flour, nutmeg, and pepper. Coat thighs with flour mixture. Heat oil in large skillet over medium-high heat. Add thighs and cook 10–15 minutes or until lightly browned, turning once. Sprinkle thyme on chicken and pour wine on top. Cover, reduce heat to medium-low and cook 30 minutes or until chicken is tender.

TARRAGON ROASTED CHICKEN

1 whole chicken (about 3 pounds)
3 tablespoons unsalted margarine
1 tablespoon minced fresh tarragon or 1½ teaspoons dried
⅛ teaspoon ground pepper
4 sprigs fresh parsley
2 cloves garlic, peeled
1 cup low-sodium chicken broth
2 tablespoons dry white wine
1 tablespoon cornstarch

NUTRITIONAL FIGURES PER SERVING
Calories, 454.
Protein, 42 grams.
Fat, 29 grams.
Carbohydrates, 3 grams.
Sodium, 138 mg.
Cholesterol, 132 mg.

Make a light, clear pan gravy for chicken by removing fat from drippings and using cornstarch instead of flour to thicken; 1 tablespoon cornstarch = 2 tablespoons flour.

♦ ♦ ♦

Remove and discard any visible fat from cavity of chicken. Remove giblets. Preheat oven to 350°F. In small saucepan, over medium heat, melt margarine; stir in tarragon and pepper. Place parsley and garlic in cavity of chicken; tie legs together. Place chicken, breast-side up, in roasting pan; brush with tarragon mixture. Roast, brushing occasionally with remaining tarragon mixture, for about 1½ hours or until juices run clear with no hint of pink when thigh is pierced. Remove chicken to serving platter; keep warm. Pour pan drippings into measuring cup. Allow to stand several minutes until clear fat drippings separate from chicken juices; discard fat drippings. Return chicken juices to roasting pan; add broth. In cup, blend wine and cornstarch; stir into roasting pan. Over medium heat, bring to a boil, stirring up brown bits from bottom of pan; boil 1 minute. Serve gravy with chicken.

CRUNCHY BAKED DRUMSTICKS

6 chicken drumsticks
1 egg white, lightly beaten
2 tablespoons lowfat milk
½ teaspoon salt or to taste
¼ teaspoon ground pepper
1 cup crunchy nutlike cereal nuggets or bran flakes, crushed

The grated lemon peel and the pepper can minimize the need for salt in this recipe. If you're on a low-salt diet, skip the salt. The nutritional analysis at the end of this recipe is per serving of one drumstick.

♦ ♦ ♦

1 teaspoon grated lemon peel
Vegetable cooking spray

Preheat oven to 350°F. In shallow bowl, beat together egg white, milk, salt, and pepper. On waxed paper, combine cereal and lemon peel. Roll drumsticks evenly in egg white mixture, then in cereal mixture, turning to coat well.

Spray a rectangular baking dish or cookie sheet with vegetable cooking spray. Arrange drumsticks in dish in a single layer. Bake 35–45 minutes or until cooked through and golden.

CAPE COD CHICKEN BREASTS

SERVES 4

4 chicken breast halves
Ground pepper to taste
1–2 tablespoons vegetable oil
   or margarine
1 medium onion, finely
   chopped
1½ cups fresh or frozen,
   thawed cranberries
¾ cup orange juice
2–3 tablespoons sugar
1 teaspoon grated fresh
   orange peel
Pinch nutmeg

The cranberries called for in this recipe are available in your supermarket produce section from September through November. If you want to have cranberries available for use at another time of the year, buy them when they're available and then freeze them in the bag they came in. Just enclose that bag in a freezer bag so the berries are double wrapped. They'll stay in good condition for about nine months.

♦ ♦ ♦

Remove skin, and season chicken on both sides with pepper. In a large skillet, over medium-high heat, heat oil. Add chicken breasts and cook for 4–5 minutes per side until golden brown. Add onion; cook 2 minutes longer, stirring often. Add cranberries, orange juice, sugar, orange peel, and nutmeg. Stir to scrape up bits from bottom of skillet; bring to a boil. Reduce heat to medium-low, cover and cook 20–25 minutes longer or until chicken is tender and cranberries are soft, stirring occasionally. Remove chicken to warm platter; keep warm. Transfer cranberry mixture from skillet to food processor or blender; cover and puree until almost smooth. To serve, pour sauce over chicken.

CHICKEN AND BELL PEPPER SAUTÉ

SERVES 4

4 boneless, skinless chicken breast halves
1 teaspoon ground cumin
1 teaspoon dried oregano
Ground pepper to taste
1–2 tablespoons olive oil
1 clove garlic, minced
1 small red bell pepper, cut into thin strips
1 small green bell pepper, cut into thin strips
1 small yellow bell pepper, cut into thin strips

NUTRITIONAL FIGURES PER SERVING
Calories, 189.
Protein, 28 grams.
Fat, 7 grams.
Carbohydrates, 3 grams.
Sodium, 79 mg.
Cholesterol, 68 mg.

This recipe is prettiest when made with red, green, and yellow bell peppers. However, your supermarket may not have the red and yellow ones available, in which case, substitute green ones. Incidentally, red bell peppers start out as green bell peppers, but as they mature, their color changes from green to red.

♦ ♦ ♦

Place chicken breasts between sheets of plastic wrap and pound to ¼-inch thickness. Sprinkle both sides of chicken with cumin, oregano, and pepper to taste, pressing to make seasonings adhere.

In large skillet, over medium-high heat, heat oil. Add chicken; sauté 1–2 minutes per side until lightly browned and almost cooked through. Remove chicken to warm platter; keep warm.

Add garlic and pepper strips to drippings in skillet; stir-fry 1 minute. Reduce heat to medium-low; cover and cook 3 minutes or until peppers are tender-crisp. Return chicken to skillet, spooning pepper mixture on top. Cover and cook 3–5 minutes longer until vegetables are tender and chicken is completely cooked through.

MEDITERRANEAN CHICKEN BREASTS

SERVES 4

4 chicken breast halves
1–2 tablespoons olive oil
Ground pepper to taste
½ cup dry red wine
4 fresh or canned plum tomatoes, seeded and coarsely chopped
2 garlic cloves, minced
½ teaspoon dried basil
½ teaspoon dried marjoram

Fresh garlic, stored in a cool, dry place, will last about as long as a fresh onion. If the cloves start to sprout, you can still use them, but they won't be quite as flavorful.

♦ ♦ ♦

Remove skin from chicken breasts. In a large skillet, over medium heat, heat 1 tablespoon oil. Add chicken breasts and cook for 5 minutes until golden, turning once. Add more oil if necessary. Stir in wine, tomatoes, garlic, basil, and mar-

½ cup pitted black olives, cut in half

¼ cup minced, fresh parsley

NUTRITIONAL FIGURES PER SERVING
Calories, 235.
Protein, 29 grams.
Fat, 10 grams.
Carbohydrates, 7 grams.
Sodium, 216 mg.
Cholesterol, 68 mg.

joram; bring to a boil. Reduce heat to low; cover and simmer 20–25 minutes or until chicken is almost cooked through. Uncover; increase heat to medium-high and cook 5 minutes longer or until liquid is reduced by one-third. Stir in olives and parsley; heat through.

INDONESIAN CHICKEN KEBOBS WITH CURRIED YOGURT DIP

SERVES 4

2 tablespoons fresh lime juice

2 tablespoons soy sauce

1 tablespoon vegetable oil

1 teaspoon brown or white sugar

1 garlic clove, crushed

4 boneless, skinless chicken breast halves

1 cup plain low-fat yogurt

¼ cup chopped scallions

1 tablespoon curry powder

1 teaspoon oriental sesame oil, optional

You can use bottled lime juice in this recipe, but it lacks the spark that fresh lime juice has. Also, you can lower the sodium content still further by using light soy sauce. *The nutritional information you'll find at the end of this recipe assumes that you're using all the marinade. Use less of the marinade and the sodium count will drop dramatically.*

♦ ♦ ♦

In a shallow bowl, combine lime juice, soy sauce, vegetable oil, sugar, and garlic; mix well. Add chicken, turning to coat with marinade. Cover and refrigerate 1 hour.

Meanwhile, in small bowl, combine yogurt, scallions, curry powder, and sesame oil. Cover and refrigerate until ready to use.

Remove chicken from marinade and cut into ¾-inch cubes; reserve marinade. On each of 10 to 12 skewers, thread 4 to 5 chicken cubes. Preheat broiler. Place skewers in broiler pan; broil 4 inches from heat source 8–10 minutes until cooked through, turning once and brushing occasionally with marinade. Serve kebobs with curried yogurt dip.

NUTRITIONAL FIGURES PER SERVING
Calories, 215.
Protein, 31 grams.
Fat, 6 grams.
Carbohydrates, 8 grams.
Sodium, 632 grams.
Cholesterol, 72 mg.

POACHED CHICKEN IN CREAMY LEMON SAUCE

4 boneless, skinless, chicken breast halves
¼ teaspoon ground pepper
½ cup chicken broth
¼ cup white wine
2 tablespoons lemon juice
1 teaspoon grated lemon peel
1 cup lowfat milk
1½ tablespoons cornstarch
1 tablespoon Dijon mustard
2 tablespoons minced, fresh parsley, optional

NUTRITIONAL FIGURES PER SERVING
Calories, 182.
Protein, 30 grams.
Fat, 3 grams.
Carbohydrates, 7 grams.
Sodium, 345 mg.
Cholesterol, 73 mg.

I'm fond of this recipe because the texture is creamy and it doesn't use cream.

♦ ♦ ♦

Season chicken with pepper. In a large, deep skillet over medium-high heat, combine broth, wine, lemon juice, and lemon peel; bring to a boil. Add chicken; reduce heat to medium-low. Cover and simmer 12–15 minutes or until chicken is cooked through. Transfer chicken to a warm serving plate and keep warm.

In a small bowl, blend milk, cornstarch, and mustard until smooth; stir into simmering liquid in skillet. Increase heat to medium; cook until mixture boils and thickens, stirring constantly. Return chicken to skillet; coat well with sauce. Sprinkle with parsley, if desired.

CHICKEN NORMANDY

1 chicken, cut in serving pieces (about 3 pounds)
Ground pepper to taste
Vegetable cooking spray
2 medium apples, cored and sliced
1 large onion, sliced
½ cup apple cider or juice
2 tablespoons fresh lemon juice
1 tablespoon vegetable oil
2 teaspoons brown sugar
¼ teaspoon ground allspice

If they're available, choose Rome Beauty apples for this recipe. Romes have a somewhat flat, mealy taste when eaten raw, but their flavor develops a wonderful richness when cooked. They're available from October until early Summer. The Golden Delicious, the Cortland, the Jonathan, and the Granny Smith are also good for baking. Red Delicious apples are only fair for cooking.

♦ ♦ ♦

Preheat oven to 350°F. Sprinkle chicken pieces with pepper to taste.

Spray 13 × 9-inch baking dish with vegetable cooking spray. Arrange chicken in baking dish; scatter apple and onion slices around and on top of chicken. In cup, combine cider, lemon juice, oil, sugar, and allspice; pour over chicken. Bake, uncovered, for about 1 hour or until chicken is cooked through and apples are tender, turning pieces once during cooking and basting occasionally with drippings. To serve, remove chicken from pan juices and spoon apples and onions on top. Remove skin before eating.

BALSAMIC CHICKEN AND MUSHROOMS

SERVES 4

1 chicken, cut in serving
    pieces (about 3 pounds)
Ground pepper to taste
Paprika
1½ to 2 tablespoons olive oil,
    divided
2 tablespoons chopped
    shallots or scallions
2 cups sliced fresh
    mushrooms (about ½
    pound)
½ cup chicken broth
2 tablespoons balsamic or red
    wine vinegar

If you can find balsamic vinegar, buy it! It's terrific in this recipe, and it's worth having on hand for salad dressings afterward.

◆ ◆ ◆

Preheat oven to 350°F. In large baking dish, place chicken, skin-side up; brush with ½–1 tablespoon oil and sprinkle with pepper and paprika to taste. Bake 40 minutes. Pour off and discard pan juices.

Meanwhile, in medium skillet over medium-high heat, heat remaining oil. Add shallots; sauté 2 minutes until slightly softened. Stir in mushrooms; cook 2 minutes longer until lightly browned, stirring constantly. Add broth and vinegar; reduce heat to medium, and cook 3 minutes or until mushrooms are tender and liquid is slightly reduced. Pour mushroom mixture over chicken; bake 20–25 minutes longer until chicken is cooked through, basting occasionally with pan drippings. Serve chicken with mushroom sauce.

HARVEST CHICKEN DINNER

1 whole roaster (about 6
    pounds)
½ cup white wine
¼ cup brown sugar
2 tablespoons cider vinegar
1 tablespoon vegetable oil
2 teaspoons dried rosemary
    leaves, crushed
1 teaspoon Worcestershire
    sauce
2 large acorn squash

NUTRITIONAL FIGURES PER SERVING
Calories, 357.
Protein, 40 grams.
Fat, 12 grams.
Carbohydrates, 21 grams.
Sodium, 131 mg.
Cholesterol, 117 mg.

Acorn squash is high in vitamin A. A single serving will more than meet your Recommended Daily Allowance for this vitamin.

♦ ♦ ♦

Preheat oven to 350°F. Remove and discard any visible fat from roaster cavity. Remove giblets. Tie drumsticks together and fold wings back. Place chicken in roasting pan. In small bowl, combine wine, sugar, vinegar, oil, rosemary, and Worcestershire; brush mixture on roaster, covering entire surface. Roast chicken 45 minutes.

Meanwhile, cut squash into quarters; remove seeds. After 45 minutes cooking time, arrange squash in roasting pan around chicken; fill cavities with a little basting mixture. Roast chicken, basting occasionally, 1¼–1¾ hours longer (depending on weight) or until juices run clear with no hint of pink when thigh is pierced.

To serve, slice chicken with degreased pan juices and accompany with squash. Remove skin before eating.

CAJUN SPICED ROASTER

1 whole roaster (about 6
pounds)
½ lemon
1 tablespoon vegetable oil
1–1½ tablespoons dried
thyme
2 teaspoons ground black
pepper
1 teaspoon salt
½–1 teaspoon Cayenne
pepper
1 clove garlic, minced
2 celery ribs, sliced (leaves
included)
1 onion, quartered
¼ cup parsley sprigs

NUTRITIONAL FIGURES PER SERVING
Calories, 288.
Protein, 40 grams.
Fat, 12 grams.
Carbohydrates, 3 grams.
Sodium, 403 mg.
Cholesterol, 117.

If roasters aren't available in your area, you can use a regular whole chicken, adjusting the cooking time. However, roasters are juicier and more tender and more flavorful, so if you've got a choice, go for a roaster.

♦ ♦ ♦

Preheat oven to 350°F. Remove and discard any visible fat from roaster cavity. Remove giblets. Rub roaster inside and out with lemon; brush oil evenly over skin.

In small bowl, combine thyme, black pepper, salt, red pepper, and garlic. Rub some of mixture into cavity of roaster; stuff with celery, onion, and parsley. Skewer or tie cavity closed and fold back wings. Rub remaining herb and spice mixture evenly into skin of roaster, covering entire surface.

Place chicken in roasting pan. Roast 2¼–2¾ hours (depending on weight) or until juices run clear with no hint of pink when thigh is pierced. Baste occasionally with pan drippings.

To serve, remove celery, onion, and parsley from cavity of roaster; discard. Skim fat from pan drippings and discard; reserve pan juices. Slice roaster and serve with pan juices. Remove skin before eating.

4

CHICKEN FOR CHILDREN

This chapter is about cooking for and by kids, but I got the idea for it when I was thinking about something entirely different. I was idly wondering, "When is Frank the absolute happiest and most content?" Part of me instantly wanted to answer, "When working, of course." I believe that for him business *is* pleasure. If it's a busy time, he'll happily get along for weeks at a time on four hours' sleep and work the rest except for meals. When it gets really busy, I've seen him get by on two hours—and still relish the work.

But there are certainly other things he enjoys. He's an avid baseball fan and the best Father's Day gift I think he ever got was tickets to go to one of the Oriole games with his son Jim and grandson Ryan. He also loves dancing. (His nickname years ago used to be "Twinkle toes.")

Still, I think the time that he looks the most relaxed and content and generally pleased with life is when the four children and twelve grandchildren are here. They're scattered from Maine to Virginia, so we don't get them often, but when we do, it's an occasion. And it's one when I want to have food that I can count on the kids' liking.

Here are some of the principles of cooking for young children that I've learned from the Perdue home economists and from Cooperative Extension. I'm guessing that if you have kids, you know their preferences pretty well, but if you're entertaining other kids, these tips may come in handy.

Cooking with school-age kids can be a lot of fun, as long as it's presented as a treat instead of a chore. You might, for a start, get them involved in planning the week's menu. I know some families who allow each child to pick the main dish for one meal a week. Older children

TIPS FOR COOKING FOR CHILDREN

- Finger foods such as chicken nuggets are always a hit. I keep a carton or two on hand for a never-fail snack food for kids—or grown-ups.
- Young children often prefer uncomplicated tastes. While some may go for elaborate sauces, it's safest to cook chicken by quickly sautéing it in your frying pan and then have any of the grown-ups' sauces available for the kids to use as an optional dip.
- Avoid highly seasoned foods for kids unless you know they're used to them.
- Frequently young children like uniform textures. Casseroles with hard and soft textures would be riskier than, say, a straightforward boned chicken breast.
- Pieces cut from a cooked Cornish hen can be a real treat for a small child. He or she eats the child-size portion, breast or leg, while the grown-ups eat regular-size broiler breast or drumsticks.
- My friends in Cooperative Extension tell me that the latest scientific research suggests thinking of a balanced diet in terms of several days rather than just a rigid 24-hour period. That means that if one of the kids in your care goes on a chicken-eating jag or a peanut butter jag or a not-eating jag, don't worry; it's okay as long as in the course of several days he or she is getting a balanced diet. Knowing this can make meal time a lot more relaxed.

actually get to cook their choice. My daughter-in-law, Jan Perdue, suggests getting kids to pick out meals with an ethnic or international theme so that mealtime is a time to explore other cultures as well as a time to eat.

Many of the recipes in this chapter are not only popular with kids, they're designed to be easy and fun for them to make. When your kids are trying these recipes, why not teach them food preparation tips that will be useful to them for the rest of their lives?

When I'm cooking with kids, my first concern is food safety. I explain to them that in most cases, food-borne illnesses don't make you violently sick (although they can); the usual episode is more likely to be simple queasiness or a headache or feeling under the weather and not knowing quite why. To avoid these nuisance illnesses as well as the possibility of more serious ones, the number-one rule is:

Wash your hands and all utensils before and after touching any raw meat.

Personally, I love having kids in the kitchen. I like the bustle and hubbub, and even though I know, as I'm sure you do too, that we parents could probably do things a lot faster without their "help," that's not the point. The point is being together and having fun doing things together.

ALLISON'S CHIX IN A BLANKET

SERVES 1

2 biscuits from a tube of buttermilk refrigerator biscuits, uncooked
1 chicken frank
1 tablespoon of grated cheddar cheese, or more, to taste

At age eight, our granddaughter Allison Perdue loves to make these. She tells me that her six-year-old brother can make them too. She got the recipe from summer camp, but changed the main ingredient to Frank's Franks. It will have much less fat than regular franks. Sometimes Ali's biscuits stay wrapped around the frank, and sometimes they open during cooking. Ali says they're okay either way.

♦ ♦ ♦

Lay the biscuits side by side with the sides touching. Pinch together the parts that are touching and then, using your palms or a rolling pin, press or roll the biscuits into a single rectangle that's hot dog–shaped, only wider. Lay a frank on the dough and then sprinkle the frank with the cheese. Pierce frank in several places with fork. Wrap the dough around the frank, pinch closed, and then bake according to the directions for cooking the biscuits.

BBQ "SPARERIBS"

MAKES 40, SERVES 8–10

8 chicken franks
1¼ cups prepared barbecue sauce
1 tablespoon finely chopped onion
1 teaspoon mustard

One of my favorite commercials is of Frank introducing the Perdue Chicken Franks. It starts out with Frank in front of a hot dog stand calling out, "Hot dogs only 25 cents." A young kid who's been made up to have a large nose and ears just like Frank's says, "Only 25 cents for a hot dog? How good could it be?" Frank answers, "I'm making it easy for people to try Perdue Chicken Franks." The kids answers, "Chicken Franks? Free would be a lot easier." When Frank answers that his franks cost less and have 25 percent less fat, the kid answers, "All right, I'll bite," and then says, "Tastes as good as a real hot dog." Frank looks at the kid, with his Perdue-shaped nose and ears, and says, "This kid's got good taste and good looks." These "spareribs" also taste good and look good.

♦ ♦ ♦

Slice each frank on the diagonal into 5 pieces. In a large bowl, combine remaining ingredients. Add frank slices and toss gently to coat well. Arrange coated franks in single layer on baking sheet and place under broiler 2 minutes. Turn and broil 2 minutes longer, or until franks are golden brown. Watch carefully to avoid burning. Serve with toothpicks, if desired.

- Before starting to cook, read the recipe carefully and gather all ingredients and equipment.
- Don't wear loose, floppy clothing or sleeves that are too long. Tie back hair if it gets in the way.
- When using a sharp knife, cut on a cutting board and point the knife away from your body.
- If you're walking around with a knife, hold it so the blade is pointed toward the floor and away from your body.
- Make sure you know how to light your stove. If a gas burner or oven doesn't light, turn the knob to "off" and ask an adult for help. Electric burners remain hot even after they're turned off, so don't touch!
- When removing lids from cooking pots, point them away from you to prevent steam burns.
- Don't let pot handles extend over the edge of the stove or counter—a little brother or sister could grab the handle and pull it down on his or her head.
- Never stick anything into an electric mixer or blender while it's running.
- Don't let any part of your potholder touch the burner; it could catch fire.
- Clean up as you go along—and don't forget the cutting board.
- Double check that stove and appliances are turned off before you leave the kitchen. Make a habit of turning off the burner before removing your pan, that way you won't forget.
- Never be embarrassed to ask for help. That's how we learn.

BIG-TOP CORN DOGS

SERVES 8

8 chicken franks
¼ cup flour
1 package (8 ounces) corn muffin mix
2 eggs
1 cup milk
Vegetable oil for deep frying
8 wooden lollipop or caramel-apple sticks

Because this involves deep-fat frying, it's probably best cooked by adults or mature teenagers only, but the end result will impress your kids.

◆ ◆ ◆

Pierce each frank in several places with a fork. Roll in flour and set aside. In a mixing bowl combine corn muffin mix, eggs, and milk; mix thoroughly. In large fryer or deep, heavy skillet, heat 1½ inches of vegetable oil to 375°F or until bread cube sizzles in it. Also, preheat oven to 375°F.

Dip each frank in batter, coating evenly. Place gently into oil; cook 3 to 4 at one time, turning until golden brown all over. Drain on paper towels. Place corn dogs on lightly oiled shallow baking sheet and bake at 375°F for 8 minutes or until thoroughly heated. Insert stick at least 2 inches into corn dog. Serve with mustard and ketchup.

BETSY'S BEST-"GETTI"

SERVES 6–8

8 chicken franks
1 pound spaghetti
3 tablespoons vegetable oil
½ clove garlic, minced
½ cup finely chopped onion
1 can (16 ounces) whole tomatoes, chopped with liquid
1 can (8 ounces) tomato sauce
1½ teaspoons minced fresh basil or ½ teaspoon dried
1 tablespoon minced fresh parsley
Grated Parmesan cheese

You can make this even simpler by using canned spaghetti. Also, if you top the casserole with thin slices of mozzarella and heat it until the mozzarella melts, you'll get a gloppy, stretchy, chewing gum—like topping that kids will adore if they're into being messy. Mine love it.

◆ ◆ ◆

Slice franks into thin rounds. In large kettle, over high heat, bring 3½ quarts salted water to boil. Add spaghetti, stir and cook until tender. Drain and place in large bowl.

In a medium saucepan over medium heat, heat oil. Add garlic and onion and cook for 3 minutes, stirring often. Add tomatoes and liquid, sauce, and herbs. Stir and add franks. Bring to boil, reduce heat to medium-low and simmer 5 minutes.

Pour sauce over spaghetti, toss to combine. Serve with Parmesan cheese.

CHICKEN DIVAN

1 package (10 ounces) frozen broccoli, uncooked
2 packages fully cooked chicken breast tenders
½ teaspoon salt or to taste
1 can (10½ ounces) cream of celery soup, undiluted
1 cup shredded Cheddar cheese

This is an easy recipe for a kid when he or she is in charge of making dinner for the family.

♦ ♦ ♦

Preheat oven to 400°F. Place broccoli across bottom of baking dish; sprinkle with salt. Arrange chicken tenders in a layer on top of broccoli. Pour soup over chicken. Sprinkle with cheese. Bake, uncovered, 20–30 minutes or until broccoli is just tender.

CHICKEN PIZZAS

6 chicken drumsticks
1 can (10½ ounces) pizza sauce
1 cup grated Mozzarella cheese
1 package (10 ounces) refrigerated Parkerhouse rolls (unbaked)

If you want something unusual for the teenagers, this is it. It's tasty and not much trouble.

♦ ♦ ♦

Preheat oven to 350°F. Pour pizza sauce in small bowl. Dip chicken in sauce; place on baking sheet. Bake, uncovered, for 30 minutes. Separate rolls and roll out one at a time to 5-inch circle. Dip chicken in pizza sauce again and roll in cheese. Place on round of dough; pull dough around chicken and pinch together. (Leave bony end of drumstick uncovered for finger eating.) Bake, uncovered, approximately 30 minutes longer or until dough is brown.

COZY KITTEN WHISKERS

16 chicken franks
1 package (13¾ ounces) hot roll mix
Butter or margarine

A shortcut for this is to use bread dough that comes in tubes in the refrigerator section of your supermarket.

♦ ♦ ♦

Preheat oven to 375°F. Pierce each frank in several places with a fork. To make "whisker" on both ends of franks, lay frank on cutting board and make 4 lengthwise cuts 1½ inches from each end. Cut carefully, rotating frank, so that 8 "whiskers" result. Repeat with all franks.

Prepare hot roll mix according to package directions. Or use the prepared bread dough that comes in tubes at the supermarket. Divide into 16 equal portions and roll each on lightly floured surface to 3×3-inch square. Starting at a corner, roll dough around middle of each frank, leaving ends of franks exposed.

Place on buttered baking sheet, tucking dough tip under frank. Arrange "whiskers" fanned out. Brush with melted butter. Bake 12–15 minutes until golden brown. Serve with mustard and ketchup in squeeze containers so children can "draw" faces.

CRISPY PEANUT BUTTER CHICKEN

SERVES 4

1 egg
½ cup peanut butter
1 teaspoon salt or to taste
½ teaspoon ground pepper
¼ cup milk
¾ cup bread crumbs
1 chicken, cut in serving
    pieces
¼ cup oil

I once heard a professor at the University of California at Davis argue that wine was the greatest cultural achievement of mankind. He's wrong, of course. It's really peanut butter. Or at least a lot of my young friends seem to think so. Did you know that there are 540 peanuts in a 12-ounce jar of peanut butter?

The first time I made this recipe, I skipped the ¼ cup oil, just to see if I could save some calories. I don't recommend skipping any of the oil. It was too dry and crusty without it.

♦ ♦ ♦

Preheat oven to 350°F. In a mixing bowl beat egg and peanut butter together; add salt and pepper. Add milk gradually, stirring well to blend. Place bread crumbs on a sheet of wax paper. Dip chicken in peanut butter mixture and roll in crumbs. Place chicken, skin side up, in single layer in shallow baking pan. Pour oil over chicken. Bake, uncovered, until fork tender. Allow 25–35 minutes for wings, 30–40 minutes for breasts, 35–45 minutes for drumsticks, and 40–50 minutes for thighs.

CROISSANT DOGS

8 chicken franks
1 package (8 ounces)
  crescent roll dough
2 tablespoons Dijon mustard
2 slices Swiss cheese, 7 × 4
  inches
1 egg beaten with 1
  tablespoon water
1½ teaspoons poppy seeds
  (optional)

I don't think I can count the number of times my son Carlos made this as a teenager. He loved the idea of serving Frank's Franks to Frank.

◆ ◆ ◆

Preheat oven to 375°F. Pierce franks all over with tines of fork. Divide crescent rolls and place on lightly floured surface. Working with one piece of dough at a time, fold tips of long side of triangle in to meet at center Then stretch triangle lightly up toward point. Cut cheese slices in half, then diagonally to form four triangular pieces. Brush dough with thin layer of mustard, top with cheese, brush with mustard again. Roll franks in the dough, starting at the bottom and rolling toward the point. Place on ungreased baking sheet so they are not touching. Brush lightly with egg wash and sprinkle with poppy seeds. Place in the middle of the oven 15–20 minutes or until dough is golden brown.

CRUNCHY MINI DRUMSTICKS

½ cup whole wheat flour
2 eggs, beaten
1 teaspoon Worcestershire
  sauce (optional)
¾ teaspoon salt or to taste
¼ teaspoon ground pepper
2 cups whole wheat or
  seasoned bread crumbs
2 tablespoons unsweetened
  wheat germ (optional)
⅓ cup vegetable oil
9 chicken wings
Paprika

Young children love miniature versions of adult food, but if you're serving this recipe to them, you might want to leave out the Worcestershire sauce.

◆ ◆ ◆

Preheat oven to 400°F. Place flour on wax paper. In shallow bowl, beat eggs with Worcestershire sauce, salt, and pepper. On another sheet of wax paper, combine bread crumbs and wheat germ, if desired.

Pour oil into a shallow roasting pan or large shallow baking dish and place in oven. With sharp knife, divide wings into 3 pieces. Reserve bony wing tips to prepare chicken broth. Roll remaining "mini drumstick" pieces first in flour, then in egg mixture, and finally in bread crumbs. Sprinkle with paprika and arrange in preheated baking dish.

Bake 10 minutes, then turn with tongs and bake 10 minutes longer. Reduce heat to 350°F; cook 10–15 minutes longer until crisp and golden brown. Drain on paper towels and serve warm or at room temperature.

DELI DOGS

8 chicken franks
1 can (16 ounces) sauerkraut
3 cups prepared biscuit mix
1 tablespoon caraway seeds
½ cup water
2 tablespoons prepared
    mustard (optional)
Flour
1 egg beaten with 1
    tablespoon water

Some teenagers love sauerkraut; some most definitely don't. This is a great dish for those who do.

♦ ♦ ♦

Preheat oven to 375°F. Pierce franks all over with tines of fork. Drain sauerkraut, thoroughly by pressing between two stacked dinner plates, then chop coarsely. In a large mixing bowl, combine biscuit mix, sauerkraut, and 2 teaspoons of the caraway seeds. Gradually add water and mix vigorously until soft, slightly sticky dough forms. Divide dough in half. Roll each half on a well-floured surface into a 7 × 16-inch rectangle approximately ¼ inch thick. Cut each rectangle into four 7 × 4-inch pieces. Brush center of each piece of dough with a thin layer of mustard, if desired, then brush the outer ½ inch of the rectangle with egg wash. Roll each frank loosely in a piece of dough. Tuck outer ends under and place seam-side down on lightly greased baking sheet so they are not touching. Brush lightly with egg wash and sprinkle with remaining caraway seeds. Bake in middle of oven for 30 minutes or until crust is golden brown. Serve with more mustard and relish if desired.

JALAPEÑO BURGERS

1 package fresh ground
   chicken (about 1 pound)
⅔ cup shredded Monterey
   Jack cheese with jalapeño
   peppers
½ teaspoon cumin
1 teaspoon salt
8 taco shells
1 tomato, thinly sliced
1 avocado, thinly sliced
1 cup salsa

This is good for older teenagers. Young kids may find the flavors too harsh.

♦ ♦ ♦

Combine chicken with cheese and seasonings. Form into 8 burgers. Grill or broil on lightly oiled surface 5 to 6 inches from heat source, 4–5 minutes per side until burgers are cooked through. Serve in heated taco shells with slices of tomato and avocado. Top with salsa.

MAPLE CRUNCH CHICKEN

1 chicken, cut in serving
   pieces
1 egg
½ cup maple syrup
½ cup uncooked oatmeal
1 teaspoon salt or to taste
¼ teaspoon ground pepper
⅓ cup oil

Maple syrup with chicken may seem a little unusual to you—but it's really good. Frank liked it so much that I've served it to him several times, once substituting boneless skinless chicken breasts. If you want to make that substitution, shorten the cooking time to about 20 minutes, or until a meat thermometer registers 170–175°F. Also, use instant oatmeal and toast it for a couple of minutes in the oven first, to compensate for the shorter time in the oven.

♦ ♦ ♦

Preheat oven to 350°F. In a shallow bowl beat egg with maple syrup. Place oatmeal, salt, and pepper on a sheet of wax paper. Dip chicken pieces in egg mixture, then oatmeal mixture. Pour oil in shallow baking pan. Place chicken, skin side down, in oil in baking pan; turn chicken pieces to coat with oil; leave skin side up. Bake, uncovered, until fork tender. Allow 25–35 minutes for wings, 30–40 minutes for breasts, 35–45 minutes for drumsticks, and 40–50 minutes for thighs.

NACHO NIBBLES

8 chicken franks
1 package (16 ounces) tortilla chips
2 cups chili
2 scallions, thinly sliced
½ cup diced green pepper, or mild to hot green chili peppers
12 ounces grated Monterey Jack or Cheddar cheese

I've made this recipe scattering the cheese and franks and other ingredients over the tortilla chips haphazardly, and I've also made it so that each individual tortilla chip has its own slice of frank, its own chili, and its own pepper and cheese. The second way looks more impressive. The first way is a lot easier. My son Jose likes to serve this at parties with his college friends.

♦ ♦ ♦

Preheat oven to 350°F. Cut franks into thin slices. Place tortilla chips on large shallow baking pan and top with frank slices. Dab chili on top, then sprinkle with scallions, peppers, and cheese.

Bake nachos 15 minutes or until cheese bubbles.

NUGGETS IN A POCKET

1 package fully cooked chicken breast nuggets
4 mini pita pockets
Prepared Thousand Island dressing or Magic Mixture Sauce (recipe follows)
½ cup shredded lettuce
8 cherry tomatoes, halved

This is an easy sandwich for teenagers to make.

♦ ♦ ♦

Bake nuggets following package directions. Slit top of pita pockets. Spoon 1 to 2 teaspoons sauce into each pocket and fill with nuggets, lettuce, tomato, and additional sauce if desired. Serve with Rick Rack Carrot Sticks and Broccoli Trees (raw cut-up pieces of carrot and broccoli).

Magic Mixture Sauce:
In small bowl, combine ¼ cup mayonnaise, ¼ cup ketchup, 1 tablespoon prepared French dressing, ⅛ to ¼ teaspoon curry powder (optional), and 1 to 2 drops Tabasco (optional).

NUTTY BUDDY CHICKEN

1 egg
2 tablespoons milk
⅓ cup all-purpose flour
1 teaspoon salt or to taste
¼ teaspoon ground pepper
⅓ cup bran buds
¾ cup finely chopped salted
    peanuts
1 chicken, cut in serving
    pieces
½ cup melted butter or
    margarine

According to the Texas Peanut Producers' Board, Americans eat 4 million pounds of peanuts each day. Tell your kids that, as they help you chop the salted peanuts for this recipe.

◆ ◆ ◆

Preheat oven to 350°F. In a shallow bowl beat egg with milk. Place flour, salt, pepper, bran buds, and peanuts on a sheet of wax paper and mix together. Dip chicken pieces in egg mixture; then flour mixture. Place chicken in single layer, skin side up, in shallow baking pan. Pour melted butter or margarine over chicken. Bake, uncovered, until fork tender. Allow 25–35 minutes for wings, 30–40 minutes for breasts, 35–45 minutes for drumsticks, and 40–50 minutes for thighs. If you want to simplify this for kids, you can just cook all the pieces 45 minutes. The breasts won't be as tender as they could be, but they'll still be acceptable.

PICNIC PACKET CHICKEN

1 chicken, cut in serving
    pieces
4 small raw carrots, cut in
    sticks
4 raw potatoes, quartered
1 teaspoon salt or to taste
¼ teaspoon ground pepper
½ teaspoon dried oregano
4 teaspoons butter or
    margarine

The whole picnic meal is ready to serve when these come out of the oven. Children love the idea of having their own packets. You can also cook this on an outdoor grill.

◆ ◆ ◆

Preheat oven to 350°F. Tear off 4 pieces heavy duty aluminum foil, approximately 18 inches square. Place 1 or 2 pieces of chicken on each piece of foil. Put 1 carrot and 1 potato on each piece of foil. Sprinkle salt, pepper, and oregano over all. Add teaspoon of butter or margarine to each. Wrap tightly. Bake for approximately 40 minutes or until fork tender.

POTATO CHIP DRUMSTICKS

SERVES 4–6

6 chicken drumsticks
⅓ cup whole wheat flour
1 container (8 ounces) plain
  yogurt (1 cup)
Salt and ground pepper to
  taste
¼ teaspoon curry powder
  (optional)
1 package (7 ounces) no-salt
  potato chips, crushed

These are wonderful for school lunch boxes. Since they're stored in the freezer, you can take them out a meal at a time and they'll defrost in the child's lunch box in time to eat later in the day.

♦ ♦ ♦

Preheat oven to 375°F. Grease a baking sheet. Remove skin from drumsticks. In small bowl, combine yogurt, salt, pepper, and curry. On wax paper, place crushed potato chips. Roll drumsticks first in yogurt mixture and then in potato chips, pressing crumbs gently onto drumsticks to coat thoroughly. Arrange drumsticks on baking sheet and place in oven. Reduce heat to 350°F and bake 45–50 minutes until crisp and golden brown. Chill drumsticks, uncovered, on baking sheet. Then wrap individually in foil and freeze. If desired, allow extra foil at ends of package and twist to form a chicken.

To pack for lunch: Freeze individual containers of juice overnight. Place frozen juice in lunch bag with well-chilled or frozen foil-wrapped drumsticks and fresh peas and cherry tomatoes in plastic bag. Frozen juice will keep other foods chilled and by lunchtime will be a "fruit slush" dessert.

Variation: Instead of potato chips, use crushed salt-free tortilla chips and substitute chili powder for curry.

PUNK PIZZA ROLLS

SERVES 8

8 chicken franks
1 cup tomato sauce or pizza
  sauce
2 tablespoons finely chopped
  onion
½ teaspoon dried oregano
8 flour tortillas
1½ cups shredded Mozzarella
  cheese

Tell your kids as they're eating this, "If you grew as fast as a chicken, you would have weighed 349 pounds by the time you were 2 months old!"

♦ ♦ ♦

Preheat oven to 350°F. Pierce each frank in several places with a fork. In a small bowl combine tomato sauce, onion, and oregano; spread equal amounts over each tortilla. Place one frank in center of each tortilla and roll up. Place rolls about 1 inch apart in shallow baking dish and sprinkle each with an equal amount of cheese. Bake about 20 minutes or until cheese melts and bubbles.

RAMAKI WRAPS

MAKES 64, SERVES 16–18

8 chicken franks
1 can (8 ounces) water
   chestnuts, drained
32 strips bacon

This is a good appetizer for a teenage party. I've served it to kids who would never go for the chicken livers called for in the original ramaki recipe. They've loved this version, made with cut-up franks.

♦ ♦ ♦

Preheat oven to 400°F. Cut each frank into 8 slices. Slice water chestnuts thinly. Halve bacon slices crosswise.

   For each ramaki, wrap frank slice and water chestnut slice with bacon; secure with toothpick. Place ramakis on a rack over large baking pan and bake 15 minutes or until bacon is crisp.

RED-EYE EGGROLLS

MAKES 16, SERVES 8

8 chicken franks
2 tablespoons vegetable oil
1 can (16 ounces) bean
   sprouts, drained
2 cups shredded Chinese
   cabbage or iceberg lettuce
1 tablespoon soy sauce
¼ cup chicken broth
16 square eggroll wrappers
   (You might find them in
   the produce section of
   your supermarket, and
   they are available in
   Oriental food shops.)
1 egg, beaten
Vegetable oil for deep frying

These take some work, but they've been a great success with both kids and adults. I've served them at parties where both have been present and the "egg rolls" vanished just about as fast as I could make them.

♦ ♦ ♦

Halve franks crosswise, set aside. In large skillet, over medium-high heat, heat oil; add vegetables, toss, and cook 2 minutes. Add soy sauce and broth. Reduce heat to medium-low and simmer, covered, 5 minutes; drain well in colander.

   Place eggroll wrapper on work surface with a corner pointing toward you; brush each corner with egg. Place 2 rounded tablespoons of vegetable mixture in center, then top with frank piece horizontally. Fold bottom corner over frank and filling, then fold right and left corners over and roll up to complete.

In a wok, fryer, or heavy skillet, heat 2 inches oil to 370°F or until a small cube of bread sizzles when placed in oil. Fry 3 to 4 eggrolls at a time until crisp all over. Drain well on paper towels.

Before serving, reheat on shallow baking pan in preheated 350°F oven 10–12 minutes. (I don't recommend reheating them in the microwave. They'll come out soggy instead of crisp.)

SPICED CREAMED CONE CHICKEN

SERVES 4

1 teaspoon salt or to taste
¼ teaspoon ground pepper
½ cup sour cream
1 tablespoon finely chopped onion
½ teaspoon ground allspice
8 ice cream cones, crushed (I use the sugar cones.)
1 chicken, cut in serving pieces
2 tablespoons shortening

This is my first choice for when our twelve grandchildren are coming. The ice cream–cone flavor is so subtle that no one has yet been able to identify it without being told. Still, the flavor is delicious.

♦ ♦ ♦

Preheat oven to 350°F. In a shallow bowl combine sour cream, salt, pepper, onion, and allspice. Place cone crumbs on a sheet of wax paper. Dip chicken in sour cream mixture; then in cone crumbs. Melt shortening in shallow baking pan; place chicken in single layer, skin side up, in pan. Bake, uncovered, until fork tender. Allow 25–35 minutes for wings, 30–40 minutes for breasts, 35–45 minutes for drumsticks, and 40–50 minutes for thighs.

TACO DOGS

SERVES 6–8

8 chicken franks
8 taco shells
1 can (15 ounces) chili with beans
1 cup shredded Monterey Jack or cheddar cheese
1 cup shredded lettuce
½ cup diced tomato

Our neighbors south of the border might be surprised at this version of their tacos, but it's quick and good.

♦ ♦ ♦

Preheat oven to 350°F. Split franks in half lengthwise and grill or fry briefly. Place franks in taco shells and top each with 2 tablespoons chili and 1 tablespoon cheese. Place tacos on baking sheet and bake 15 minutes, or until chili is hot and cheese is melted. Top with taco sauce, lettuce, tomato, and remaining cheese. Serve immediately.

SPICY SOUTHWESTERN CASSEROLE

SERVES 6–8

8 chicken franks
2 cans (15 ounces) chili
1 cup yellow cornmeal
2 teaspoons baking powder
1 teaspoon salt or to taste
2 eggs
⅔ cup melted butter or
    margarine
1 cup sour cream
1 can (16 ounces) niblets-
    style corn, drained
¼ pound grated Monterey
    Jack or Cheddar cheese
1 can (4 ounces) chopped,
    mild green chilies, drained

Your teenage cook could make this for the family dinner one night this week.

♦ ♦ ♦

Preheat oven to 375°F. Cut franks in half lengthwise. Place chili in bottom of a buttered 7 × 14 × 2-inch baking dish. Arrange franks, cut side down, on top of chili. In medium-size mixing bowl, mix dry ingredients. Add eggs, butter, and sour cream and blend thoroughly. Fold in corn. Sprinkle half of the cheese and green chilies over the layer of franks. Top with half of the corn mixture. Sprinkle with remaining cheese and chilies and finish with a layer of corn mixture. Smooth the top with a spatula. Bake in the middle of oven 35–40 minutes, or until top is lightly browned and toothpick inserted in corn layers comes out clean.

SWEET AND SOUR CHICKEN

SERVES 4

1 chicken, cut in serving
    pieces
1 bottle (8 ounces) Russian
    salad dressing
1 envelope (1⅜ ounces) dry
    onion soup mix
1 jar (10 ounces) apricot
    preserves

This is one of the National Chicken Cooking Contest winners, and it's easy enough for the beginning cook. The original recipe called for adding a teaspoon of salt to the sweet and sour mixture, but I found that the salt in the salad dressing and the onion soup mix was enough. If your kids like foods salty, they may want to sprinkle more on at the end.

♦ ♦ ♦

Preheat oven to 350°F. Place chicken, skin side up, in single layer in large shallow baking dish. In a large measuring cup combine remaining ingredients and pour over chicken. Bake, uncovered, until fork tender. Allow 25–35 minutes for wings, 30–40 minutes for breasts, 35–45 minutes for drumsticks, and 40–50 minutes for thighs.

TATER FRANKS

8 chicken franks
3 tablespoons melted butter
    or margarine, divided
1½ tablespoons milk
1 teaspoon salt or to taste
ground pepper to taste
3 cups cooked riced potatoes
    or very firm prepared
    instant mashed potatoes
2 egg yolks
2 egg whites, lightly beaten
    with 1 tablespoon water
2½ cups cornflake crumbs

This is inexpensive and easy to like.

♦ ♦ ♦

Preheat oven to 375°F. Pierce franks all over with a fork. Pour half of butter into a mixing bowl. Add milk, salt, and pepper, then add riced potatoes and beaten egg yolks. (If using instant mashed potatoes, omit milk.) Beat thoroughly with wooden spoon until well blended; chill until firm enough to handle. Divide potato mixture into eight parts. using your hands, form an even layer of potato (about ½-inch thick) around each frank. If mixture is sticky, flour hands lightly. Roll first in cornflake crumbs, then in egg white and water mixture, and again in crumbs. Place tater franks on buttered baking sheet so they are not touching, and drizzle with remaining melted butter. Bake in the middle of the oven 30 minutes or until crisp and golden brown. Serve immediately.

TEAM-SPIRIT HEROS

8 chicken franks
8 hero rolls
4 tablespoons vegetable oil
1 onion, thinly sliced
2 green peppers, cut into thin
    strips
1½ cups tomato sauce
1 tablespoon fresh, minced
    basil or 1 teaspoon dried
1 tablespoon minced fresh
    parsley
12 slices Provolone cheese,
    cut into ½-inch strips.

Your teenagers can make this one. If they don't like peppers or onions, it's fine to skip them.

♦ ♦ ♦

Pierce each frank in several places with a fork. Cut rolls lengthwise, leaving the 2 halves attached. In a large skillet over medium-low heat, heat oil. Add onions and peppers and cook 10 minutes, stirring often. Add sauce and herbs; stir and simmer 5 minutes. Preheat oven to 350°F. Place 1 frank in each roll, spoon equal amounts of sauce mixture over franks. Close roll and wrap securely in foil.

Heat 20 minutes, turning packages after 10 minutes.

5

CHICKEN FOR BARBECUING

America's Love Affair with an Old Flame Is Heating Up!

Are you about to barbecue something? Then you're participating in an ancient tradition. Barbecuing is actually man's oldest form of cooking; the outdoors was man's first kitchen and an open fire his first stove. The earliest cooks simply laid their food on smoldering embers or impaled it on sticks held over a fire or dying coals.

It wasn't until the 1950s, however, that backyard barbecuing as we know it began to catch on. It may surprise you, but auto mogul Henry Ford played a major role in this—and it had nothing to do with his automobiles. In the late 1920s, it was Ford who had the idea of grinding charcoal, combining it with a starch, and re-forming it into uniform pillow-shaped briquets. These charcoal briquets burned more consis-

- Start with a clean grill. Removing old ashes assures good air circulation, and cleaning away any cooked-on bits of food results in better flavor and quality.
- Be sure to wash everything after handling raw meat. Don't use the same plate for the cooked meat that you used for the uncooked meat unless you've washed it in between.
- Coat grate with vegetable cooking spray, or brush with cooking oil to prevent food from sticking.
- If the basting sauce contains oil, however, do not grease the grill; too much oil causes flare-ups.
- Prepare the fire a half hour or more before grilling. For quick lighting, use a chimney starter with crumpled newspaper in the bottom and briquets or charcoal above. Or stack the charcoal in a pyramid shape and light with a liquid or electric starter, following the manufacturer's directions. Charcoal is ready for cooking when it's 80 percent ashy gray in daylight, glowing red at night. This usually takes 25–30 minutes.
- Toss a handful of aromatic wood chips such as mesquite, hickory, alder, or fruitwood chips over the coals once they're fully lit. They'll create a whole new dimension of flavor without adding any extra calories.
- Check the temperature of the fire before cooking food to prevent over- or under-cooking. For most of the recipes in this chapter, the fire should be medium-hot with a single, even layer of coals lightly covered with gray ash. It's relatively simple to judge the temperature of a charcoal fire. To do this, hold your hand, palm side down, at cooking height:

    HOT—You can hold your hand over the coals for only 2 seconds.
    MEDIUM-HOT—You can hold your hand over the coals 3–4 seconds.
    MEDIUM—You can hold your hand over the coals 4–5 seconds.

- Be patient. If the fire hasn't cooled down adequately, do not be tempted to put your chicken on to cook—unless you like "blackened bird" a lot more than I do.
- If you're dieting and want to remove the chicken's skin, do so after cooking, not before. Without some kind of covering, the chicken will dry out and toughen before it finishes cooking.
- Turn chicken frequently, about every 5 minutes to insure even doneness and to prevent blistering.
- If flare-ups occur, remove the food for a few moments and sprinkle water lightly over the flames, or smother them by covering the grill. A friend of mine who works for a volunteer fire department keeps a laundry squirt bottle handy for flare-ups.

- To increase the heat, you can push coals together, add more coals, lower the grilling surface, or fan the fire and tap the ashes from the coals.
- To decrease heat, raise the cooking grid or sprinkle coals with a little water.
- Cook white-meat poultry until juices run clear and the meat reaches an internal temperature of 170–175°F and dark meat to 180–185°F on a meat thermometer.
- Grill smaller poultry parts and Cornish game hens directly over a single layer of coals on an open grill or hibachi.
- Grill whole birds and larger parts using this indirect method in a covered grill. Place a drip pan directly on top of the coals beneath the grate and the bird; the pan should be slightly larger than the bird. Fill the pan halfway with water, and surround it with a double layer of coals to provide longer, slower, ovenlike cooking. Add extra coals to the outer edge of the fire as needed to extend grilling.
- To reduce the chance of overbrowning, apply tomato-based sauces or those containing sugar or other sweeteners only during the last 20–30 minutes of grilling.
- To make breast quarters grill more quickly and evenly, cut through the wing joint to break it and bring the wing closer to the grill.
- Chicken should be well-done. If you're in a hurry, cook your chicken partially in the microwave and then finish it on the grill.
- The basic guidelines for timing chicken on the grill are:
  - PARTS—Cook dark meat 30 minutes, white meat 15 minutes, basting and turning every 5 or so minutes.
  - HALVES—First, grill skin side down 5 minutes, then cook covered, skin side up, 35–40 minutes.
  - WINGS—10 minutes per side.
  - WHOLE—(About 3-1/2 pounds) 1-1/4–1-1/2 hours in a covered grill, 1½–2 hours on rotisserie.
- Use tongs rather than a fork to turn food gently without losing juices.
- If you plan to use marinade as a sauce to be served with chicken during the meal, be sure to cook it before using. You want to avoid the cross-contamination that can come from contact with the uncooked chicken. Temperatures over 140°F will destroy any microbes.

tently and more evenly than randomly sized and shaped lumps of charcoal.

People began using charcoal briquets for industrial purposes. In the 1950s, when backyard grills became widely available, outdoor cooking really began to take off. Today, according to a Barbecue Industry Association survey, seven out of ten American households own a barbecue grill, and we use them a total of about 1.5 billion times a year.

Frank and I also barbecue but it took some learning on my part. In spite of being someone who loves to cook, before marrying Frank, I'd never barbecued. I'd never even thought to buy an outdoor grill.

What I'd been missing! Frank does own a barbecue, a nice handsome one that can manage chickenburgers for our combined eighteen children and grandchildren all at once. I love it, because we can all be outdoors, playing volleyball or watching the young ones, with their arsenal of squirt guns, as they gang up on Frank—and the beauty of it all is that no one has to miss a moment of the fun by having to go into the kitchen to fuss with dinner.

If you've been barbecuing for years, skip ahead to the recipes. But if you're like me and still new at it, here are some tips that can help you get uniformly good results. The tips come from the Perdue food scientists and home economists, from Cooperative Extension and from the Barbecue Industry Association.

MARINADES AND BASTES

Basting has no tenderizing qualities, but it does add a special flavor to poultry. Marinating for half an hour or more will enhance both flavor and tenderness.

BEER MARINADE

MAKES ABOUT 2 CUPS

3 tablespoons spicy brown
    mustard
3 tablespoons brown sugar
3 tablespoons vegetable oil
1 tablespoon Worcestershire
    sauce
1 teaspoon Tabasco
1 teaspoon salt or to taste
½ teaspoon ground pepper.
1 can (12 ounces) beer
1 extra-large onion, peeled
    and sliced into rings

In large, shallow baking dish, combine first 7 ingredients; stir in beer. Add onion and 4–6 pounds chicken to marinade. Cover and refrigerate 1 hour or longer, turning occasionally. To grill, drain poultry and use marinade for basting. Onion rings may be grilled 2–3 minutes per side and served with poultry.

CHUTNEY BARBECUE SAUCE

1 jar (8½ ounces) mango
   chutney
⅓ cup wine vinegar
1 tablespoon spicy brown
   mustard
1 tablespoon brown sugar
¼ teaspoon Cayenne pepper

You'll get a deeply browned chicken with this recipe.

♦ ♦ ♦

In small bowl, combine all ingredients. Use as basting sauce for grilling 4–5 pounds of chicken during last 10–15 minutes cooking. Lightly oil poultry before cooking, and turn often to avoid burning.

FIREHOUSE BARBECUE SAUCE

1 egg
1 cup vegetable oil
1 cup cider vinegar
3 tablespoons salt or to taste
1 tablespoon poultry
   seasoning
½ teaspoon ground pepper

This barbecue recipe was developed by Robert Baker of Cornell University in 1946, then published by New York's state Extension Service with directions for quantity grilling. Dr. Baker's updated version of the recipe is somewhat lower in salt. You can refrigerate the extra sauce for several weeks.

♦ ♦ ♦

In blender or medium-size bowl, blend or beat egg. Add oil and beat again. Stir in remaining ingredients. Use as a basting sauce for grilling 8–10 pounds of chicken, basting frequently. For milder, less salty flavor, baste less often.

Chicken-in-Every-Pot Soup

Chapter 1: Chicken for Every Day
page 17

Drumsticks Little Italy Style

Chapter 2: Chicken for the Microwave
page 67

Greek Lemon Chicken

Chapter 3: Chicken for Dieters
page 85

Potato Chip Drumsticks

Chapter 4: Chicken for Children
page 113

Hawaiian Glazed Wings

Chapter 5: Chicken for Barbecuing
page 133

Citrus Chicken Bouquet

Chapter 8: Chicken for Holidays
page 193

Stuffed Chicken Jardiniere

Chapter 9: Chicken for Very
Important Occasions
page 227

Chicken Pot Pies Rediscovered (from top):
Fancy Chicken Puff Pie *(page 244)*;
Cajun Pie *(page 242)*;
Empanada Pie *(page 243)*;
Chicken Hash Pie *(page 241)*

Chapter 10: Chicken for Planovers

ORIENTAL MARINADE

¾ cup pineapple juice
¼ cup soy sauce
3 tablespoons peanut or vegetable oil
2 tablespoons minced fresh ginger
1 tablespoon brown sugar
2–3 garlic cloves, minced
½ teaspoon crushed red pepper (optional)
½ teaspoon salt or to taste

If you're using this marinade for kebobs, avoid a sticky cleanup by using disposable wooden skewers; to prevent burning, soak skewers in water for 30 minutes before use.

♦ ♦ ♦

In wide, shallow bowl, combine all ingredients. Add 3–4 pounds chicken to marinade; cover and refrigerate 1 hour or longer, turning occasionally. To grill, drain poultry and use marinade for basting.

TRADITIONAL BARBECUE SAUCE

1 cup chili sauce
½ cup brown sugar
¼ cup vegetable oil
2 tablespoons cider vinegar
2 tablespoons soy sauce
1 tablespoon spicy brown mustard
1½ teaspoons minced fresh oregano, or ½ teaspoon dried
1–1½ teaspoons liquid smoke (optional, but I recommend it, if you can find it)

Barbecue sauces differ from marinades in how they are used. A marinade is used to flavor meat before cooking and for basting during grilling. Barbecue sauces are used for basting during cooking and are frequently re-cooked and later served as a sauce at the table.

♦ ♦ ♦

In small bowl, combine all ingredients. Use as basting sauce for grilling 4–5 pounds chicken during last 10–15 minutes of cooking. Turn poultry often to avoid scorching.

WINE AND GARLIC MARINADE

1 cup dry white wine
¼ cup olive oil
6–8 garlic cloves, minced
3 lemon slices
1 tablespoon minced, fresh
    thyme or 1 teaspoon dried
1 tablespoon minced, fresh
    basil, or 1 teaspoon dried
1 teaspoon salt or to taste
1 bay leaf (optional)
½ teaspoon ground pepper

In wide, shallow bowl, combine all ingredients. Add 3–4 pounds chicken to marinade; cover and refrigerate 1 hour or longer, turning occasionally. Grill poultry and use marinade for basting.

BEER-BE-CUED CHICKEN

1 can (12 ounces) beer
1 tablespoon dark molasses
1 tablespoon onion juice
2 tablespoons lemon juice
½ cup ketchup
1 teaspoon salt or to taste
1 chicken, cut in half
    lengthwise

This is one of the National Chicken Cooking Contest winners. It's been adapted slightly, and this version has the reputation of being particularly popular with men.

♦ ♦ ♦

In a shallow dish combine beer, molasses, onion juice, lemon juice, ketchup, and salt. Add chicken, cover, and marinate 3 hours or longer, refrigerated. Grill chicken 5 to 6 inches above medium-hot coals 35–45 minutes or until cooked through. Turn and baste with marinade every 10–15 minutes.

BONELESS BREASTS TANDOORI

SERVES 4–6

8 boneless, skinless chicken
  breast halves
1 cup plain yogurt
½ cup butter or margarine
¼ cup fresh lemon juice
2 large cloves garlic, minced
1 teaspoon cinnamon
1 teaspoon ground cumin
1 teaspoon ground ginger
1 teaspoon turmeric
2 teaspoons ground coriander
Salt and ground pepper to
  taste
Lemon wedges for garnish
½ cup melted butter

In many eastern countries, yogurt is a favorite ingredient for marinades. One of the most famous of these recipes is India's Tandoori Chicken, which takes its name from the clay stove called a tandor in which it is cooked.

♦ ♦ ♦

In large bowl combine yogurt, butter, lemon juice, garlic, and spices. Place chicken breasts in mixture and turn to coat well. Cover and marinate for 3 hours or longer, refrigerated. Remove chicken from marinade and grill 5 to 6 inches above medium-hot coals 7–15 minutes. Turn and baste two or three times with marinade. Serve with lemon wedges.

BRANDY-ORANGE BARBECUED CORNISH

SERVES 2–4

2 fresh Cornish hens
1 tablespoon vegetable oil
2 tablespoons fresh lemon
  juice, divided
½ teaspoon ground ginger,
  divided
Salt and ground pepper to
  taste
¼ cup orange marmalade
1 tablespoon brandy

When choosing the brandy for this, I'd recommend a California brandy in preference to an imported one. The California ones tend to be lighter and fruitier and more appropriate for this recipe.

♦ ♦ ♦

With kitchen string, tie drumsticks together. Rub hens with oil and 1 tablespoon lemon juice; sprinkle with ¼ teaspoon ginger, salt, and pepper. In small bowl, combine marmalade, brandy, remaining lemon juice and ginger; set aside. Place hens on grill breast side up. Grill, covered, 5 to 6 inches above medium-hot coals 45–60 minutes. After 40 minutes, brush hens with brandy-orange sauce. Turn if bottom begins to char. Cook, basting three to four times, until juices run clear with no hint of pink when thigh is pierced.

CHICK KEBOBS

6 boneless, skinless chicken
  breast halves
¼ pound small, fresh
  mushrooms
1 can (7½ ounces) whole
  white onions
1 green pepper, cut in 1-inch
  squares

Marinade:
¼ cup oil
2 tablespoons vinegar
1 can (8 ounces) crushed
  pineapple
1 cup ketchup
2 tablespoons soy sauce
1 teaspoon curry powder
¾ teaspoon minced fresh
  rosemary or ¼ teaspoon
  dried
2 tablespoons brown sugar
1½ teaspoons salt or to taste
2 teaspoons ground pepper
1 tablespoon fresh lemon
  juice
1 tablespoon cornstarch
½ cup water

These chick kebobs go wonderfully with rice. As someone who grows rice commercially, it hurts me to say this, but for this recipe, I recommend a kind of rice I don't grow, the long-grain kind that cooks up fluffy with each grain separate. (I grow short- or medium-grain rice, which is always sticky, no matter how you cook it.)

◆ ◆ ◆

Cut chicken breasts into 1-inch cubes. Alternate chicken on skewers with mushrooms, onions, and green pepper, then lay flat in shallow baking dish. Combine marinade ingredients except flour and water. Pour marinade over skewers. Cover and store in refrigerator 3–4 hours or overnight. Baste kebobs with marinade and grill 4 to 5 inches above medium-hot coals 6–8 minutes, turning occasionally until chicken is lightly browned and cooked through. In a small bowl dissolve cornstarch in water. Place remaining marinade in a small saucepan. Stir in cornstarch and heat, stirring until sauce is slightly thickened. Serve sauce over kebobs and rice.

CHICKEN ALMONDINE

8 boneless, skinless chicken
  breast halves
1½ teaspoons salt or to taste
½ teaspoon paprika
6 tablespoons sesame seeds
8 tablespoons butter or
  margarine, melted
8 tablespoons sliced almonds
8 tablespoons dry vermouth
Aluminum foil

You can save money buying sesame seeds in bulk, either from your supermarket or health food store. Keep sesame seeds refrigerated or frozen if you won't be using them within a week or so. They have a limited shelf life and at room temperature, they can become rancid quickly.

◆ ◆ ◆

Season chicken with salt and paprika; then roll in sesame seeds. Place each chicken piece in center of piece of foil; fold sides up to vertical position to hold liquids. Place 1 tablespoon butter, 1 tablespoon almonds and 1 tablespoon vermouth on each chicken piece. Close foil over chicken and seal well. Place packets on grill 5 to 6 inches above hot coals. Cook 15–20 minutes, turning two or three times until chicken is fork tender.

CHICKEN TARRAGON

SERVES 4

1 chicken, quartered
½ cup fresh lime juice
¼ cup vegetable oil
½ cup chopped onion
⅓ cup chopped fresh tarragon
    or 2 tablespoons dried
Salt and ground pepper to
    taste

To make breast quarters grill more quickly and evenly, remember to cut through the wing joint to break it and bring the wing closer to the grill.

◆ ◆ ◆

Working from the cut side of breast and thigh quarters, carefully use fingers to separate skin from flesh and form a "pocket." In large bowl, combine lime juice and remaining ingredients. Place chicken in marinade and spoon some marinade between skin and flesh. Cover and refrigerate 1 hour or longer. Drain chicken, reserving marinade. Grill chicken, uncovered, 5 to 6 inches above medium-hot coals 35–45 minutes or until cooked through, turning and basting frequently with marinade.

CHUTNEY BURGERS

SERVES 4–6

1 package fresh ground
    chicken (about 1 pound)
2 tablespoons chutney
1 tablespoon fresh lemon
    juice
¼ cup chopped scallion
1 teaspoon salt
6 individual pita pockets

Try this Yogurt Sauce along with the Chutney Burgers. In a small bowl combine ½ cup yogurt, 2 tablespoons chopped scallions, 2 teaspoons lemon juice, ½ teaspoon sugar, ¼ teaspoon salt and a dash of Cayenne pepper.

◆ ◆ ◆

In a mixing bowl, combine chicken and remaining seasonings. Form into 4 to 6 burgers. Grill on lightly oiled surface, 5 to 6 inches above medium-hot coals, 5–6 minutes per side, or until burgers are cooked through. Serve in lightly toasted pita pockets topped with Yogurt Sauce.

CONFETTI BURGERS

SERVES 4–6

1 package fresh ground
  chicken (about 1 pound)
¼ cup oat bran or bread
  crumbs
¼ cup finely chopped onion
¼ cup diced tomato
¼ cup finely chopped carrot
¼ cup finely chopped celery
¼ cup finely chopped green
  pepper
1 tablespoon Worcestershire
  sauce
1 tablespoon fresh lemon
  juice
1 teaspoon salt
½ teaspoon dried thyme
¼ teaspoon ground black
  pepper
6 Kaiser rolls

A neat accompaniment for Confetti Burgers is halved Kaiser rolls, brushed with olive oil flavored with garlic. Place on outer edges of grill a few minutes until lightly toasted.

◆ ◆ ◆

In a mixing bowl combine chicken with vegetables and seasonings. Form into 6 burgers. Grill on lightly oiled surface 5 to 6 inches above medium-hot coals, 4–6 minutes per side or until burgers are cooked through. Serve on toasted Kaiser rolls.

CHINESE GRILLED DRUMSTICKS

SERVES 2–4

5 roaster drumsticks
Salt and ground pepper to
  taste
¼ cup hoisin sauce
2 tablespoons dry sherry
2 tablespoons cider vinegar
2 tablespoons honey
1 teaspoon minced fresh
  ginger
1 clove garlic, minced

Hoisin sauce is available in Chinese groceries. It's slightly sweet, and thick, somewhat like ketchup.

◆ ◆ ◆

Season chicken to taste with salt and pepper. In a shallow bowl combine remaining ingredients. Roll drumsticks in sauce, reserving excess. Wrap drumsticks individually in aluminum foil, adding a spoonful of sauce to each package. Grill 6 to 8 inches from hot coals, or bake 1 hour at 375°F, turning once. Unwrap drumsticks and place on grill. Pour drippings from foil packages and remaining sauce into a small saucepan and heat. Grill drumsticks turning and basting frequently with sauce for additional 15 minutes or until fork tender.

FIRE-EATERS' CHICKEN

SERVES 4

4 boneless, skinless chicken breast halves
3 tablespoons fresh lemon juice
2 tablespoons olive oil
2 garlic cloves, minced
1 teaspoon paprika
½–1 teaspoon crushed red pepper or to taste
½ teaspoon salt or to taste
Lemon wedges (optional)

This recipe gets its name from the rather large quantity of red pepper. If children and other non–fire-eaters will be eating this, you will probably want to decrease the amount of red pepper substantially.

◆ ◆ ◆

In shallow dish, combine lemon juice, olive oil, garlic, paprika, pepper, and salt. Add chicken to marinade, turning to coat both sides. Cover and refrigerate 1 hour or longer.

Drain chicken, reserving marinade. Grill chicken breasts, uncovered, 5 to 6 inches above medium-hot coals 5–8 minutes on each side until fork tender, basting occasionally with marinade. To serve, garnish with lemon wedges.

GAME HENS PESTO

SERVES 4

2 fresh Cornish game hens
¼ cup olive or salad oil
¼ cup minced fresh basil or 1 tablespoon dried basil
¼ cup minced fresh parsley
2 tablespoons grated Parmesan cheese
1 small clove garlic, minced
½ teaspoon salt or to taste
1 can (8 ounces) minced clams, drained
2 tablespoons dry white wine (optional)

Pesto is a sauce made with basil, parsley, garlic, olive oil, and Parmesan cheese. If you're looking for a shortcut, you might be able to find ready-made Pesto in your supermarket.

◆ ◆ ◆

Halve hens lengthwise and remove backbones. Place a half on each of four 14-inch squares of heavy-duty aluminum foil. Turn up edges of foil. In bowl, blend oil, basil, parsley, cheese, garlic, and salt. Add clams and wine. Divide among packets, spooning over hens. Bring two opposite sides of foil together and close packets securely using several folds and turning up ends to seal. Cook 4 to 6 inches above hot coals, 30–40 minutes, until cooked through, turning packets twice. Packets may also be baked at 400°F for about 30 minutes.

GRILLED BREAST STEAK SALAD

1 roaster boneless breast
3 tablespoons butter or
  margarine, melted
1½ teaspoons Worcestershire
  sauce
¼ teaspoon paprika
Salt and ground pepper to
  taste
¼ cup red wine vinegar
2 teaspoons Dijon mustard
¾ cup olive or vegetable oil
3 tablespoons minced red
  onion
3 cups spinach leaves, sliced
  into ½-inch strips
3 cups thinly sliced red
  cabbage

*U*se the leftovers in a sandwich.

◆ ◆ ◆

Flatten breast halves slightly between sheets of plastic wrap. Combine butter, Worcestershire sauce, paprika, salt, and pepper. Brush sauce liberally over chicken. Grill 5 to 6 inches above medium-hot coals 8–10 minutes on each side or until cooked through. Remove and slice thinly on the diagonal. Combine vinegar and mustard in a small bowl. Slowly whisk in oil. Add red onion and season with salt and pepper. Place 2 cups spinach and 2 cups cabbage in a salad bowl. Arrange half of the chicken slices over top and spoon half of the dressing over all.

GRILLED CORNISH WITH VEGETABLES

2 fresh Cornish game hens
Salt and ground pepper to
  taste
2 tablespoons butter or
  margarine
1 medium carrot, cut into
  thin strips
1 small leek, cut into thin
  strips
1 rib celery, cut into thin
  strips
¼ cup apple juice
1 tablespoon minced fresh
  parsley

*Y*ou can skip tying the hen's legs together—they just won't hold their shape as well and will look more relaxed. The advantage is that you may feel more relaxed.

◆ ◆ ◆

Season hens inside and out with salt and pepper. Tie legs together and fold wings back. Place each hen on an 18-inch square of heavy-duty aluminum foil. Dot with butter. Divide vegetables and apple juice among foil pieces. Fold edges up and seal tightly. Place packets on grill 5 to 6 inches above hot coals. Cook 50–70 minutes, turning two or three times until hens are cooked through. Or bake 375°F 1 hour or until juices run clear with no hint of pink when thigh is pierced. Open foil packages carefully and sprinkle with parsley.

GRILLED CUTLETS COSTA DEL SOL

4 roaster boneless thigh cutlets
⅓ cup dry sherry
1 teaspoon paprika
1 teaspoon ground cumin
1 teaspoon sugar
1 teaspoon white vinegar
Salt and ground pepper to taste
1 clove garlic, minced

This is one of Perdue's most popular and most requested recipes.

♦ ♦ ♦

Place cutlets between sheets of plastic wrap and pound to ½-inch thickness. In a shallow dish combine remaining ingredients. Add chicken and marinate for 1 hour or longer, refrigerated. Grill chicken 4 to 6 inches above medium-hot coals 3–4 minutes on each side or until cooked through. Turn and baste with glaze two or three times.

GRILLED CUTLETS GREEK STYLE WITH OLIVE OIL

4 roaster boneless thigh cutlets
2 cloves garlic, minced
2 tablespoons fresh lemon juice, divided
6 tablespoons olive oil, divided
⅓ cup plain yogurt
1 teaspoon dried oregano
Salt and ground pepper to taste
4 ripe tomatoes, cut into wedges (3 cups)
2 cucumbers, peeled, halved, and cut into ½-inch slices (¾ cup)
1 red onion, sliced
½ cup pitted ripe olives
Salt and ground pepper to taste
2 tablespoons minced, fresh parsley or mint

Olive growers like to point out that the lowest mortality rates due to cardiovascular disease are found on the Greek island of Crete where olive oil consumption is highest.

♦ ♦ ♦

Place cutlets between two sheets of plastic wrap and pound to ¼-inch thickness. In a shallow dish whisk together garlic, 1 tablespoon lemon juice, 2 tablespoons olive oil, yogurt, oregano, salt, and pepper. Add cutlets and turn to coat with marinade. Cover and marinate for 3 hours or longer, refrigerated grill cutlets 4 to 6 inches above medium-hot coals 3–4 minutes on each side or until cooked through.

In a large bowl, combine tomatoes, cucumbers, red onion, black olives, remaining lemon juice, 4 tablespoons olive oil, and salt and pepper to taste. Sprinkle with parsley or mint before serving. Cutlets may be served hot with salad as a side dish or served cold, sliced and added to salad.

GRILLED DRUMSTICKS WITH FRUIT MUSTARD

5 roaster drumsticks
Salt and ground pepper to
    taste
8 ripe apricots, or 1 can (16
    ounces) drained and
    coarsely chopped
1 tablespoon fresh lemon
    juice
¼ cup Dijon mustard
3 tablespoons dark brown
    sugar
¼ cup brandy
1 teaspoon Worcestershire
    sauce

Do you remember in the early 1980s a fast food chain had a popular advertising campaign based on the slogan, "Where's the beef?" One of my favorite Perdue ads is a full-page ad showing Frank holding a drumstick with a big bite missing. He's looking out at you, his eyebrows raised quizzically as he asks, "Who cares where the beef is?"

This recipe will make you not care.

♦ ♦ ♦

Season drumsticks with salt and pepper. Toss apricots with lemon; add remaining ingredients and toss. Wrap drumsticks individually with aluminum foil, adding a spoonful of sauce to each package. Grill 5 to 6 inches above hot coals 20–30 minutes, turning once. Unwrap drumsticks and place on grill. Add drippings from foil packages to remaining sauce. Grill drumsticks turning and basting frequently with sauce for 15 minutes or until cooked through.

GYPSY BURGERS

1 package fresh ground
    chicken
¾ cup chopped scallion,
    divided
½ cup sour cream, divided
2 teaspoons paprika
1 teaspoon salt
¼ teaspoon ground pepper
Pinch Cayenne pepper
8–12 slices Italian or French
    bread

What I like best about chicken burgers, as opposed to hamburgers, is that chicken burgers don't shrink much when you cook them.

♦ ♦ ♦

In a mixing bowl, combine chicken, ⅓ cup scallions, 2 tablespoons sour cream, paprika, and remaining seasonings. Form into 4 to 6 burgers. Grill on lightly oiled surface 5 to 6 inches above medium-hot coals, 5–6 minutes per side or until cooked through. Serve on toasted slices of Italian or French bread, topped with remaining sour cream and scallions.

HAWAIIAN GLAZED WINGS

10 chicken wings
½ cup vegetable oil
2 tablespoons fresh lemon
    juice
½ teaspoon seasoned salt or
    to taste

**Marmalade Pineapple
    Glaze:**
¼ cup orange marmalade
¼ cup pineapple preserves
½ cup soy sauce
1 teaspoon Dijon mustard
2 tablespoons white wine
    vinegar

The natural juiciness of chicken wings makes them a good choice for barbecuing. This can make either a nice meal for a few, or appetizers for several.

♦ ♦ ♦

In a large bowl toss wings with vegetable oil, lemon juice, and seasoned salt. In a small bowl combine glaze ingredients. Drain wings and grill 6 to 8 inches above medium-hot coals for about 20 minutes or until golden brown and cooked through. Turn and baste two or three times with glaze.

HERB BARBECUED BREASTS

SERVES 4

4 chicken breast halves
½ cup softened butter or
    margarine
2 tablespoons chopped
    scallions
2 tablespoons minced, fresh
    parsley
1½ teaspoons minced, fresh
    rosemary, or ½ teaspoon
    dried
½ teaspoon salt or to taste
1 small clove garlic, minced
⅛ teaspoon ground pepper

Frank always removes the skin from chicken, and often, that means losing some of the herbs and spices. I like this recipe because even if you remove the skin at the end of the barbecuing, the flavoring is still there.

♦ ♦ ♦

Working from the wide "neck end" of breasts, use fingertips to carefully separate skin from meat to form a pocket. In a small saucepan combine remaining ingredients. Place about 2 tablespoons of butter mixture in pocket of each breast. Close skin flap at neck edge with a small skewer or toothpick. Melt remaining butter mixture and reserve for basting. Grill chicken 6 to 8 inches above medium-hot coals 15–25 minutes or until fork tender, turning and basting chicken several times with butter.

"KUNG FU" CUTLETS

SERVES 4

4 boneless, skinless chicken
    breast halves
2 sweet potatoes, scrubbed
    but not peeled
8 scallions, trimmed
1 tablespoon soy sauce
1 teaspoon sesame or
    vegetable oil
½ teaspoon ground pepper
½ cup tonkatsu sauce (recipe
    follows, or use bottled
    version)

Many people wonder if there is a difference between sweet potatoes and yams. And if there is a difference, does it matter? According to sweet potato grower Tom Archibald from California, there is and it does. The sweet potato's texture is close to an Irish potato's, while the yam is moister and less firm and doesn't hold up as well. Also, the sweet potato is light-skinned, while the yam has a bronze-colored or reddish skin.

♦ ♦ ♦

Place chicken breasts between sheets of plastic wrap and pound to ½-inch thickness. Skip previous step if using thin-sliced roaster breast. Cut sweet potatoes into ½-inch slices. Place chicken and potatoes in a shallow bowl with scallions, soy sauce, oil, and pepper; toss well. Grill scallions and potato slices 6 to 8 inches above medium-hot coals 5–10 minutes, turning once, until tender. Grill cutlets 2–3 minutes per side until cooked through. Serve grilled cutlets and vegetables with tonkatsu sauce as condiment; add a favorite cole slaw as side dish.

Tonkatsu Sauce:
In small bowl, combine ¼ cup sweet and sour sauce, 1 tablespoon soy sauce, 2 teaspoon white vinegar, and 1 teaspoon Worcestershire sauce.

HONEY MUSTARD GRILLED HENS

SERVES 2

2 fresh Cornish game hens
Salt and ground pepper to taste
4 tablespoons butter or margarine
2 tablespoons honey
1½ tablespoons Dijon mustard
1 tablespoon Worcestershire sauce

I've found that hens cook a little faster and are more attractive when served if you remove the backbone before cooking.

♦ ♦ ♦

Halve hens and remove backbones. Season with salt and pepper. In a small saucepan, melt butter; stir in remaining ingredients. Grill hens 6 to 8 inches above hot coals 20–30 minutes or until cooked through, turning often. Baste with sauce during last 10 minutes of cooking time.

HOT AND SPICY PICK-OF-THE-CHICK

SERVES 4–6

1 jar (5 ounces) roasted peppers, drained
1 can (4 ounces) mild green chilies, drained
2 tablespoons brown sugar
2 tablespoons vegetable oil
2 tablespoons lime juice
1½ teaspoons Tabasco
1 teaspoon ground cumin
1 teaspoon salt or to taste
2–3 sprigs fresh coriander (optional)
1 package chicken parts (about 3 pounds)

The spice cumin is the dried fruit or seed of a plant in the parsley family. It's sometimes substituted for caraway seed and is a principal ingredient in both curry powder and chili powder.

♦ ♦ ♦

In food processor or blender, combine all ingredients except chicken; puree until smooth. Set aside ½ cup sauce. Grill chicken, uncovered, 5 to 6 inches above medium-hot coals, allowing 20 minutes for wings, 15–25 minutes for breasts, 20–30 minutes for thighs and drumsticks. Baste with remaining sauce three or four times during grilling. Serve reserved ½ cup sauce as a condiment with grilled chicken.

LEMON SPECIAL CHICKEN

1 chicken, cut in half
    lengthwise
4 tablespoons butter or
    margarine, melted
½ teaspoon paprika
2 tablespoons sugar
2 tablespoons fresh lemon
    juice
1 teaspoon Worcestershire
    sauce
1 teaspoon salt or to taste
½ teaspoon ground pepper

If you don't want to barbecue a half chicken, substitute chicken parts. See table on pages xxii–xxiii for amounts to equal a whole chicken.

◆ ◆ ◆

Grill chicken halves 5 to 6 inches above medium-hot coals 35–40 minutes or until cooked through. In a small saucepan combine remaining ingredients. Make sauce of butter or margarine, paprika, sugar, lemon juice, and Worcestershire. Turn and baste chicken with butter sauce two or three times.

MAHOGANY BARBECUED HENS

2 fresh Cornish game hens
¼ cup mustard
¼ cup grape jelly
2 tablespoons oil

People often ask Frank if a Cornish game hen is a separate breed from regular chickens. The answer is mostly no and a little bit yes. Cornish game hens are young chickens, usually around five weeks. But Perdue Cornish come from the Roaster breed which Perdue geneticist Norman Lupean developed, and which is only available through Perdue. Both Perdue Cornish and the Oven Stuffer Roasters were bred to have the broadest, meatiest breasts in the industry.

◆ ◆ ◆

Halve hens and remove backbones. In a small bowl combine remaining ingredients. Grill 5 to 6 inches above medium-hot coals 20–30 minutes until cooked through, turning two or three times. Baste with mustard mixture during last 15 minutes.

MEXICALI CHICKEN

⅓ cup fresh lime juice
⅓ cup white vinegar
½ teaspoon cumin
1 teaspoon chili powder
1 teaspoon salt or to taste
¼ teaspoon ground pepper
1 whole roaster breast
2 tablespoons chopped, mild
   green chilies
¼ cup ketchup
Tabasco

When you buy a chili powder for use in a Mexican dish like this one, you can be pretty sure that as long as you stick with the same brand, it will taste about the same, year after year. This kind of quality control is difficult for manufacturers to achieve because there are more than 5,000 known varieties of chilies, each with their own degree of "heat" and the same variety grown in a different climate or different year will vary considerably. The chili powder manufacturers get a consistent product by adjusting the formulations each year.

◆ ◆ ◆

In large bowl, combine lime juice, vinegar, cumin, chili powder, salt, and pepper. Place breast in marinade; cover and refrigerate 1 hour or longer. When coals are hot, arrange around drip pan filled halfway with water, close all vents. Drain breast, reserving marinade. Place breast skin side down on grill over drip pan. Grill, covered 50–55 minutes, turning occasionally. Meanwhile, in small saucepan over medium-high heat, combine reserved marinade, green chilies, ketchup, and Tabasco to taste; bring to a boil. Reduce heat to low; simmer until slightly thickened. Remove from heat and brush over chicken during last 10 minutes of cooking time. Serve chicken with remaining sauce.

MEXICALI CUTLETS

1 package breaded chicken
   breast cutlets, ready to eat
4 slices Monterey Jack or
   mild cheddar cheese
8 flour tortillas
1 ripe tomato, sliced
1 ripe avocado, sliced
½ cup sour cream
¼ cup Mexican salsa

You could just heat the cutlets in the microwave, but the smoke from the barbecue will produce a particularly delicious result.

◆ ◆ ◆

Grill cutlets 5 to 6 inches above hot coals, 3–4 minutes on each side, or until crisp, browned, and sizzling. In last 3–4 minutes, place a slice of cheese on each cutlet to melt. While cutlets are grilling, sprinkle tortillas with a few drops of water and wrap in aluminum foil. Warm tortillas along edge of grill. To serve, remove grilled cutlets to serving plates and top with tomato and avocado slices; add dollops of sour cream and salsa. Pass warm tortillas.

MISSISSIPPI SMOKY BARBECUED DRUMSTICKS

SERVES 2

5 roaster drumsticks
Salt and ground pepper to taste
¼ cup finely chopped onion
¼ cup finely chopped green pepper
½ cup ketchup
1 tablespoon Worcestershire sauce
1½ teaspoons liquid smoke (optional)
2 tablespoons dark brown sugar
2 tablespoons cider vinegar
½ teaspoon cinnamon
8–12 drops Tabasco, or to taste

Try serving these with drumsticks frills for a special decorative touch. Fold heavy white paper (7 × 9 inches) in half, lengthwise. Fold in half lengthwise again and tape long edges closed. This produces a strip measuring 9 × 1¾ inches. Cut strip into two 4½-inch strips. On each, make 1-inch cuts at ¼-inch intervals along the entire length of the untaped folded edge. To "fluff" frills, press down on the folded tops of cut edge. Tape frills in place around drumsticks just before serving.

◆ ◆ ◆

Season drumsticks with salt and pepper. In a shallow dish combine remaining ingredients. Roll drumsticks in sauce, reserving excess. Wrap drumsticks individually in aluminum foil, adding a spoonful of sauce to each package. Grill in packet 6 to 8 inches from hot coals for about 45 minutes, turning once. Unwrap drumsticks and place on grill. Add drippings from foil packages to remaining sauce. Grill drumsticks turning and basting frequently with sauce 15 minutes or until cooked through.

PEPPERY GRILLED THIGH SALAD

SERVES 4

4 boneless roaster thigh cutlets
1 teaspoon coarsely ground or cracked black pepper
3 tablespoons Worcestershire sauce, divided

The arugula called for in this recipe is not essential and you can substitute watercress or even iceberg lettuce if you have to. But if you can find it, it's a fresh, attractive taste. I used to grow arugula in my backyard garden, using seeds a friend brought back for me from Italy.

◆ ◆ ◆

½ cup olive oil or vegetable oil, divided
Salt to taste
1 tablespoon Dijon mustard
2 tablespoons wine vinegar
1 tablespoon minced shallot or scallion
1 small head bibb or Boston lettuce, torn into pieces
1 bunch arugula, well rinsed, torn into pieces
1 head Belgian endive, torn into pieces
½ pound green beans, cooked tender-crisp
1 tablespoon minced fresh basil (optional)
1 tablespoon minced fresh parsley

Open cutlets and flatten slightly to even thickness; press pepper into both sides of cutlets and place in a shallow baking dish. Add 2 tablespoons Worcestershire sauce; turn chicken to coat well. Cover and refrigerate 1 hour or longer. Remove cutlets from marinade; brush with 1 tablespoon oil and sprinkle lightly with salt. Grill cutlets, uncovered, 5 to 6 inches above medium-hot coals 3–4 minutes per side until chicken is cooked through, turning occasionally.

In salad bowl, combine mustard, vinegar, and shallot. Gradually whisk in remaining oil. Slice warm cutlets and add any meat juices to dressing. Arrange greens around edges of four dinner plates. Toss chicken and beans with dressing and mound equal portions in middle of greens. To serve, drizzle salads with any remaining dressing and sprinkle with minced herbs.

SANTA FE CHICKEN HERO

SERVES 4–5

1 package roaster thin-sliced boneless breast or 4 skinless, boneless chicken breast halves, butterflied
1 tablespoon vegetable oil
Salt and ground pepper to taste
Cayenne
Chili powder
5–6 thin slices Monterey Jack cheese with chilies
5–6 slices French or Italian bread
2 tablespoons melted butter or margarine
5–6 leaves Romaine lettuce
1 tomato, thinly sliced
1 avocado, peeled, pitted, sliced and tossed with lemon juice
½ cup prepared salsa

Thin-sliced roaster breast couldn't be easier or faster to grill for this hearty update of the submarine/hoagy/hero sandwich. This is a complete Tex-Mex meal in one.

♦ ♦ ♦

Rub chicken lightly with oil and season with salt, pepper, Cayenne, and chili powder. Grill, 5 to 6 inches above medium-hot coals about 2 minutes on each side. Top chicken with slices of cheese; grill 1–2 minutes longer or until cheese is melted.

Brush bread with melted butter; grill alongside chicken 1–2 minutes on each side until golden brown. To serve, place a lettuce leaf on each toasted bread slice. Evenly divide chicken, slices of tomato, and avocado on top. Serve sandwiches open-faced with salsa.

NORTH CAROLINA GRILLED CHICKEN

SERVES 4–6

2 chickens, cut in half
   lengthwise
1 cup butter or margarine (2
   sticks), melted
2 envelopes (6 ounces each)
   Italian salad dressing mix
½ cup fresh lime juice
1 teaspoon salt or to taste

This was a National Chicken Cooking Contest winner.

♦ ♦ ♦

Place chicken in a shallow dish. Melt butter or margarine in saucepan. In a measuring cup combine butter and remaining ingredients and pour over chicken; cover and refrigerate. Marinate, turning occasionally, 3–4 hours or overnight. Grill chicken 5 to 6 inches above medium-hot coals 35–45 minutes or until cooked through. Turn and baste with marinade every 10–15 minutes.

PRAIRIE BARBECUED CHICKEN

SERVES 2–4

½ cup butter or margarine,
   melted
½ cup cider vinegar
1 bottle (15 ounces) ketchup
1 teaspoon salt or to taste
1 teaspoon ground pepper
1 cup water
1 chicken, cut in half
   lengthwise

Besides adding flavor, vinegar makes an excellent tenderizing agent in this—or any—marinade.

♦ ♦ ♦

In a shallow dish combine butter, vinegar, ketchup, salt, pepper, and water. Add chicken and turn to coat well; cover and refrigerate. Marinate chicken several hours or overnight. Grill 5 to 6 inches above medium-hot coals 35–45 minutes or until cooked through. Baste with marinade and turn three or four times.

PROVENÇALE HERB DRUMSTICKS

SERVES 2–3

6 chicken drumsticks
½ cup red wine
⅓ cup water
1 tablespoon wine vinegar
2 garlic cloves, minced

The flavorful combination called "herbes de Provence," consisting of basil, thyme, oregano, and other herbs, is typically used in marinades in the south of France, where grilling is often done over cuttings from grape vines.

♦ ♦ ♦

1½ teaspoons minced fresh
basil or ½ teaspoon dried
1½ teaspoons minced fresh
thyme or ½ teaspoon
dried
1½ teaspoons minced fresh
oregano or ½ teaspoon
dried
1 bay leaf
1 tablespoon tomato paste
2 teaspoons anchovy paste
(optional)
½ teaspoon salt or to taste
¼ teaspoon ground pepper
1 tablespoon olive oil

With fork, pierce drumsticks to help seasonings to penetrate. In large bowl, combine remaining ingredients except oil; whisk in oil. Add chicken to marinade; cover and refrigerate 1 hour or longer. Grill drumsticks, uncovered, 5 to 6 inches above medium-hot coals 35–45 minutes or until cooked through, turning and basting frequently with marinade.

RUSSIAN GRILLED CORNISH

SERVES 2–3

2 fresh Cornish game hens
6 tablespoons fresh lemon
juice
1 clove garlic, minced
1 tablespoon vegetable oil
Kosher salt and pepper to
taste
Lemon wedges (optional)

For a traditional Russian Cornish, use a heavy iron skillet to weight hens while grilling. Called tabaka-style in Russia, pressed chicken is popular because it browns quickly and holds its shape well.

♦ ♦ ♦

With poultry shears or sharp knife, cut along both sides of backbone and remove. On flat surface, spread hens skin side up and press down on breast bones to flatten.

In a dish combine lemon juice and garlic. Add hens to marinade, turning to coat well. Cover and refrigerate 1 hour or longer.

Remove hens from marinade, rub lightly with oil and sprinkle with salt and pepper. Place hens on grill, skin side up, and top with a heavy iron skillet or other pan filled with 1-pound heat-proof object, to flatten. Grill 5 to 6 inches above medium-hot coals. After 15 minutes turn hens and replace weight. Continue grilling another 15–20 minutes or until hens are well browned and cooked through. To serve, garnish hens with lemon wedges.

SEASONED BARBECUED CHICKEN

SERVES 2–4

1 chicken, cut in half
   lengthwise
1 cup Sauterne wine
½ cup oil
½ cup fresh lemon juice
¼ cup soy sauce
1 tablespoon onion juice
1 clove garlic, minced
½ teaspoon salt
½ teaspoon ground pepper

This recipe calls for Sauterne wine, which is a fairly sweet wine. You can use another white wine if you can't find Sauterne; the results will still be good, just different.

♦ ♦ ♦

Place chicken in a shallow dish and add remaining ingredients. Turn chicken to coat with marinade. Cover and refrigerate 3 hours or longer. Grill chicken 5 to 6 inches above medium-hot coals 35–45 minutes or until cooked through. Turn and baste with marinade three or four times.

SOY AND SESAME THIGH KEBOBS

SERVES 4

4 roaster boneless thigh
   cutlets
1 teaspoon minced, fresh
   ginger or ½ teaspoon dried
2 cloves garlic, minced
2 tablespoons sesame seeds
⅓ cup soy sauce
1 tablespoon white vinegar
4 tablespoons vegetable oil
Tabasco, to taste

Thigh meat is a good choice for barbecuing because it's naturally juicy and doesn't easily dry out or toughen. If you want to grill some vegetables at the same time, reserve some of the marinade and baste the vegetables with it. Try serving the kebobs over rice.

♦ ♦ ♦

Flatten cutlets slightly with a meat pounder. Cut each thigh into 6 or 8 pieces. In a shallow dish, combine remaining ingredients. Add thigh pieces and toss to coat well. Cover and marinate 1 hour or longer, refrigerated. Thread chicken onto skewers; reserve marinade. Grill kebobs 5 to 6 inches above medium-hot coals 10–15 minutes until cooked through. Turn and baste often with marinade.

SWEET AND SOUR
ROASTER BREASTS

1 roaster boneless breast
½ cup diced onion
¼ cup soy sauce
2 tablespoons vegetable oil
2 tablespoons minced fresh
  ginger
½ cup brown sugar
1 tablespoon cornstarch

Boneless roaster breasts grill quickly and make an impressive dish for guests. Because they are skinless, they absorb marinades well, but should be turned and basted often to keep the meat moist. Without basting, they can quickly get dry and tough.

♦ ♦ ♦

In a shallow dish, combine onions, soy sauce, oil, and ginger. Place chicken in marinade; cover and refrigerate 1 hour or longer, turning occasionally. Drain chicken, reserving marinade. Grill breasts 5 to 6 inches above medium-hot coals 15–20 minutes, turning frequently until cooked through.

Meanwhile, in small saucepan over medium heat, combine marinade with sugar and cornstarch; bring to a boil. Reduce heat to low; simmer 5–6 minutes or until thickened. Baste chicken generously with sauce during last 10 minutes of cooking time. To serve, spoon remaining sauce over chicken.

SWEET AND SOUR
DRUMSTICKS

¾ cup apricot preserves
¾ cup chili sauce
⅓ cup brown sugar
¼ cup red wine vinegar
2 tablespoons vegetable oil
2 tablespoons grated onion
1 tablespoon fresh grated
  orange rind
2 tablespoons fresh orange
  juice
12 chicken drumsticks

Chicken drumsticks are wonderfully tasty to eat by hand at all outdoor functions. If you've ever wondered about the etiquette of eating chicken with your fingers, Frank says, "When in doubt, do!"

♦ ♦ ♦

In a large measuring cup combine all ingredients except for chicken. Reserve half of sauce to serve with cooked chicken. Brush remaining sauce over legs and grill 5 to 6 inches above medium-hot coals 25–30 minutes until cooked through. Turn and baste with sauce two or three times. Transfer to serving dish and serve with remaining sauce.

SYRIAN GRILLED BREAST

SERVES 4

1 roaster boneless breast or 1 package roaster thin-sliced boneless breast
2 tablespoons fresh lemon juice
¼ cup olive oil
1 tablespoon fresh mint or 1 teaspoon dried
1 small clove garlic, minced
Salt and ground pepper to taste
½ cup chopped pistachios

I like pistachios in recipes because they are relatively low in saturated fats and lower in calories than most other nuts. Weight Watchers International endorses pistachios for just this reason.

♦ ♦ ♦

Cut breast pieces in half, removing tenderloin pieces. Place pieces, including tenderloin pieces, between sheets of plastic wrap and pound to ¼-inch thickness to form cutlets. Or use the already sliced roaster breast and skip the cutting and pounding. In a shallow dish combine lemon juice, olive oil, mint, garlic, salt, and pepper. Add chicken to marinade. Cover and refrigerate 1 hour or longer, turning occasionally. Grill cutlets 4 to 5 inches above medium-hot coals 2–3 minutes per side until cooked through, brushing often with the marinade. Sprinkle with pistachios before serving.

SZECHUAN WINGS

SERVES 4

24 chicken wings
3 tablespoons soy sauce
3 tablespoons chili sauce
3 tablespoons white vinegar
1 tablespoon vegetable oil
1 tablespoon minced fresh ginger
1 tablespoon sugar
1 tablespoon crushed red pepper (less if you don't like it hot)
Salt to taste

If you buy chicken wings from Perdue, the odds are that they won't have any tiny hairs on them. The singeing machines at the processing plants should burn the little hairs off, but the birds being processed are wet and often hairs that are stuck down are missed by the flame. Seeing this, Frank told the engineers at the processing plant, "You know when you wash your hands in the restroom and they have those hot-air driers? Design one that's got an engine like a 747. We'll hit the wing with that and dry the hairs so they'll stand up." After the initial effort, the machines still missed one or two hairs. For research into the solution to this minor detail, the company has spent more than $100,000 over the years.

♦ ♦ ♦

Fold wing tips behind tip of large joints to form triangles. In large bowl, combine soy sauce and remaining ingredients.

Place wings in marinade; cover and refrigerate 1 hour or longer.

Grill wingettes 5 to 6 inches above medium-hot coals 15–20 minutes or until cooked through. Turn and baste frequently with marinade.

TEXAS TWISTER BARBECUED CUTLETS

SERVES 4

4 roaster boneless thigh
   cutlets
1 tablespoon vegetable oil
Salt and Cayenne pepper to
   taste
1 clove garlic, minced
¼ teaspoon ground cumin
1 tablespoon brown sugar
½ cup ketchup
¼ cup cider vinegar
⅛–¼ teaspoon Tabasco, to
   taste

There are a number of tips for keeping brown sugar soft. My stepdaughter, Sandy Spedden, recommends adding a slice of fresh apple to the box once you've opened it. Close the box with the apple slice inside, and put in a sealed plastic bag.

♦ ♦ ♦

Flatten cutlets slightly with a meat pounder. Rub lightly with vegetable oil and sprinkle with salt and Cayenne pepper. In a small mixing bowl, combine garlic, cumin, brown sugar, ketchup, vinegar, and Tabasco. Grill cutlets 4 to 5 inches above medium-hot coals 15–20 minutes until cooked through. Turn and baste two or three times with sauce.

6

CHICKEN FOR CROWDS

Do you have a wedding coming up? A school reunion? Or you just want to have the crowd over? Well guess what! I recommend chicken for the menu! Seriously, it's a good choice because it's on almost everyone's diet, most people like it, and it's probably the most economical main course that can be served to crowds.

Frank and I both enjoy entertaining. There are many months in the year when we entertain fifty associates (that's the term used at Perdue Farms for employees) each week, and at Christmas time, as many as three hundred.

People ask me why I don't have our parties catered. The fact is, I don't want to hire somebody to do what I enjoy doing anyway.

Besides, catered affairs don't fit in with our lifestyle. Frank is actually a frugal and down-to-earth man. He travels economy class, is careful to turn the lights off when we leave the house, and before we married, he cooked for himself and washed his own dishes. (Now I do it.) It's a real compliment when Frank says that someone is "tight as the bark on an oak tree."

Still, we're all busy, so I'm in favor of any shortcuts that help save time even if they cost a little extra. Although, as a former New England Yankee, I am always in favor of spending money carefully.

TIPS ON COOKING FOR CROWDS

- Plan a simple menu with everything done in advance, except simple heating or reheating. Most cookbooks suggest that you have only a few dishes that require last-minute work, but I don't want the hassle of worrying about any. Other last-minute things always come up, and it's wonderful to know that they're not going to upset your schedule or leave you in a state of frazzlement. I work harder the day *before* the party than the day of the party.
- Check that you've got refrigerator or freezer space for all perishables.
- Check that you have the pots and pans and storage containers for the foods you'll be preparing.
- Write a detailed schedule for yourself including the menu and shopping list. I like to have a copy of the menu visible on my refrigerator. It gives me confidence as I check off each dish as it's completed. I remember one party when I forget a dish and was faced with leftover string beans for thirty.
- This tip has nothing to do with poultry, but it's worked so well for me I'll share it anyway. When the occasion is special enough that you're using a florist, (a wedding? an anniversary?) your flower budget will go further if you'll call the florist a week ahead and tell him or her your color scheme and what you're willing to spend. The florist will know which flowers are in over supply and therefore a bargain, and given a week, he or she will have the time to place an order with the wholesaler. You won't necessarily spend less, but you're likely to get considerably more for your money.
- Keep food safety in mind as you work. Keep perishable food, such as chicken, in the refrigerator except when you're working with it. Prepare food in batches and have out only what you're using. When refrigerating foods, have them in small enough batches so that they'll cool quickly.

- If you're serving wine, make it white wine rather than red wine. I say that not because white wine is supposed to go with chicken (some of the more robust recipes for chicken go beautifully with red wine), but because white wine is less of a menace to your carpets.
- If it's a buffet and people will be balancing plates on their laps, serve foods that are already bite-sized and that don't require cutting with a knife and fork.
- Just because you're not having it catered doesn't mean you have to do it all yourself. If you're near a college campus, see if the food service people at the student cafeteria would be willing to make the vegetables or other side dishes. Also, check the cafeteria at a local factory or processing plant. Sometimes these people will moonlight and make large batches of your favorite recipe for you. They've got the equipment, and in my experience, they're pleased to have the extra income. Also, they're apt to be much, much less expensive than a caterer.
- A crowd seldom consumes more than 3 ounces of cooked protein total, per person, and that includes whatever protein is part of the appetizers as well as the main course. However, I usually have closer to 4 ounces per person available, just for "sociable security." If you plan on just under 4 ounces each, you'll almost certainly have leftovers, but at least you won't run out. Another way of calculating is that a breast and a wing per person will insure that you'll have more than enough. (Adjust this depending on whether you're entertaining toddlers or professional football players or—the biggest eaters—older teenage boys.) Also, keep in mind how much else you're serving. I'll always have some leftovers if I allow a half cup serving per person of each of the following: starches, vegetables, and salad, plus a serving and a quarter of bread. That's assuming that there have been a couple of small appetizers before, and that the main course will be followed by dessert.
- When you're multiplying recipes, keep in mind that cooking times may have to be increased. Adjust accordingly.

CHICKEN "NIBBLES" TAKE THE HEAT OUT OF SUMMER ENTERTAINING

Summer parties come in all shapes and sizes. Some are small and happen on the spur of the moment. Others are great boisterous affairs that roll across the lawn or down the beach. They're fun. They're happy. They also can be lots of work. One of the nicest shortcuts I know is the pre-cooked nuggets, tenders, or wings. Straight from the package or warmed for serving, they're extra tasty dunked into a quick dip. I sometimes have an assortment of store-bought mustards available, each in a pretty dish. When there's more time, use one of these Perdue recipes for dips.

COOL AND CREAMY AVOCADO DIP

MAKES ABOUT 1½ CUPS

1 ripe avocado, peeled and seed removed
¼ cup chopped scallions
1 tablespoon lime or lemon juice
½ teaspoon salt or to taste
½ cup sour cream

Home economist Pat Cobe developed many of the dips for Perdue. She starts out by imagining all the dips she's sampled at restaurants or food conventions or parties, or ones she's read about in magazines and cookbooks, and puts together the best ideas from all of them. The only ones she actually recommends to Perdue, have to meet her criteria of being "real food for real people"—like this one.

♦ ♦ ♦

In small bowl with fork, mash avocado. Add green scallions, lime juice, and salt; blend well. Stir in sour cream. Serve immediately or refrigerate until ready to serve.

CREOLE DIP

⅔ cup bottled chili sauce
1 tablespoon prepared
  horseradish (optional)
1 tablespoon Worcestershire
  sauce
1 tablespoon minced fresh
  parsley
1 tablespoon minced scallion
1 tablespoon minced celery

In small bowl, combine all ingredients. If time allows, let stand at room temperature 1 hour for flavors to blend.

GARLICKEY SWEET-SOUR DIP

⅔ cup packed brown sugar
⅓ cup chicken broth
1 tablespoon soy sauce
1 clove garlic, minced
2 tablespoons cider vinegar
1 tablespoon cornstarch

In small saucepan, combine brown sugar, broth, soy sauce, and garlic; mix well. In cup, blend vinegar and cornstarch until smooth; stir into saucepan and place over medium heat. Bring to a boil; cook 3–5 minutes until mixture thickens and becomes slightly reduced, stirring frequently. Serve warm or at room temperature.

MEXICALI CHEESE DIP

1 can (11 ounces) condensed
  Cheddar cheese soup
1 cup shredded Monterey
  Jack cheese with Jalapeno
  peppers
½ teaspoon ground cumin
½ cup sour cream
¼ cup chopped pimentos or
  tomatoes
Tabasco (hot pepper sauce),
  optional

In small saucepan, combine undiluted soup, shredded cheese, and cumin. Place over low heat and cook until cheese is completely melted, stirring constantly. Remove from heat; stir in sour cream, pimentos, and hot pepper sauce to taste, if desired. To serve, keep warm in fondue pot, chafing dish, or heatproof bowl set on warming tray.

RED PEPPER DIP

MAKES ABOUT 1⅓ CUPS

1 jar (7 ounces) roasted red
    peppers, drained
1 clove garlic, quartered
½ teaspoon ground cumin
1 cup plain lowfat yogurt

In blender or food processor, puree red peppers, garlic, and cumin. Add yogurt; blend or process a few seconds just until mixed. Chill several hours or overnight to blend flavors.

SPICY CRANBERRY-ORANGE DIP

MAKES ABOUT 1 CUP

1 cup prepared cranberry
    sauce
2 tablespoons fresh orange
    juice
1 tablespoon port or Marsala
    wine (optional)
1 tablespoon fresh lemon
    juice
¾ teaspoon dry mustard
½ teaspoon ground ginger

In blender or food processor, puree all ingredients. If time allows, let stand at room temperature 1 hour for flavors to blend.

APPETIZERS

CHICKEN COCKTAIL PUFFS

MAKES 36 PUFFS

Cocktail Puffs:
¼ cup water
3 tablespoons butter or
    margarine
⅛ teaspoon salt
¼ cup flour
1 egg, unbeaten
¼ cup grated Swiss cheese

Filling:
2 cups cooked chicken,
    minced
¼ cup minced celery
3 tablespoons minced canned
    pimento
2 tablespoons fresh lemon
    juice
1 tablespoon finely chopped
    onion
1 tablespoon minced fresh
    tarragon or basil
¼ cup mayonnaise or salad
    dressing
½ teaspoon salt or to taste
⅛ teaspoon ground pepper

The cocktail puff is great when stuffed with chicken. I sometimes keep these puffs, unfilled, in the freezer to have available when I need something on short notice. You don't need to thaw them before stuffing.

♦ ♦ ♦

Preheat oven to 350°F. In a saucepan over medium heat, heat butter in water until melted. Add salt and flour all at once and stir vigorously until ball forms in center of pan. Remove from heat and let stand 5 minutes. Add egg and beat until smooth, add cheese. Mixture should be very stiff. Drop by teaspoonful on baking sheet and bake for about 40 minutes or until surface is free from beads of moisture. Turn off oven and prop door open slightly by putting a pot holder in the crack. Allow puffs to cool in oven. Slice crosswise for stuffing.

In a mixing bowl combine chicken, celery, pimento, lemon juice, onion, and tarragon lightly with mayonnaise. Season with salt and pepper. Fill each puff with about 2 teaspoons of filling.

CHICKEN LIVER PÂTÉ

MAKES 12

12 chicken livers (about 1
    pound)
½ cup butter or margarine
1 medium onion, finely
    chopped
4 eggs, hard cooked
½ teaspoon Tabasco (hot
    pepper sauce)
Salt and pepper to taste

I like this on rye crackers.

♦ ♦ ♦

In a large skillet over medium heat, melt butter. Add livers and onions and sauté 8–10 minutes. Put all ingredients in blender or food processor and blend until smooth.

CHICKEN FRANK CARAWAY & KRAUT ROLL-UPS

2 tubes (10 ounces each)
    refrigerated white dinner
    loaf
2 tablespoons German-style
    mustard
1 can (7 ounces) sauerkraut,
    drained
1 egg, beaten, for glaze
8 chicken franks
4 tablespoons caraway seeds

You can reheat the Roll-Ups by toasting briefly under the broiler after slicing.

♦ ♦ ♦

Preheat oven to 350°F. Meanwhile, gently unroll loaf into a 12-inch square, pinching slashed portions together to seal. With sharp knife, cut dough into quarters. Spread each piece of dough with mustard and a thin layer of sauerkraut to within ½ inch of edge. Brush edge lightly with egg. Place a frank on left side of 1 piece of dough and roll up tightly. Place roll, seam side down, on a greased baking sheet. Repeat with remaining franks and dough. Brush rolls with egg and sprinkle with caraway seeds.

Bake for 15 minutes until golden brown. Remove rolls to a cutting board and allow to cool several minutes. With serrated knife, slice each roll into 8 small Roll-Ups. Serve immediately.

CHICKEN LIVER LOVERLIES

12 chicken livers (about 1
    pound)
¾ cup butter or margarine,
    divided
1 cup water
1 cup flour
4 eggs, unbeaten
1 envelope (1⅜ ounces)
    dehydrated onion soup
    mix

It's not quite a cookie. It's not quite a puff. It's not quite a fritter. It's just something very special.

♦ ♦ ♦

In a large skillet over medium heat, melt ¼ cup butter. Add chicken livers and sauté 6–8 minutes; chop finely. In a saucepan over medium heat, melt remaining butter with water. Add flour all at once and stir vigorously until ball forms in center of pan. Add eggs, one at a time, beating after each egg. Stir in livers and soup mix. Preheat oven to 375°F. Drop by teaspoonful on baking sheet and bake 25–30 minutes until puffed and golden brown.

CHICKEN PARTY SANDWICH FILLING

1 cup cooked, ground chicken
½ teaspoon salt or to taste
¼ cup mayonnaise or salad
  dressing
2 tablespoons fresh lemon
  juice
2 tablespoons milk
1 teaspoon sugar

Try using different shaped cookie cutters or use different colors of bread. It's nice on open sandwiches—garnished with an olive slice or a lemon sliver.

♦ ♦ ♦

In a bowl combine all ingredients. Spread on bread or salted crackers.

CHICKEN QUICHE

1 tablespoon butter or
  margarine, softened
2 pie shells (approximately 9
  inches)
1 cup cooked chicken cut in
  small pieces
1 cup grated Swiss cheese
12 slices crisp, cooked
  bacon, crumbled
4 eggs, slightly beaten
2 cups heavy cream
½ teaspoon salt or to taste
⅛ teaspoon nutmeg
⅛ teaspoon sugar
⅛ teaspoon Cayenne pepper
⅛ teaspoon ground pepper

For an attractive and professional presentation, make miniature quiches by lining the inside bottom of your muffin pans with pie dough, forming little tart shells. Then add the filling. I see a lot of these at Washington parties.

♦ ♦ ♦

Preheat oven to 425°F. Rub butter or margarine on pie shells. Put chicken, grated cheese, and bacon in pie shells. In a mixing bowl combine all remaining ingredients and pour into shells. Bake 15 minutes. Reduce heat to 300°F and bake 40 minutes longer, or until filling is set. Cut in narrow pie wedges for serving.

CURRIED CHICKEN AND FRUIT KEBOBS WITH YOGURT SAUCE

MAKES 25–30

1 roaster boneless breast
2 tablespoons curry powder
¼ teaspoon salt or to taste
1 tablespoon vegetable oil
1 can (20 ounces) pineapple
  chunks, well drained
½ pound (about 60) seedless
  grapes
60 cocktail toothpicks
Yogurt Sauce in Zucchini
  Cups (recipe follows)

This looks good as well as tastes good.

♦ ♦ ♦

Cut breast into 50 to 60 bite-size chunks. Place chicken chunks in large bowl; add curry powder and salt; toss together. In a large, heavy non-stick skillet over medium heat, heat oil. Add curried chicken chunks; reduce heat to low and sauté 10 minutes, turning to cook all sides. Cover and remove from heat; cool.

Thread cooled chicken onto toothpicks with a chunk of pineapple and a grape. Serve with Yogurt Sauce as dip.

YOGURT SAUCE IN ZUCCHINI CUPS FOR CURRIED CHICKEN AND FRUIT KEBOBS

1 container (16 ounces) plain
  yogurt
3 tablespoons honey
2 tablespoons minced fresh
  coriander (also called
  cilantro or Chinese
  parsley) or ½ teaspoon
  ground coriander seed
1 teaspoon ground ginger
1 tablespoon fresh lemon
  juice
4 or 5 medium-sized
  zucchini, optional

In medium-size bowl, combine yogurt, honey, coriander, ginger, and lemon juice. If desired, spoon into individual zucchini cups for each guest. To make cups, slice each zucchini into 1½-inch rounds. Use a melon baller to scoop out centers from one end of each piece.

ORIENTAL MINI DRUMSTICKS

30 chicken wings
1 bottle (5 ounces) teriyaki
  sauce
¼ cup peanut or vegetable oil
¼ cup honey
1 tablespoon white vinegar
1 teaspoon ground ginger
2 cups lightly toasted, finely
  chopped peanuts or
  pecans

If the honey you're planning on using for this recipe has crystallized, you can re-liquify it by heating the opened jar gently in hot water or microwave it at low power. Take the honey out of the microwave as soon as it becomes liquid again. Some of the delicate flavor can be lost from overheating.

♦ ♦ ♦

With sharp kitchen knife, divide wings into three sections, cutting between joints—not bone. Reserve first and middle joints for mini drumsticks; set wing tips aside for stock or another use.

To make mini drums from the first joint: Using a small sharp knife, cut around the narrower end to loosen meat. Then, use knife blade to gently scrape meat and skin down toward the larger, knobby end of bone, turning meat inside out and tucking beneath the skin. To make mini drums from middle joints: Cut around the narrower end; cut tendons away and loosen meat. Then use knife blade to gently scrape meat and skin along both bones toward the larger end. Pull out smaller bone, detaching with knife if necessary. Turn meat inside out tucked under the skin around knob of remaining bone.

In large bowl, combine teriyaki sauce, oil, honey, vinegar, and ginger; mix well. Add chicken and coat well. Cover and marinate overnight in refrigerator. Preheat oven to 325°F. Grease two large baking sheets with sides; arrange chicken on baking sheets. Bake 35 minutes or until cooked through. Remove and roll in chopped nuts. Serve hot or at room temperature.

SANTA FE CHICKEN QUESADILLAS (Kay-sa-dee-yas)

4 roaster boneless thigh
   cutlets
2 cloves garlic
2 teaspoons ground cumin
1 teaspoon salt or to taste
¼ teaspoon ground pepper
2 tablespoons vegetable oil
2 cans (4 ounces each)
   chopped mild green chilies
1 minced, canned or fresh
   Jalapeno pepper (optional)
16 flour tortillas (8 inches
   each)
8 tablespoons minced fresh
   coriander (also called
   cilantro or Chinese
   parsley), optional
1 pound Monterey Jack or
   Cheddar cheese, grated
Mexican salsa or slivers of
   avocado sprinkled with
   lemon juice
Chopped tomato and
   coriander sprigs

If you want to make this way ahead of time, you can cool and then freeze the ungarnished quesadilla wedges between layers of aluminum foil. Reheat in preheated 300°F oven 20 minutes and then add the garnish.

♦ ♦ ♦

Cut each thigh into 4 pieces. In container of food processor fitted with steel blade, finely mince garlic. Gradually add chicken pieces, cumin, salt, and pepper; grind to a fine texture.

In a large, heavy, non-stick skillet, heat oil. Add ground chicken mixture and cook over medium heat, stirring often. Cook 8–10 minutes or until meat is no longer pink.

Preheat oven to 300°F. Drain chilies and add to cooked chicken. Place 8 tortillas on 2 large baking sheets and brush lightly with water. Divide chicken mixture among the 8 tortillas, spreading a thin layer almost to the edges. Sprinkle with chopped coriander and grated cheese; top with remaining tortillas, pressing down edges to seal. Brush lightly with water and bake 15 minutes. Remove from oven and cut each quesadilla into 8 wedges. If desired, serve with Mexican salsa or top with avocado, tomato, and coriander.

SHERRY-FRIED CHICKEN LIVERS

12 chicken livers (about 1
  pound)
2 tablespoons butter or
  margarine
1½ teaspoons salt or to taste
¼ teaspoon ground pepper
½ cup dry sherry

People who don't think they will ever like chicken livers can be won over when the flavor of sherry wine is added.

♦ ♦ ♦

In a large skillet over medium heat, melt butter. Add chicken livers and sauté 6–8 minutes. Sprinkle with salt and pepper. Add sherry, cover, and simmer 5 minutes longer or until cooked through. Serve on toothpicks.

BLEU CHEESE CHICKEN SPREAD

1 cup cooked, ground chicken
1 jar (5 ounces) bleu cheese
  spread
½ cup drained, crushed
  pineapple
½ cup chopped almonds,
  lightly toasted
Salt and ground pepper to
  taste

Although I usually prefer fresh products to canned ones, in this case I recommend using canned pineapple. Fresh pineapple contains an enzyme called bromelin which breaks down protein. The bleu cheese in this recipe is rich in protein and fresh pineapple would not work well with it. Canned pineapple, on the other hand, doesn't have enough active bromelin to cause a problem.

♦ ♦ ♦

Makes approximately 40 party sandwiches (1 tablespoon per sandwich).

In a bowl, combine chicken with remaining ingredients. Use as a filling for party sandwiches.

MAIN COURSES

CHICKEN CORDON BLEU FOR A CROWD

SERVES 15–20

20 boneless, skinless chicken breast halves
1 cup butter or margarine, melted
⅓ cup minced, fresh parsley
20 slices Canadian bacon or ham
20 slices sharp or Swiss cheese
3 eggs, beaten
2 cups bread crumbs

There are many recipes for Chicken Cordon Bleu, but I like this one because you can do everything the day before except the frying. Also, don't hold it in the refrigerator for longer than a day.

♦ ♦ ♦

Slice each breast half almost in half lengthwise and then open like the wings of a butterfly. Brush with melted butter and sprinkle with parsley. Place slice of bacon or ham and slice of cheese in each chicken breast, folding to fit. Roll, jellyroll fashion, and secure with toothpicks. Dip in beaten eggs and roll in bread crumbs. Fry in deep fat at 350°F 10–15 minutes or until golden brown and cooked through. Remove toothpicks before serving.

CHICKEN SALAD HAWAIIAN

SERVES 12–15

6 cups cooked chicken, cut in chunks
1½ cups mayonnaise or salad dressing
2 cups chopped celery
2 tablespoons soy sauce
1 can (20 ounces) pineapple tidbits, drained
½ cup slivered almonds, lightly toasted, divided

This recipe is good for a summer lunch. You should keep it cold until serving, but contrary to popular belief, mayonnaise itself isn't particularly dangerous from a food safety point of view. Mayonnaise in its usual commercial formulations is acid enough to be mildly protective against harmful microorganisms. But it's not protective enough, so don't take chances and do keep this refrigerated until you need it.

♦ ♦ ♦

In a large mixing bowl combine chicken, mayonnaise, celery, and soy sauce. Gently fold in pineapple and half of almond slivers. Serve salad on a platter lined with lettuce leaves. Garnish with remaining almonds.

CREAMED CHICKEN VICTORIA

2 whole roast breasts, 2½–3
    pounds each
8 cups chicken broth
½ cup butter or margarine
1 pound fresh mushrooms,
    sliced
½ cup flour
2 teaspoons dry mustard
Salt to taste, depending on
    saltiness of the broth
½ teaspoon Cayenne pepper
    or to taste
2 cups light cream or half and
    half
1 cup dry sherry
¼ cup grated Parmesan
    cheese
¼ cup minced fresh parsley
Puffed Pastry Hearts (recipe
    on next page) or
    toast points

This is a good buffet dish because your guests don't have to cut anything while balancing their dinner plates on their laps. I've expanded it to feed as many as 60 people, and it always draws raves. You can use leftover chicken and skip cooking the roaster breasts; I've done it and it works just fine. The original recipe called for twice as much mustard. If you like your foods quite spicy, you may want to use the four teaspoons of mustard that the original recipe called for.

◆ ◆ ◆

In 4-quart Dutch oven or large, deep skillet over high heat, bring chicken broth to a boil. Add roaster breasts and enough water to cover, if necessary. Reduce heat to low; simmer 70 minutes. Cool breasts in broth. Remove and cut into ½-inch dice; discard bones and skin. Reserve 2 cups broth for recipe; save remainder for another use.

In same Dutch oven or skillet over medium-high heat, melt butter; add mushrooms and sauté 30 seconds. Add diced chicken and sauté 30 seconds longer. Stir in flour until dissolved. Add seasonings, 2 cups reserved broth, and cream; bring to a simmer. Reduce heat to low and simmer 5 minutes, stirring frequently. Add sherry, Parmesan cheese, and parsley. Simmer 1 minute longer. Serve chicken with warmed Puff Pastry Hearts or toast points.

PUFF PASTRY HEARTS TO GO WITH CHICKEN VICTORIA

1 package (17½ ounces) frozen puff pastry
1 heart-shaped cookie cutter (3-inch)
1 whole egg beaten with 1 tablespoon water

You can bake the Puff Pastry Hearts 1 or 2 days in advance. Store thoroughly cooled hearts in an airtight container.

♦ ♦ ♦

Defrost pastry 20 minutes at room temperature. Preheat oven to 375°F. Open one sheet at a time onto a lightly floured board. Cut hearts from pastry and place on two dampened cookie sheets. Pierce hearts with tines of a fork. Then, using the back of a small knife, decorate tops and edges. Brush tops lightly with egg wash. Bake 20 minutes or until golden.

CURRIED CHICKEN RAJ

SERVES 10–12

2 whole roaster breasts 2½–3 pounds each
½ cup butter or margarine
8 cups chicken broth
¾ cup raisins
¼ cup curry powder
½ cup flour
1¼ teaspoons salt or to taste
¼ teaspoon Cayenne pepper or to taste
¼ teaspoon ground pepper
2 cups light cream or half and half
¼ cup minced fresh parsley
Puffed Pastry Hearts (see above) or toast points
Chutney, slivered toasted almonds, other condiments, optional

This is another dish that works well for a buffet.

♦ ♦ ♦

In 4-quart Dutch oven or large, deep skillet over high heat, bring chicken broth to a boil. Add roaster breasts and enough water to cover, if necessary. Reduce heat to low; simmer chicken for 70 minutes. Cool chicken in broth. Remove meat and cut into ½-inch cubes; discard skin and bones. Reserve 3 cups broth for recipe; save remainder for another use.

In same Dutch oven or skillet over medium-high heat, melt butter, stir in chicken, raisins, and curry powder; sauté 1 minute. Stir in flour, seasonings, reserved 3 cups broth, and cream; bring to a simmer. Reduce heat to low and simmer 5 minutes, stirring frequently. Stir in parsley. Serve chicken with Puff Pastry Hearts or toast points, accompanied by chutney, toasted almonds, or other condiments, if desired.

JUST PLAIN BARBECUED CHICKEN

SERVES 50

50 chicken breast halves
25 chicken drumsticks
2 quarts oil
2 quarts vinegar
8 tablespoons salt or to taste
3 tablespoons ground pepper

If you visit the Delmarva Peninsula (Delaware, Maryland, Virginia) in summer, you may come across some of the chicken barbecues that take place here. This is one of the popular recipes for crowds.

♦ ♦ ♦

In a 2-gallon container, combine oil, vinegar, salt, and pepper. Marinate chicken 2 hours. Grill chicken 5 to 6 inches above medium-hot coals until fork tender. Allow 15–25 minutes for the split breasts and 15–25 minutes for the drumsticks. Turn and brush with sauce every 5–10 minutes.

SWEET 'N' SMOKEY CHICKEN

SERVES 30–40

8 medium onions, sliced
30 chicken breast halves
15 chicken drumsticks
15 chicken thighs
2 quarts ketchup
1 cup prepared mustard
2 cups vinegar
1 quart maple syrup
¼ cup hickory smoked salt or
   to taste
2 teaspoons ground pepper

My stepdaughter-in-law, Jan Perdue, says that when Frank's son Jim was courting her, he invited her over for dinner and served Sweet 'n' Smokey Chicken for two. Jan was enchanted with his culinary skill and thought that this would be a sample of what marriage to him would be like. She learned later that this is just about the only thing he cooks. Fortunately, she enjoys cooking and doesn't mind.

♦ ♦ ♦

Preheat oven to 350°F. Place chicken in a single layer, skin side up on top of onion slices in the bottom of two to three large baking pans. If possible keep breast halves in a separate pan from legs and thighs as they will cook more quickly. In a 2-gallon container combine remaining ingredients and pour over chicken. Bake chicken, uncovered, until fork tender. Allow 25–35 minutes for wings, 30–40 minutes for breasts, 35–45 minutes for drumsticks, and 40–50 minutes for thighs.

TREASURE ISLAND CHICKEN

SERVES 30–40

30 chicken breast halves
15 chicken drumsticks
15 chicken thighs
½ pound butter or margarine
½ cup flour
¾ cup sugar
1 teaspoon dry mustard
2 teaspoons cinnamon
½ teaspoon ground ginger
1 quart orange juice
2 tablespoons salt or to taste

A school-lunch chicken recipe contest produced this one. The winner adapted it from an old family recipe.

♦ ♦ ♦

Preheat oven to 350°F. Place chicken in single layer, skin side up, in two to three large baking pans. Keep breast halves in a separate pan as they will cook more quickly than the legs and thighs. In a large saucepan over medium heat, melt butter. Stir in flour, sugar, spices, orange juice, and salt and cook, stirring constantly until thickened. Pour sauce over chicken. Bake, uncovered, until fork tender. Allow 25–35 minutes for wings, 30–40 minutes for breasts, 35–45 minutes for drumsticks, and 40–50 minutes for thighs.

TEXAS BARBECUED BREASTS

SERVES 10–16

1 cup tomato sauce
¼ cup red wine vinegar
¼ cup chili sauce
¼ cup brown sugar
3 tablespoons grated onion
2 tablespoons Worcestershire sauce
1 tablespoon Dijon mustard
½ teaspoon chili powder
1 teaspoon paprika
½ teaspoon Tabasco (hot pepper sauce) optional
16 chicken breast halves

Turn chicken breasts with tongs instead of a fork, which could pierce the meat and cause it to lose some of its juiciness.

♦ ♦ ♦

In a large saucepan over medium heat combine all ingredients except chicken and bring to a boil. Grill chicken 5 to 6 inches above medium-hot coals 15–25 minutes or until fork tender. Turn and baste three or four times with sauce during cooking.

7

CHICKEN FOR TOMORROW— OR NEXT WEEK

In an ideal world, we'd always have food at its freshest and we'd eat it right after it was prepared. In the real world, though, there are many, many times when cooking ahead is useful. You're giving a party and you don't want to be frazzled the day of the event. Or you've got a busy week coming up and you want to do better by your family than just giving them calorie-laden, greasy take-out food. Or you're having house guests, and you want to spend the time with them instead of in the kitchen. Or maybe there's only one or two of you at home, and you've discovered that it's simpler to make a recipe for four and freeze part of it for use later.

My freezer is always full. One reason is that Frank often invites people over at the last minute, and it helps to have emergency food on hand. Equally often, I've made the meal and he'll call at 6:00 P.M. to tell me we're eating out with one of the poultry distributors or suppliers. As I wrap the food in foil and wedge it into the freezer, I remind myself, "This meal isn't going to waste, it's a head start on a future one."

When you know the principles for successful freezing, you can freeze just about any of the recipes in this cookbook. The recipes in this chapter are different because they not only *can* be cooked ahead, often they *should* be cooked ahead. Some of them require marination, others improve with age, and still others adapt so well to cooking the day before that they belong in this chapter. Use this chapter for recipes to use when you want to cook a day or so ahead of time and for tips on how to freeze foods successfully.

If you'll follow the suggestions above, you'll find that most of the foods you cook can be prepared ahead of time and if necessary, frozen. This means that, with the exception of fried foods, just about all the recipes in this book can be considered cook-ahead foods.

CRISPY CORNISH À LA BLEU

SERVES 2

2 fresh Cornish game hens
Oil for deep frying
½ cup mayonnaise
¼ cup sour cream
¼ cup minced onion
¼ cup crumbled bleu cheese
1 small clove garlic, minced
Celery sticks

There are easily 50 varieties of bleu vein cheeses for sale in this country. Probably the most famous are the French Roquefort, the Italian Gorgonzola, the English Stilton, and the American Treasure Cave. Personally, I like the American varieties best.

♦ ♦ ♦

Cut hens into 8 pieces each. Fry in deep hot oil at 375°F, turning once, until golden brown on both sides, about ten minutes. Drain well on paper towels. Refrigerate if not serving right away.

In a small bowl combine remaining ingredients except celery. Cover and chill. Serve hens warm, at room temperature, or cold with bleu cheese dip and celery sticks.

- The biggest boon to food preparation is the freezer. Everything freezes from the point of view of food safety, but there's a lot of variation in palatability. For best flavor and texture, don't freeze the following foods in your home freezer:
  - Milk products—they'll curdle.
  - Boiled eggs—the whites get watery.
  - Custards—they'll lose texture, get lumpy.
  - Mayonnaise—it may separate.
  - Most foods that you fry at home (except french fries and onions)—they can get an unattractive "warmed-over" taste. It's actually the fats turning slightly rancid.
  - Cooked potatoes—they darken and get an unattractive texture. (If you're going to freeze stew, add cooked potatoes later on when you're reheating the stew.)
  - Fresh greens, celery, and carrots—they get limp.
  - Fresh tomatoes—their high water content causes them to collapse when thawed. (However, you can freeze tomatoes if you're going to use them in a cooked form, such as in a pasta sauce.)
  - Gravy—the fat will separate out and puddle. (If you must freeze gravy, cut way back on the fat when you're making the gravy, and stir constantly when you're reheating it so as to keep the fat from separating.)
  - Heavily spiced foods—most herbs, salts, onions, fade away, but garlic and cloves will seem more intense. Pepper has a tendency to turn bitter. Curry takes on a musty flavor.
  - Synthetic flavors—use real vanilla rather than synthetic because synthetic vanilla can have an off-flavor after freezing.
  - Highly salted foods—salt tends to attract moisture and uneven freezing may result because salt slows down the freezing process.
- Even if you're freezing food for only a couple of days, be careful of packaging. Air left in the package will affect the color, flavor, and texture. The container should be airtight, or the food will get freezer burn and lose nutritional value and palatability.
- It's critical to have both your refrigerator and freezer cold enough. The best indicator of a good freezer temperature is brick-hard ice cream. If ice cream stored in your freezer is soft, turn the control to a colder setting. As for the

refrigerator, check the drinking temperature of milk. If it's very cold, you've probably hit 40°F, which is what you're aiming for. If the milk isn't cold enough, or if it sours too quickly, move the control to a colder setting.

- Here's a great tip if you're freezing chicken in a polyethylene bag: lower the bag, with the chicken in it, into a pan of water to force out the air. Be sure the bag opening is above water. Press entire surface area of bag to squeeze out air bubbles. Twist end of bag and fold over. Secure with fastener and label.

- Here's a convenient way to freeze casseroles for later use that Joy Schrage from Whirlpool Corporation told me:

    1. Line the casserole dish with foil, leaving 2-inch collar all around.
    2. Add casserole ingredients and bake.
    3. Cool and freeze in uncovered casserole
    4. When frozen, lift casserole and foil out in one piece
    5. Cover with foil or place in a polyethylene freezer bag. Press air out, then seal tightly, label, date, and freeze. Place in a second polyethylene freezer bag.
    6. To thaw, take frozen casserole out of bag and foil, and place in the casserole dish it was originally baked in.

    This type of freezing frees the casserole dish for other uses while the casserole is in the freezer.

- Homemade "TV" dinners: Place leftovers in serving portions on sectioned plastic trays. Cover, chill, wrap tightly with plastic wrap and seal. Then wrap entire tray in foil. Label, date, and freeze. To reheat, remove foil, puncture plastic wrap to make steam vents, and heat dinner in microwave.

- To keep chicken pieces from sticking together in your freezer so you can take out just what you need, spread the pieces in a single layer on a cookie sheet and place them unwrapped in the freezer. Once frozen, remove the chicken pieces from the cookie sheet and place them in a polyethylene freezer bag. Press the air out, and seal tightly. Label and date the bag and place it in freezer.

- Freezing tip—use freezing tape to seal freezer wrap or suitable plastic wrap. Freezer tape is made with a special adhesive designed to stick at low temperatures.

- Whole birds to be roasted should be thawed before cooking. Broilers and birds to be cooked by other methods can start being cooked when thawed enough for pieces to separate.

CHICKEN SOUFFLÉ

SERVES 4

4 eggs, beaten
1 teaspoon minced, fresh thyme or ¼ teaspoon dried
1 teaspoon minced, fresh basil or ¼ teaspoon dried
Ground pepper to taste
2 cups cooked, shredded chicken
¼ pound ham, roughly chopped
1 tablespoon minced, fresh parsley
½ cup grated Parmesan cheese, divided
3 cups chicken broth
½ loaf (5 ounces) Italian bread, roughly torn into chunks
1 cup grated mozzarella cheese

This is really best if stored overnight in the refrigerator before baking so the flavors have a chance to blend.

◆ ◆ ◆

In a mixing bowl combine eggs, thyme, basil, and pepper. Add chicken, ham, parsley, ¼ cup Parmesan cheese, and broth. Combine thoroughly and set aside. Butter an 8 × 12-inch baking dish. Place bread chunks in the bottom. Cover with egg mixture followed by Mozzarella cheese and remaining Parmesan. Refrigerate 1 hour or longer. Preheat oven to 350°F. Bake 45 minutes until puffed and golden brown.

CHICKEN AND STUFFING

SERVES 6

2 cans (10½ ounces each) condensed cream of chicken soup, divided
1 can (10½ ounces) chicken broth
2 eggs, beaten
1 package (7½ ounces) herb seasoned stuffing mix
3 cups cooked chicken, cut in chunks
1 teaspoon salt or to taste
⅛ teaspoon ground pepper
½ cup milk
2 tablespoons chopped canned pimento

I wouldn't serve this to a gourmet club, but it's an easy, cook ahead dish for a relaxed family meal when you don't want to spend a lot of time in the kitchen. It's also an ideal way to have the taste of stuffed chicken—with easier serving qualities. You can make it ahead of time, up to the point of baking.

◆ ◆ ◆

Preheat oven to 350°F. In a mixing bowl whisk together one can of undiluted cream soup, broth, and eggs. Add stuffing mix and toss. Place stuffing in bottom of a baking dish. Arrange chicken on top of stuffing and sprinkle with salt and pepper. In a large measuring cup combine remaining can of soup and milk and pimento and pour over all. Bake, uncovered, 35–45 minutes or until hot and bubbling.

CHICK-O-TATO CASSEROLE

SERVES 4–6

1/3 cup vegetable oil
1/2 cup chopped onion
1/2 cup chopped celery
1/2 cup chopped green pepper
1/2 cup ketchup
1/2 cup water
2 tablespoons vinegar
2 tablespoons sugar
1 tablespoon Worcestershire sauce
1 tablespoon prepared mustard
1 teaspoon salt or to taste
1/4 teaspoon ground pepper
1 chicken, cut in serving pieces
4 medium potatoes, peeled and thickly sliced

This tastes better reheated, after the flavors have had a chance to blend.

♦ ♦ ♦

Preheat oven to 350°F. In a large skillet, over medium heat, heat oil. Add onion, celery, and green pepper and cook, stirring often, 6–8 minutes or until softened. Add ketchup, water, vinegar, sugar, Worcestershire sauce, mustard, salt, and pepper, and simmer at low heat for about 15 minutes. Place chicken in bottom of a baking dish and tuck potatoes around chicken pieces. Pour sauce over all. Bake, covered, 50–60 minutes or until cooked through. If planning to reheat, remove from oven when slightly under cooked.

CHOICE CHEESY CHICKEN

SERVES 4–6

1 clove garlic, peeled
1/2 cup (1 stick) butter or margarine
1 cup bread crumbs
1/2 cup grated sharp Cheddar cheese
1/4 cup grated Parmesan cheese
1 teaspoon salt or to taste
1/8 teaspoon ground pepper
6 skinless, boneless chicken breast halves

There's no last-minute attention required for this recipe. Prepare it a day ahead, right up to the point of baking.

♦ ♦ ♦

With the broad side of a large kitchen knife crush garlic slightly to release flavor. In a small saucepan over low heat melt butter with garlic clove. Set butter aside for a half-hour for maximum garlic flavoring. On a sheet of wax paper combine bread crumbs, cheese, salt and pepper. Dip chicken in garlic butter, then roll in cheese mixture. Tuck sides under to form a neat roll. Arrange chicken in a large shallow baking pan and drizzle with any remaining butter. Cover and refrigerate if making ahead. When ready to bake, preheat oven to 350°F. Bake chicken 15–25 minutes or until golden and fork tender.

COLD CHICKEN TONNATO

SERVES 6–8

8 chicken cutlets (about 2 pounds skinless, boneless chicken breast halves, pounded thin, or 2 thin-sliced boneless roaster breasts)
½ cup flour, seasoned with salt and ground pepper to taste
½ cup (1 stick) butter or margarine
2 cans (13 ounces) tuna, drained
8 anchovies
2 cloves garlic, peeled
1 cup olive oil
4 tablespoons white vinegar
4 tablespoons light cream
2 tablespoons capers

This is an elegant company recipe, and it works well if you make it the day before. I've made it with water-packed tuna, but oil-packed would work also.

♦ ♦ ♦

Dip cutlets in flour to coat lightly, shake off excess. In a large skillet over medium-high heat, melt butter. Add cutlets and sauté until cooked through, about 5 minutes; turn once. Drain cutlets on paper towels. Chill. In a blender or food processor, combine tuna, anchovies, garlic, oil, vinegar, and light cream. Blend until pureed. Pour sauce over cold cutlets, sprinkle with capers. May be loosely covered and refrigerated overnight before serving.

EASY CHICKEN CORDON BLEU

SERVES 4

4 skinless, boneless chicken breast halves or 1 package thin-sliced boneless roaster breast
4 tablespoons butter or margarine
1 tablespoon minced, fresh parsley
4 slices ham
4 slices sharp cheese
1 egg, beaten
1 cup bread crumbs

This is another recipe that can be fixed, except for frying, on the day before. For variation, try Swiss cheese and Canadian bacon. A white sauce made with chicken broth is a nice accompaniment. If you're in a hurry, undiluted cream of chicken soup makes a handy substitute. Garnish with parsley sprig.

♦ ♦ ♦

Place chicken between sheets of plastic wrap and pound to ¼-inch thickness. Skip the preceding step if you're using the thin sliced boneless roaster breast. Spread chicken with butter and sprinkle with parsley. Place a slice of ham and a slice of cheese on each chicken breast, folding to fit. Roll, jellyroll fashion, and secure with toothpicks. Dip chicken in beaten egg and roll in bread crumbs. Fry in deep fat at 350°F 12–15 minutes or until golden brown and cooked through. Remove toothpicks before serving.

FIESTA TORTILLA STACK

6–8 SERVINGS

1 cup cooked, shredded
    chicken
½ cup mayonnaise
3 tablespoons chopped, fresh,
    cilantro (also called
    coriander or Chinese
    parsley), if available
½ teaspoon salt
1 package (8 ounces) cream
    cheese
1 can (7 ounces) whole
    kernel corn, drained
2 tablespoons taco seasoning
    mix
1 dozen 8-inch flour tortillas
Cherry tomatoes
1 small head lettuce

The flavors in this recipe blend and get better if you make it the day before, but I have also served it the same day when I was in a hurry. It does need at least a couple of hours for the flavors to develop. I've made this recipe with coriander and without; it works well either way. Coriander is also known as cilantro, or Chinese parsley.

♦ ♦ ♦

In a mixing bowl combine chicken, mayonnaise, cilantro, and salt. In a separate small bowl combine cream cheese, drained corn, and taco seasoning mix. Place 2 flour tortillas, one on top of other. Spread with ⅓ of chicken mixture, then 2 tortillas and corn mixture. Continue until mixtures are used up.

Chill for at least 4 hours to develop flavors. Remove from refrigerator half an hour before serving. Cut in 6–8 wedges. Garnish with tomatoes and serve on a bed of lettuce.

GARDEN BREAST CHÈVRE

SERVES 4

1 whole roaster breast, bone
    in
Salt and ground pepper to
    taste
6 ounces mild creamy goat
    cheese or cream cheese,
    softened
1 medium carrot, coarsely
    grated
1 small zucchini, unpeeled
    and coarsely grated
¼ cup snipped fresh or frozen
    chives
2 teaspoons minced fresh
    rosemary or ½ teaspoon
    dried
1 tablespoon vegetable oil

Chèvre means goat in French, and the name of this recipe comes from the goat cheese in it. Frank loves goat cheese, so this is a special treat for him.

♦ ♦ ♦

Preheat oven to 375°F. Working from the top of the breast use fingertips to carefully loosen the skin from the meat on the breast to form a pocket. Do not detach skin on sides or at base of breast. Combine cheese, carrot, zucchini, chives, rosemary, and salt and pepper. Stuff vegetable mixture evenly under skin of breast. Brush with oil and place skin side up in a roasting pan. Bake about 1 hour and 15 minutes or until juices run clear with no hint of pink when a cut is made near the bone. Chill, wrap tightly, and refrigerate if not serving immediately. Serve at room temperature or reheated.

COLD CORNISH

2 fresh Cornish game hens
2 tablespoons olive oil
2 large tomatoes, coarsely
    chopped, or 1 can (16
    ounces) whole tomatoes,
    chopped, drained
1 medium zucchini, sliced
1 cup fresh green beans, cut
    into 2-inch lengths
4 scallions, sliced
¼ cup minced fresh basil or 1
    tablespoon dried
1 teaspoon salt or to taste
⅛ teaspoon ground pepper
1 cup chicken broth
⅓ cup Feta cheese (optional)

Choose green beans that are fresh and young. The bean growers say that if the bean is fresh, it will snap easily when broken. If it bends instead of snapping, the bean has been around too long. Also, if the seeds bulge inside the pods they are too mature and you can count on the beans being tough and leathery.

♦ ♦ ♦

Quarter hens, remove backbones. In a large skillet, over medium-high heat, heat oil. Add hens and brown on all sides, 12–15 minutes. Add remaining ingredients Cover and simmer 20 minutes or until hens are cooked through. Refrigerate. Serve cold, sprinkled with cheese.

KICK-OFF KEBOBS

6 skinless, boneless chicken
    breast halves
¼ cup flour
1 teaspoon salt or to taste
⅛ teaspoon ground pepper
1 egg, slightly beaten
2 tablespoons water
½ cup fine dry bread crumbs
¼ cup grated Parmesan
    cheese
3 tablespoons butter or
    margarine

Frank is an avid sports fan, and he constantly astonishes his friends by knowing obscure facts and dates concerning the various players and games. This is an easy dish to serve your sports fans.

♦ ♦ ♦

Preheat oven to 375°F. On a sheet of wax paper, combine flour, salt, and pepper. In a shallow dish beat together egg and water. On a separate sheet of wax paper blend bread crumbs and cheese. Dip chicken into flour, then egg, then bread crumb mixture turning to coat well on both sides. Arrange chicken in a buttered baking dish. Dot with remaining butter. Bake 15 minutes. Turn and bake 5 minutes longer or until cooked through. Cut each breast half into 4 pieces and thread onto wooden skewers. Wrap in foil or place in plastic container and refrigerate until needed. Serve with assorted dips.

Herbed Sour Cream Dip:

In a small bowl combine 1 cup sour cream, 3 tablespoons minced fresh parsley, 1 teaspoon dried tarragon, 2 tablespoons minced scallions, 2 tablespoons snipped fresh or frozen chives, and ½ teaspoon salt or to taste.

Instant Spiced Dip:

In a small bowl blend together 1 cup mayonnaise, ¼ cup bottled French dressing, ¼ cup chili sauce, 1 teaspoon horseradish sauce, 1 teaspoon Worcestershire sauce, ½ teaspoon dry mustard, 2 cloves garlic, minced, and salt to taste. (If you're in a hurry, substitute ½ teaspoon garlic salt for the fresh garlic and the salt.)

OVEN-BRAISED ROASTER BREAST WITH VEGETABLES

SERVES 4–6

1 whole roaster breast, bone in
2 tablespoons vegetable oil
8 small white onions (about ½ pound)
1½ cups low-sodium chicken broth
⅓ cup dry white wine
1 tablespoon minced, fresh tarragon or 1 teaspoon dried
¼ teaspoon ground pepper
8 small potatoes, peeled
8 baby carrots
2 cups broccoli florets
¼ cup milk
1½ tablespoons cornstarch

Making this dish the day before has a couple of advantages. Any fat will rise to the top where it's easy to remove, and also the wine and herbs "marry" with the other flavors.

♦ ♦ ♦

Preheat oven to 350°F. In 5-quart oven-proof Dutch oven or saucepot over medium-high heat, heat oil. Add roaster breast; cook 15–20 minutes, turning until browned on all sides. Remove and set aside. Add onions, cook 2–3 minutes or until lightly browned, stirring frequently. Remove onions; pour off excess fat. Return roaster breast to Dutch oven. Add broth, wine, tarragon, and pepper; bring to a boil. Add potatoes; cover and bake 20 minutes. Add onions and carrots; cover. Bake 20 minutes longer or until roaster breast and vegetables are almost tender. Add broccoli; cover. Bake 8–10 minutes longer or until roaster breast is cooked through and vegetables are tender. (Prepare to this point and refrigerate overnight, if desired.) Remove roaster breast and vegetables to serving platter; keep warm. In small bowl, stir together milk and cornstarch until smooth; stir into liquid in

Dutch oven. Over medium heat, bring to boil; boil 1 minute, stirring constantly. Serve sauce with roaster breast and vegetables.

PARMESAN BREAST

SERVES 4

1 whole roaster breast, bone in
2 cups cooked rice
1 cup fresh chopped spinach (or ½ package frozen, thawed and drained)
½ cup minced fresh basil, or 2 tablespoons dried
1 clove garlic, minced
¼ cup toasted pine nuts
1 egg
2 tablespoons milk
2 tablespoons olive oil, plus 1 tablespoon for basting
¼ cup grated Parmesan cheese
Salt and ground pepper to taste

Parmesan cheese is a "cooking cheese" and is usually used in its grated form in the United States. When young, it's mild and nutty, but with age it acquires a sharply tangy flavor. It can get too old, so check the shelf life on the container. When in doubt, taste it.

♦ ♦ ♦

Preheat oven to 375°F. Season breast to taste with salt and pepper. In a mixing bowl combine remaining ingredients. Stuff breast cavity with rice and place a sheet of aluminum foil over cavity to hold in stuffing. Carefully turn breast over and place skin side up in a roasting pan. Spoon any remaining rice around breast. Baste chicken with oil and bake for about one hour or until juices run clear with no hint of pink when a cut is made near the bone. Chill, wrap tightly, and refrigerate 24 hours to give flavors a chance to blend. You can serve it warm or at room temperature.

PISTACHIO SMOKED CHICKEN SPREAD

SERVES 4

1 package cream cheese (8 ounces), room temperature
1 cup finely chopped cooked chicken
½ teaspoon salt or to taste
⅛ teaspoon liquid smoke
¼ cup chopped pistachios
3 teaspoons fresh lemon juice

The green color and the crunch of the pistachios add a lot to this spread. Be sure to store the pistachios in an airtight container after purchase. Exposure to air causes the nuts to become soggy.

♦ ♦ ♦

In a mixing bowl combine ingredients thoroughly. Refrigerate 24 hours while flavors blend. Serve on crackers. For a rich and delicious lunch, serve it on croissants or bagels.

SALISBURY CHICKEN BREASTS

8 skinless, boneless chicken
  breast halves
½ cup flour
1½ teaspoons salt or to taste
¼ teaspoon ground pepper
1 cup bread crumbs
¾ teaspoon minced, fresh
  sage or ¼ teaspoon dried
¾ teaspoon minced, fresh
  rosemary or ¼ teaspoon
  dried
¾ teaspoon minced, fresh
  thyme or ¼ teaspoon
  dried
2 eggs
½ cup (1 stick) butter or
  margarine, melted
½ cup Sauterne wine
8 slices mozzarella cheese

The name Salisbury, when used with steak, means that the beef will be chopped or ground. This recipe has nothing to do with chopped meat; in this case Salisbury refers to the town on Maryland's Eastern Shore where the Perdue Farms headquarters is located. You can prepare this a day ahead of time right up to the point of baking.

♦ ♦ ♦

Preheat oven to 350°F. On a sheet of wax paper, combine flour, salt, and pepper. In a shallow bowl beat eggs. On a separate sheet of wax paper, combine bread crumbs and seasonings. Dip chicken in flour mixture, then eggs, then crumb mixture. Roll and secure with toothpicks. Place in large shallow baking pan. Pour melted butter over chicken. Cover and bake 15 minutes. Remove cover. Pour Sauterne over chicken. Bake, uncovered, 15–20 minutes or until cooked through. Fold slices of cheese in half; place one on top of each roll for last 3 minutes or until cheese is melted.

SECRETARIES' SALAD

1 head lettuce, shredded
1 cup chopped celery
1 large green, red, or yellow
  pepper, chopped
1 cup thinly sliced carrots, or,
  if it's summer, 1 cup
  chopped tomato
1 cup chopped scallions
1 cup frozen peas, room
  temperature, not cooked
2 cups cooked, shredded
  chicken
1½ cups mayonnaise
2½ cups shredded Cheddar
  cheese

Perdue home economists developed most of the recipes in this book, but this recipe is one of the few that is mine. I served it first at what Frank and I jokingly call the "Perdue High Holiday," National Secretaries' Day. That's the day when we honor the people who we know really make the world go 'round. We usually have about twenty-five of the top secretaries from Perdue Headquarters for dinner along with their husbands to celebrate the day.

♦ ♦ ♦

In a large clear glass bowl, layer ingredients in the order given. It should look like layers in a parfait glass. Refrigerate 24 hours to develop flavors. Do not toss before serving.

SPICY CORNISH HEN TIDBITS

2 fresh Cornish game hens
1 teaspoon chili powder
½ teaspoon garlic powder
½ teaspoon onion salt
¼ teaspoon celery salt
¼ teaspoon lemon pepper or
    black pepper
1 cup vegetable oil or as
    needed
1 cup bottled garlic cheese
    dressing

This is another of the recipes included in the Perdue Cornish Hen packages that people have requested from Frank dozens and dozens of times over the years. I'm including the recipe exactly as it originally appeared, but you may want to substitute fresh garlic (1 clove), fresh onion (1 tablespoon, finely chopped), and fresh celery (2 tablespoons, finely chopped), for the garlic powder, onion salt, and celery salt. If you make these substitutions, be sure to add salt to taste afterward.

♦ ♦ ♦

Cut hens into serving pieces. Combine dry spices and toss hens in spices to coat evenly. Heat oil in large skillet over medium heat and fry Cornish pieces about 8 minutes on each side until tender and golden. Remove and drain on paper towels. Arrange on a serving dish. Cover and refrigerate overnight. To serve, dip Cornish pieces into bottled dressing. Serve at room temperature.

8

CHICKEN FOR HOLIDAYS

If we were back in the 1920s right now, and you were planning a holiday meal, it would almost certainly not include chicken—unless you were either lucky or rich. Back then, chicken on the menu was either a sign of affluence or that you lived on a farm and had your own chickens. When Herbert Hoover was using "a chicken in every pot" as a campaign slogan back in the late 1920s, chicken was such a rare and expensive treat that most people thought Hoover's promise was about as realistic as promising them pie in the sky.

All this changed because of a fortunate accident that happened near where Frank grew up on the Eastern Shore of Maryland. In 1923, when Mrs. Wilmer Steele, of nearby Sussex County, was ordering baby chicks for her laying flock, someone processing the order got a zero wrong. Instead of the fifty chicks she was counting on, Mrs. Steele received five hundred baby chicks. She found herself faced with the expense of feeding so many birds and the hassle of trying to sell more eggs than the market in Sussex County could possibly absorb.

The solution she came up with changed the eating patterns not just of Sussex County, but of most of the world as well. It also had a lot to do with Frank's future career. Up until then, chicken production was no more than an adjunct to egg production. When someone had chicken to eat, it was most likely a "spent hen," a tough old bird which no longer laid a sufficient number of eggs to pay her feed costs. Mrs. Steele transformed all this by deciding to sell her extra baby chicks for meat when they were only a few months old and hadn't yet cost her too much in feed.

The young and tender meat from these birds made them an instant success. Mrs. Steele discovered that raising chickens for meat was a lucrative business.

Other egg producers, including Frank and his father, Arthur W. Perdue, eventually switched over to growing chickens for meat rather than for eggs. Progressive farmers like the Perdues were soon breeding their chickens for larger size, faster growth, and better conversion of feed to meat—something no one had thought about when chickens were grown only for egg production. As a result of this specialization, the poultrymen were able to bring the cost of chicken down far enough so that it became affordable for everyone.

In 1923, Americans barely consumed a pound of broiler chicken per person in a year; today we're each eating about seventy pounds per year. And where once only the rich could feature chicken for a holiday meal, now everyone can and many do.

The holiday recipes that follow were developed by the Perdue home economists. You'll find them arranged by date, beginning with January. I've included the sample menus that accompanied the original recipes. My favorite among them is the Fourth of July menu that comes from Frank's family.

CHINESE NEW YEAR CELEBRATION IS DO-IT-YOURSELF FEAST

I wonder if any nationality can compete with the Chinese on the art of eating well. The last empress of China, for instance, was known to order two hundred dishes prepared daily. From these, she chose two for dinner.

Even average Chinese families, when they can afford it, serve an array of dishes at meal time. I took a Chinese cooking course and my teacher explained the philosophy behind it. The idea is that the taste buds quickly tire of one taste sensation and therefore, the meal is more enjoyable if you have many flavors and textures.

At Chinese celebrations such as those that welcome the lunar New Year, chicken plays an important role. It represents renewal and rebirth, and it appears in several different dishes. In China, the Oven Stuffer

---

CHINESE NEW YEAR FEAST

Cold Platter of Prepared Meat and Fish
(Abalone, Smoked Fish, Smoked Ham)

◆

Boiled Rice

◆

Oysters

◆

Egg Rolls

◆

Wonton Soup

◆

*Poached Soy Roaster

◆

*Stir-Fry in Noodle Basket

◆

*New Year Lo Mein

◆

*Peking Cornish Hens with Scallion Sauce

◆

*Stir-Fried Vegetables over Chow Mein Noodles

---

*Recipe follows

Roaster included here would be served complete with head and feet to symbolize completeness—but my husband isn't selling them that way right now, so I'm not going to be completely authentic! Other symbolic foods include oysters to represent good fortune, fish to symbolize plenty, and mein (noodles) to represent long life.

For those who don't want to make all these dishes from scratch, some of them, like the egg rolls or wonton soup, can be gotten canned or frozen from your supermarket.

POACHED SOY ROASTER

SERVES 8–10

1 whole roaster
10 cups water
3 cups dark soy sauce
1 cup dry sherry
2 tablespoons sugar
1½ teaspoons five-spice
   powder
4 slices peeled, fresh
   gingerroot
Shredded cabbage (optional)
Carrot curls (optional)
Hot pepper flowers (optional)

Remove giblets; set aside. Remove and discard fat from cavity. Tie legs together and fold wings back.

In 8-quart kettle or Dutch oven, place roaster, breast-side down; add giblets and next 6 ingredients. Over high heat, bring to a boil. Reduce heat to low and cover; simmer 30 minutes. Uncover and turn roaster over gently, being careful not to tear skin. Over high heat, return to a boil; cover and simmer over low heat for another 30 minutes or until leg joint moves easily and juices run clear with no hint of pink when thigh is pierced. Remove roaster and cool slightly; cut into small pieces. Serve hot, at room temperature or chilled, arranged on a bed of cabbage and garnished with carrot curls and hot pepper flowers. Soy sauce mixture may be boiled and then passed as a dipping sauce.

Note: Sauce mixture can be used over and over again. Skim off fat; refrigerate up to a week or freeze several months. Bring to a boil before reusing.

STIR-FRY IN A NOODLE BASKET

1 boneless roaster breast, cut into ½-inch cubes (about 4 cups)
6 tablespoons soy sauce, divided
2 tablespoons dry sherry
2 tablespoons cornstarch, divided
4 scallions, cut into ½-inch slices (¾ cup)
2 teaspoons minced fresh gingerroot
2 cloves garlic, minced
3 tablespoons cider vinegar
2 teaspoons sugar
2 teaspoons Chinese sesame oil
¼ teaspoon Cayenne pepper
5 tablespoons vegetable oil, divided
3 cups broccoli flowerets (1 small bunch), blanched
1½ cups sliced carrots (about 3), blanched
¾ cup sliced water chestnuts
1 can (8 ounces) straw mushrooms, drained, or 1 can (8 ounces) whole button mushrooms, drained
½ cup dry roasted cashew nuts
Noodle Basket (recipe follows)

In large bowl, combine breast cubes, 2 tablespoons soy sauce, sherry, and 1 tablespoon cornstarch; toss until well mixed and set aside. On small plate, combine scallions, ginger, and garlic; set aside. In small bowl, mix well remaining 4 tablespoons soy sauce, 1 tablespoon cornstarch, vinegar, sugar, sesame oil, and Cayenne; set aside.

In a wok or large, heavy skillet over high heat, heat 3 tablespoons oil until hot, but not smoking. Add breast cubes and cook, stirring quickly and frequently (stir-fry), 3 minutes. Remove breast cubes with slotted spoon. Add remaining 2 tablespoons oil to skillet and heat. Add scallions, ginger, and garlic; stir-fry about 30 seconds. Add broccoli, carrots, water chestnuts, mushrooms, and cooked breast cubes; stir-fry 2 minutes longer. Pour soy sauce mixture into skillet and cook 1 minute longer or until slightly thickened. Stir in cashews. Serve hot in noodle basket.

Note: Dish may be made up to 1½ hours ahead, but do not add cashews; add just before serving. Place mixture in oven-to-table serving dish; partially cover and reheat in preheated 325°F oven for 20 minutes. Or reheat in top of double boiler over hot water 15 minutes, stirring occasionally.

NOODLE BASKET

1 package (8 ounces)
  spaghetti
Oil for deep frying

Cook spaghetti as package directs. Run cooked spaghetti under cold water; drain. Gently toss spaghetti with a little oil. Over index finger, fold five or six spaghetti strands in half. Drape folded spaghetti over edge of 7- ×3½-inch sieve, so that loops fall to outside of sieve and ends into center. Continue to place folded spaghetti (5 to 6 strands at a time) around edge of sieve. Intertwine ends of spaghetti in center to form a woven pattern that will make the noodle basket stronger and prevent spaghetti from separating during frying. Extra spaghetti can be added in center of sieve to reinforce pattern. When basket is complete, place another sieve on top to hold in place. In large saucepan, pour enough oil to cover sieve; over medium-high heat, heat to 375°F or until a small piece of spaghetti sizzles and turns golden when placed in oil. Submerge sieves, with spaghetti between, and deep-fry until noodle basket is lightly browned; remove and drain on paper towels. Makes 1 large basket or 3 small baskets (4 × 2¼ inches)

Note: To make smaller baskets, drape spaghetti over a sieve measuring 4 × 2¼ inches; repeat for 3 baskets.

NEW YEAR LO MEIN

SERVES 8–10

Water
5 tablespoons soy sauce,
  divided
3 tablespoons cornstarch,
  divided
4 roaster boneless thigh
  cutlets, cut into thin slices
  or strips
2 teaspoons Chinese sesame
  oil
1 teaspoon sugar
5 tablespoons vegetable oil,
  divided
1 cup chopped scallions
  (4–5)
2 cloves garlic, minced

In medium-sized bowl, combine 2 tablespoons water, 2 tablespoons soy sauce, and 1 tablespoon cornstarch. Add thigh pieces and toss until well coated; set aside. In small bowl, mix well ⅔ cup water, remaining 3 tablespoons soy sauce, remaining 2 tablespoons cornstarch, sesame oil, and sugar; set aside. In large skillet or wok over medium-high heat, heat 2 tablespoons oil until hot but not smoking. Add thigh mixture; stir-fry over high heat 3 minutes. Remove thigh meat with slotted spoon; set aside. Heat remaining 3 tablespoons oil in skillet. Add scallions and garlic; stir-fry about 30 seconds. Add celery cabbage, celery, carrots, mushrooms, and snow peas; stir-fry over medium heat 5 minutes or until vegetables are tender-crisp. (Add 1–2 tablespoons water, if needed). Add bean sprouts, water

3 cups sliced celery cabbage
   (¼ medium head)
2 cups sliced celery (3 ribs)
2 cups carrots cut in julienne
   strips (3), blanched
2 cups sliced mushrooms (½
   pound)
1 cup snow peas, trimmed,
   cut into 1-inch pieces
3 cups bean sprouts
¾ cup sliced water chestnuts
¾ cup bamboo shoots cut in
   julienne strips
½ pound fine egg noodles or
   thin spaghetti broken into
   fourths, cooked, rinsed,
   and drained

chestnuts, and bamboo shoots; stir-fry 2 minutes. Stir in thigh meat and spaghetti. Add cornstarch mixture and cook until sauce has thickened. Serve immediately.

PEKING CORNISH HENS WITH SCALLION SAUCE

SERVES 4

4 fresh Cornish game hens
6 cups water
¼ cup honey
4 ¼-inch-thick slices fresh
   ginger
4 skewers (approximately 8
   inches long)

Remove giblets. Bring water to a boil in large saucepan. When boiling, add honey, and stir. One at a time, lower each bird into honey bath, quickly turning it completely over to evenly coat with liquid. Immediately remove and place a slice of ginger in each bird. Let hens dry on metal rack for 10 minutes. Place in roasting pan with wings folded back. Push tail into body cavity, then run skewer through meaty part of drumsticks underneath bone, skewering the tail. (If wood skewers are used, cover ends with foil to prevent burning.) Cook in preheated 350°F oven for 1 hour until tender. Combine sauce ingredients, heat, and serve with hens.

SCALLION SAUCE

½ cup soy sauce
2 tablespoons dry sherry
2 tablespoons fresh orange
   juice
1 teaspoon grated orange rind
1 teaspoon sugar
2 scallions thinly sliced

In small bowl, combine all ingredients. Serve with Cornish hens.

STIR-FRIED VEGETABLES

½ cup bias-cut bite-size
carrot pieces
2–3 tablespoons peanut oil
1 clove garlic peeled and
lightly crushed
1 ¼-inch thick slice fresh
ginger
½ cup broccoli flowerets
½ cup bias-cut green beans
½ cup celery thinly sliced at
an angle
½ cup snow peas
Soy sauce to taste

Stir-frying is a classic Chinese cooking technique in which food is quickly cooked over high heat to retain flavor and crispness.

◆ ◆ ◆

In a saucepan bring 1 quart of water to a boil, add carrots, and cook 2 minutes. Drain and rinse under cold running water, then pat dry with paper towels.

To a heated wok or iron skillet add 2 tablespoons peanut oil, garlic, and ginger. When oil is hot, add well dried carrots and sauté 2 minutes. Quickly remove carrots with a slotted spoon and arrange on a serving platter, then continue in the same manner cooking the broccoli and green beans, each for 2 minutes and the celery and snowpeas each for 1 minute. Add more oil as necessary and remove garlic and ginger if they start to burn. When all of the vegetables have been arranged, sprinkle lightly with soy sauce and serve immediately.

ELEGANT DINNER FOR TWO

There's a hearts-and-Valentines connection today that great-grand-mother never considered. Given what we now know about diet and heart disease, it's more true than ever that the way to a man's heart really is through his stomach.

In the case of my husband, I think it's certainly true. To be honest, Frank is not what you'd call a heavy-duty romantic. On Valentine's Day he does give me roses, but I've wondered if the flowers appear because his secretary, Elaine Barnes, puts him up to it. I also get a wonderfully romantic Valentine's card, but for all I know Elaine may choose it for him. (I got curious and asked her. She doesn't.) In my heart of hearts, I think he enjoys Valentine's Day, but is more turned on by the health aspect of the menu that follows than by any flowers or valentines.

February has been celebrated as National Heart Month since 1962. What better time than February to pamper a loved one's heart—or your own—than the season for lovers? Here's a special February 14 dinner for your Valentine, one with an elegant menu for two that encourages love, devotion, and good health.

To star at the meal, serve Cornish Hens Scheherazade, a romantic choice because fresh hens, like love birds, come in pairs. They also are low in calories, fat, cholesterol, and sodium. Surrounding the birds with beauty and good nutrition, are brown-rice pilaf, sweet-flavored miniature vegetables, and a salad studded with deep-red beets cut in tiny hearts. For dessert? Forbidden Fruit Soufflé.

MENU

*Cornish Hens Scheherazade
with Miniature Vegetables

◆

*Curried Brown Rice Pilaf

◆

*Tender Hearts Salad

◆

*Forbidden Fruit Soufflé

---

*Recipe follows

CORNISH HENS SCHEHERAZADE

2 fresh Cornish game hens
4 tablespoons fresh lemon
    juice (reserve shell)
2 teaspoons soybean oil
½ teaspoon ground ginger
½ teaspoon ground cumin
Ground pepper to taste, and
    salt, if you must
Paprika to taste
4 whole cloves
2 small onions, halved
6 fresh or frozen baby carrots,
    lightly steamed
½ cup combined fresh or
    frozen baby peas and pearl
    onions, lightly steamed
Curried Brown Rice Pilaf
    (recipe follows)

Place hens in large shallow bowl. In small bowl, combine lemon juice, oil, ginger, cumin, pepper, salt, and paprika. Pour into and over Cornish hens. Cover and marinate in refrigerator 30 minutes or longer.

Preheat oven to 350°F. Stick cloves into onion halves. Place 2 onion halves and ¼ of the squeezed lemon inside each hen. Tie legs together and fold back wings. Sprinkle with pepper and paprika. Roast about 60 minutes or until juices run clear with no trace of pink when thigh is pierced. Serve hens with vegetables and Curried Brown Rice Pilaf.

CURRIED BROWN RICE PILAF

1 teaspoon soybean oil
⅓ cup chopped onion
1 teaspoon curry powder
¼ teaspoon ground ginger
⅛ teaspoon ground cumin
⅛ teaspoon ground turmeric
Ground pepper to taste, and
    salt, if you can't do
    without it
Dash Cayenne
½ cup uncooked brown rice
1 tablespoon raisins
    (optional)
1 can (10 ounces) low-
    sodium chicken broth
½ cup water
1 tablespoon snipped fresh or
    frozen chives

Preheat oven to 350°F. In small, non-stick skillet over medium-low heat, heat oil. Sauté onion, spices, and salt, if you're using it, in hot oil 2–3 minutes until tender but not browned. Stir in rice and raisins; remove from heat and set aside.

In an ovenproof saucepan, over high heat, bring chicken broth and water to a boil. Stir in rice mixture; cover and boil 5 minutes. Place covered saucepan in oven and continue to cook 45–50 minutes until rice is tender and liquid has been absorbed. To serve, toss pilaf with chives.

TENDER HEARTS SALAD

1 can (8 ounces) low-sodium fancy sliced beets
2 teaspoons cider vinegar
1 teaspoon Dijon mustard
1 tablespoon soybean oil
Ground pepper to taste
Pinch ground cinnamon to taste
2 small heads Bibb or Boston lettuce with outside leaves removed
2 teaspoons snipped fresh or frozen chives

Drain beets, reserving 2 tablespoons liquid. Using small heart-shaped cookie cutter or cardboard pattern, cut hearts out of beet slices. Prepare dressing; in small bowl, combine reserved beet liquid, vinegar, and mustard. Whisk in oil in a slow stream; season with pepper and cinnamon. Toss beets with dressing and set aside.

Trim base of lettuce heads, if necessary, so they sit flat; gently spread leaves open like a flower. Carefully wash lettuce in cold water; pat dry with paper towels. On each of the two salad plates, place one lettuce head; arrange beet hearts decoratively among leaves. To serve, drizzle with dressing and sprinkle with chives.

FORBIDDEN FRUIT SOUFFLÉ

2 large unblemished cooking/eating apples
½ lemon
1 cup unsweetened applesauce
2 teaspoons honey
Ground cinnamon to taste
Ground nutmeg to taste
2 tablespoons applejack or Calvados, divided (optional)
1 large egg white
Confectioners' sugar

Preheat oven to 375°F. Lightly grease baking dish. Wash apples and, if necessary, cut a thin slice off bottom of each apple to make it stand upright. Cut a ½-inch slice off tops of apples. Using a small, sharp knife and a grapefruit spoon, hollow out apples, leaving a shell ¼ inch thick. Rub inside and top edges of apple shells with lemon to keep them from discoloring. In small, heavy-bottomed saucepan over low heat, combine applesauce, honey, cinnamon, nutmeg, and 1–2 teaspoons applejack. Cook, stirring often, until heated through but not boiling. In small bowl, with mixer at high speed, beat egg white until stiff but not dry. Into medium-size mixing bowl, pour hot applesauce. Add half the egg white; fold in with a rubber or wooden spatula. Add remaining egg white and fold in gently.

Sprinkle inside of apple shells lightly with additional cinnamon and nutmeg. Place apple shells in prepared baking dish; carefully fill with applesauce mixture, doming the top. Bake in center of oven 15–17 minutes or until soufflés have risen and are very lightly browned on top. Remove soufflés from oven and sprinkle lightly with confectioners' sugar. To flame soufflés, in small saucepan, heat remaining applejack until barely warm. Using a long match, light applejack and pour over soufflés. Serve at once.

DRUMSTICK CROWN ROAST FOR A WHIMSICAL EASTER FEAST

The symbols of Easter are happy ones—spring flowers and spring greens, new clothes, cuddly animals and their chocolate look-alikes, jelly beans, fancy breads and cakes, colored eggs, and Easter egg hunts. Catching the spirit of the day, Perdue Farms' home economists developed a playful main course to "crown" the Easter meal. It is a roast of drumsticks fashioned into an edible crown by baking them upright around a coffee can. When baking is complete, a cornbread stuffing replaces the can. The technique is not difficult and the can actually helps brown the outside of the chicken.

Pilaf-Stuffed Crown Roast with Herb Gravy could be the centerpiece to a Greek Easter feast, including a classic Greek soup, artichoke casserole, and salad with feta cheese. Traditional touches such as a garnish of red-dyed hard-cooked eggs and luscious rich baklava from the bakery will add authenticity to the celebration. For an American-style meal, serve Cornbread-Stuffed Crown Roast of Drumsticks with Madeira Sauce. Either way, Happy Easter!

MENU

Hot Sherried Consommé

♦

*Pilaf-Stuffed Crown Roast of Drumsticks with
Herb Gravy
or
*Cornbread-Stuffed Crown Roast of Drumsticks
with Madeira Sauce

♦

Creamy Cole Slaw

♦

Maple Candied Sweet Potatoes

♦

Wilted Lettuce Salad

♦

Golden Chiffon Cake

---

*Recipe follows

PILAF-STUFFED CROWN ROAST OF DRUMSTICKS WITH HERB GRAVY

SERVES 4–6

10 roaster drumsticks
1 empty coffee can (12–16 ounces) with ends removed and outside greased
Kitchen twine
1/3 cup olive oil
Salt and ground pepper to taste
1½ teaspoons minced, fresh oregano or ¾ teaspoon dried, divided
1½ teaspoons minced, fresh thyme, or ¾ teaspoon dried
¼ cup flour
1 clove garlic, minced
2 cups chicken broth
4 hard-cooked eggs, dyed red, optional garnish
Fresh bay leaves, thyme, oregano, and marjoram, optional garnish
Greek Easter Pilaf (recipe follows)

Preheat oven to 375°F. Place coffee can in center of a round 9- or 10-inch cake pan. Arrange drumsticks around can, narrow ends up. With twine, tie drumsticks securely around the can in three places, starting at the middle, then bottom, then top. In a small bowl, combine oil with salt, pepper, half of oregano, and half of thyme; brush onto drumsticks. Roast drumsticks 1 hour, 10 minutes, basting halfway through cooking time with any remaining oil. Meanwhile, prepare Greek Easter Pilaf; keep warm.

Using two spatulas, remove roast with can to a warm 12-inch platter or chop plate. Pour ¼ cup pan juices into a small saucepan. Whisk in flour and cook over medium heat 10 minutes, stirring constantly. Add garlic, broth, and remaining oregano and thyme; bring to a boil, whisking constantly. Season to taste with salt and pepper; strain gravy into a warm sauceboat.

To serve roast, spoon pilaf into coffee can. Carefully lift off can and gently press drumsticks against pilaf. Garnish, if desired, with dyed eggs and fresh herbs.

GREEK EASTER PILAF

¼ cup (½ stick) butter or
  margarine
½ cup chopped onion
¼ cup pine nuts (pignoli)
1½ cups converted rice
2¼ cups chicken broth or
  water
½ teaspoon salt or to taste
¼ teaspoon ground pepper
½ cup currants or raisins
¼ cup minced, fresh parsley

In a saucepan over medium heat, melt butter. Sauté onion, pine nuts, and rice in hot butter 10 minutes, stirring constantly. Stir in broth, salt, pepper, and currants and bring to boil. Cover pot with tightly fitting lid; reduce heat to low. Cook rice 20 minutes or until tender. Fluff with a fork and toss with parsley.

CORNBREAD-STUFFED CROWN ROAST OF DRUMSTICKS WITH MADEIRA SAUCE

SERVES 6

10 roaster drumsticks
1 empty coffee can (12–16
  ounces) with both ends
  removed and outside
  greased
Kitchen twine
½ cup (1 stick) butter or
  margarine, melted
Salt and ground pepper to
  taste
1 teaspoon ground sage
Dixie Cornbread Stuffing
  (recipe follows)
¼ cup flour
2 tablespoons Madeira wine
2 cups chicken broth

Preheat oven to 375°F. Place coffee can in center of a round 9- or 10-inch cake pan. Arrange drumsticks around can, narrow ends up. With twine, tie drumsticks securely around the can in 3 places, starting at the middle, then bottom, then top. In a small bowl, combine butter with salt, pepper, and sage; brush onto drumsticks. Roast for 1 hour, 10 minutes, basting halfway through cooking time with any remaining butter. Meanwhile, prepare Dixie Cornbread Stuffing, cover, and bake in oven with roast during last 20 minutes of cooking time.

Using two spatulas, remove roast with can to a warm 12-inch platter or chop plate. Pour ¼ cup pan juices into a small saucepan. Whisk in flour and cook over medium heat 10 minutes, stirring constantly. Add Madeira and broth; bring to a boil, whisking frequently. Season to taste with salt and pepper; strain gravy into a warm sauceboat.

To serve roast, spoon stuffing into coffee can. Carefully lift off can and gently press drumsticks against stuffing.

DIXIE CORNBREAD STUFFING

¼ pound lean bacon, diced
½ cup chopped onion
½ cup chopped celery
¼ cup (½ stick) butter or
    margarine
½ pound fresh spinach, kale,
    or collard greens, cooked,
    well drained and chopped*
1 package (8 ounces)
    cornbread stuffing mix
1 cup chicken broth or water
Salt and ground pepper to
    taste

In a medium-size ovenproof skillet, over medium heat, sauté bacon, onion, and celery 5–10 minutes or until bacon is cooked. Add butter and heat until melted. Stir in greens, stuffing mix, and broth; toss well. Season with salt and pepper.

---

*Note: You can substitute ½ package (10 ounces) frozen chopped spinach, kale, or collard greens, thawed and drained.

MOTHER'S DAY DINNER— WITH LOVE FROM THE KIDS

Mother's Day became a national holiday in 1914. Since then, it's a day of love and memories, with no gifts more appreciated than the "I made it myself" or "I cooked it myself" variety.

I remember well the fledgling attempts by my oldest child to cook for Mother's Day. José wasn't much more than a toddler when he got the idea to make hot cocoa for a Mother's Day treat. While I was still in bed, he went into the kitchen, turned on the electric stove, and started to make the cocoa by setting a china cup full of water directly on the hot burner. I came into the kitchen just in time to prevent a disaster. As you can imagine, a quick lesson on kitchen safety followed.

Be sure your kids don't have a similar close call and warn them to stay away from the stove unless there's adult supervision. Assuming that there's an adult around to help, children can participate in making a wonderful treat for their mother.

The recipe that follows is "a dinner bouquet for Mom." Grade-school and older children can create a bouquet of chicken kebobs, helping to thread fruit and fresh boneless thigh meat on skewers and to "plant" them

MENU

*Citrus Chicken Bouquet
or
*Drumstick Blossoms
♦
Stewed Tomatoes
♦
Idaho Baked Potatoes with Sour Cream
♦
Succotash
♦
Dinner Rolls
♦
Berries and Cream

*Recipe follows

in rice. For younger children, even toddlers, Drumstick Blossoms are an easy alternate recipe in which drumsticks are rolled in Parmesan-flavored crumbs. Any age child can help scrub vegetables and spoon sherbet into orange cups. Teenagers can enjoy creating radish roses, making stir-fry rice, and scalloping orange baskets to hold the sherbet.

CITRUS CHICKEN BOUQUET

4 roaster boneless thigh cutlets
¼ cup fresh orange juice
2 tablespoons vegetable oil
2 tablespoons soy sauce
2 tablespoons honey
1 tablespoon grated orange peel
2 cloves garlic, minced
1½ teaspoons minced, fresh ginger or ½ teaspoon ground
2 medium-size green peppers, cut into 1-inch squares
2 tangerines or small oranges, peeled and pulled into sections
1 medium-size clean, glazed ceramic flowerpot
Garden Fried Rice (see recipe page 194) or 5–6 cups cooked rice

Cut chicken thighs into 1-inch chunks. In shallow bowl or non-metal container, combine orange juice, oil, soy sauce, honey, orange peel, garlic, and ginger; mix well. Cover and marinate chicken for 1 hour or longer, refrigerated.

Drain chicken; reserve marinade. Preheat broiler. On each of 4 to 6 12-inch skewers, alternately thread chicken, green pepper, and tangerine or orange sections. Broil kebobs, about 5 inches from heat, 10–15 minutes or until chicken is cooked through, turning occasionally and basting with marinade. To serve, spoon rice into flowerpot. Stand skewers in rice. Makes about 4 servings

Note: Kebobs can also be barbecued on an outdoor grill. Cook over medium-hot coals 10–15 minutes or until cooked through, turning occasionally and basting with marinade.

DRUMSTICK BLOSSOMS

6 tablespoons butter or
   margarine, melted
⅓ cup grated Parmesan
   cheese
⅓ cup seasoned bread
   crumbs
¼ cup sesame seeds
½ teaspoon paprika
Salt and ground pepper to
   taste
12 chicken drumsticks
1 medium-size clean, glazed
   clay flowerpot
1 small head Boston lettuce
   or green leaf lettuce
Parsley sprigs, optional

Children can make this Mother's Day "bouquet" of drumsticks. Served in a flowerpot it's whimsical and fun.

♦ ♦ ♦

Preheat oven to 375°F. Place butter in a baking dish. On wax paper, combine Parmesan cheese, bread crumbs, sesame seeds, paprika, salt, and pepper. Roll each drumstick in melted butter, then in crumbs until well coated. Arrange drumsticks in same baking dish, alternating direction of drums to accommodate all pieces. Bake about 45 minutes or until cooked through and golden brown.

   To serve, separate lettuce into leaves; wash and dry. Line bottom and sides of flowerpot with lettuce, allowing leafy edges to extend above rim of flowerpot. Place drumsticks, bone end down, on lettuce in flowerpot to resemble flowers. Garnish with parsley sprigs, if desired.

GARDEN FRIED RICE

2 tablespoons vegetable oil
½ cup peeled carrots (about 2
   small carrots) cut in ¼-
   inch dices
1 cup diced mushrooms
   (about 6 medium-size
   mushrooms)
½ cup chopped scallions
   (about 3 scallions)
½ cup diced summer squash
   (about 1 small squash)
½ cup diced celery (1 large
   rib)
½ cup diced red pepper (½
   medium-size pepper)
½ cup fresh or frozen peas
2½ cups cooked rice
2–3 tablespoons soy sauce

In large skillet over medium heat, heat oil. Sauté carrots in hot oil about 3 minutes, stirring frequently. Add remaining vegetables, cook, stirring, 3–5 minutes longer until all vegetables are tender-crisp. Stir in rice and mix well, cook until heated through. Stir in soy sauce and mix thoroughly.

FRANK PERDUE'S FOURTH OF JULY MENU

Frank has warm memories of his childhood, growing up on his father's poultry farm on the Eastern Shore of Maryland. He's been part of the family business since the time "he had to hold an egg with two hands." Like any other farm family on Maryland's Eastern Shore, the Perdues did not often get to enjoy a tender young broiler; that was strictly springtime eating, when there were small birds to spare. The rest of the year, chicken dinner meant long, slow cooking of one of the venerable hens.

"If a holiday came along," says Frank, "we could be sure my mother's big cast iron kettle would come out and it would be time to cook up one of the older hens. That was great eating!"

Here's the kind of Fourth of July menu that Frank grew up with. Since you probably don't have an old stewing hen, try an Oven Stuffer Roaster. Roasters are old enough to have a lot of flavor, but young enough not to be too tough.

If you're unfamiliar with slippery dumplings, they are more like noodles or wonton wrappers than conventional dumplings. Sweet Potato

MENU

*Eastern Shore Chicken with Slippery
Dumplings
♦
Turnip Greens
♦
Corn on the Cob
♦
Zucchini Parmesan
♦
*Sweet Potato Biscuits
♦
Iced Tea
♦
Peach Cobbler

*Recipe follows

Biscuits are a typical accompaniment, and Frank is so particular about them that the first six months of our marriage, I probably tried ten different recipes before hitting on the one that accompanies this Eastern Shore Chicken recipe.

Enjoy this Eastern Fourth of July feast.

EASTERN SHORE CHICKEN WITH SLIPPERY DUMPLINGS

SERVES 6–8

Poached Roaster:
1 whole roaster or 1 soup and
  stew hen
½ lemon
1 medium-size yellow onion
2 whole cloves
Salt and ground pepper to
  taste
6 cups chicken broth or more
  if desired
Water
1 bay leaf
1 pound small white onions,
  peeled
1 pound carrots (about 6),
  peeled and cut into 1½-
  inch lengths

Rub roaster inside and out with lemon. Cut onion in half and stick with cloves; place in cavity of roaster. Truss bird by lacing up cavity and tying legs together. Season with salt and pepper, and place in an 8-quart Dutch oven. Pour in chicken broth and enough water to reach halfway up sides of roaster; add bay leaf. Place over medium heat; bring liquid to a simmer. Reduce heat to medium-low. Cover and simmer, allowing 20 minutes per pound for a roaster and 40 minutes per pound for a stew hen. (To keep meat tender, do not allow to boil.) During last 45 minutes of cooking time, add onions and carrots. Roaster is done if juices run clear with no hint of pink when thickest part of thigh is pierced. (Hen should be cooked beyond this time to tenderize.) Remove bird and vegetables to serving platter and keep warm.

Add more broth or water to poaching liquid, if necessary, to bring it halfway up sides of Dutch oven; bring to a boil. Meanwhile prepare dumplings.

Slippery Dumplings:
2 cups flour
1 cup warm water
1 teaspoon salt or to taste

In mixing bowl, combine flour, warm water, and salt. Turn onto a well-floured surface and knead dough 4–5 minutes until it becomes elastic; reflour board as necessary. Roll out kneaded dough as thinly as possible. With sharp knife, cut into 1½- to 2-inch squares. Add to boiling poaching liquid and cook 5–7 minutes until "al dente." Remove dumplings to a serving bowl.

Over high heat, cook poaching liquid until reduced. This takes about 5 minutes. For a thicker gravy, add a small amount of flour—no more than 3 tablespooons—blended with cold water to poaching liquid. To serve, pour some gravy other dumplings; pass the rest separately. Carve roaster and serve with vegetables, dumplings, and gravy.

Note: You can substitute wonton skins for dumpling dough. A typical side dish for this dinner would be greens sautéed with onion and a little salt pork.

SWEET POTATO BISCUITS

1 cup drained, canned sweet potatoes
¼ cup syrup from canned sweet potato biscuits
2 tablespoons vegetable shortening
1 tablespoon sugar
1 cup flour
2 teaspons baking powder
½ teaspoon salt, or to taste

This is how I cook sweet potato biscuits for Frank. You may prefer the biscuits with a little more salt.

♦ ♦ ♦

Preheat oven to 425°F. Grease a baking sheet. Rice or mash potatoes until smooth; place in small saucepan and stir in syrup. Cook over medium heat, stirring constantly, until just warm. Stir in shortening and sugar; mix well. In a mixing bowl, sift together flour, baking powder, and salt. Stir in sweet potato mixture; mix well with wooden spoon or knead with hands for 1 minute. On floured surface, roll or pat out dough to ¾-inch thickness. With 1½- to 2-inch round biscuit cutter, cut out dough. Bake 12–15 minutes until golden on top and cooked through. Serve warm.

SAY "BRAVO, CRISTOFORO COLOMBO" AND CELEBRATE ITALIAN STYLE

Columbus Day has been a national holiday in this country since 1971. Its first official celebration, however, dates to 1792, the three hundredth anniversary of the exploration that brought Columbus and a crew of 120 sailors to the New World. The 1792 celebration took place in New York City, where today's Italian-American population equals the population of Genoa.

The first Columbus Day celebration included a gala banquet—a thoroughly appropriate way to mark the event that changed the eating habits of the Old World forever. The enriching exchange of foods between the Old and New World affected all the cuisines of Europe, but none more than that of Italy. Imagine Italian cuisine without tomatoes or peppers or corn.

REGIONAL ITALIAN COLUMBUS DAY MENU

Antipasto

◆

*Brodo Genovese

◆

*Chicken and Eggplant Agrodolce Siciliana

◆

*"Rice Birds" Piedmontese in Wine and Cream Sauce

◆

Broccoli Florets Parmigiano

◆

Crusty Italian Bread

◆

*Coppa da Festa Cristoforo Colombo

◆

Café Espresso

---

*Recipe follows

To many of us "eating Italian" is a favorite experience, and what could be a better excuse for a "festa Italiana" than "Cristoforo Colombo Day." Here's a complete menu for just such a holiday dinner. There's a choice of main courses—one with the color, spice, and flare of southern Italy, the other with the rich creaminess of the North.

Because large numbers of immigrants came from southern Italy, especially from Naples and Sicily, lively southern Italian dishes are most familiar to Americans. These typically include tomatoes, olive oil, garlic, spices such as cinnamon, raisins, and olives. Layered pastas and pizza come from the South.

In the North, foods are lighter, more varied, and are frequently delicate in flavor. Many dishes call for butter, cream, or cheese, and filled pasta and rice are also served. Chicken is suited to either style of cooking, and boneless Oven Stuffer Roaster thigh meat is as delicious with a spicy tomato sauce as with wine and cream. In all parts of Italy, fresh vegetables, fruit, and herbs are important. Columbus' own city of Genoa is most closely associated with the use of fresh basil.

Whether inspired by the North or the South, Columbus Day is a time to wave the flags, both our red, white, and blue and the Italian red, white, and green, and to salute Christopher Columbus with a meal to remember.

BRODO GENOVESE: CHICKEN BROTH WITH PASTA, CHEESE, AND BASIL

SERVES 6–8

7 cups homemade chicken stock or 4 cans (13¾ ounces each) chicken broth
1 cup small pasta such as tubetti (tiny tubes), farfalle (bow ties), or conchiglie (shells)
¼ cup minced fresh basil or Italian parsley
1 cup freshly grated Parmesan cheese

In large saucepan or Dutch oven over high heat, bring chicken stock to a boil. Add pasta and cook until tender, stirring occasionally, 8–10 minutes. To serve, ladle hot soup into bowls; sprinkle with basil or parsley and pass the grated cheese.

CHICKEN AND EGGPLANT AGRODOLCE SICILIANA

SERVES 6–8

1 large eggplant (about 1½ pounds), cut into 1½-inch cubes
8 roaster boneless thigh cutlets
Salt and ground pepper to taste
½–¾ cup olive oil, divided
2 cups sliced red onions
¼ cup balsamic vinegar or red wine vinegar
4 cloves garlic, minced
½ teaspoon ground cinnamon
2 tablespoons honey
Grated rind of 2 oranges
1 can (16 ounces) whole plum tomatoes, drained and cut into thin strips
Minced, fresh parsley and basil (optional)

Sprinkle eggplant with salt; let stand 30 minutes to extract liquid; rinse and pat dry. Trim off any fat from thighs and cut into 2-inch pieces.

Preheat oven to 350°F. In large heavy skillet over medium heat, heat 2 tablespoons oil. Add chicken, half at a time; sauté 2–3 minutes until lightly browned, adding more oil if necessary. Remove pieces with slotted spoon to large, covered casserole or baking dish. Add 2–4 tablespoons oil to skillet; stir in eggplant and cook 5 minutes until golden, adding more oil if necessary. Add to casserole.

Pour vinegar into skillet, scraping and stirring to remove pan glaze; add garlic, cinnamon, honey, orange rind, and salt and pepper to taste. Pour vinegar mixture into casserole. Cover and bake 15 minutes. Stir in tomato strips, recover and bake 15 minutes longer. Garnish with minced parsley and basil, if desired. Serve with hot crusty Italian bread.

COPPA DA FESTA CRISTOFORO COLOMBO

SERVES 8

Amarettini (small almond-flavored biscuits) or large Amaretti, crushed
1 pint each strawberry, vanilla, and pistachio ice cream
Amaretto liqueur (optional)
Colored candy sprinkles or nonpareils
16 cocktail toothpick flags of Italy and U.S.A. (8 each)

For each serving: In bottom of large, stemmed glass, place 1 teaspoon Amarettini biscuit. Alternately scoop strawberry, vanilla, and pistachio ice cream on top, sprinkling about 1 teaspoon Amarettini between each scoop. Pour a little Amaretto or other liqueur on ice cream, if desired. Top with sprinkles and insert a flag of Italy and of the U.S.A. Repeat with remaining ingredients. Serve immediately or place coppas in freezer until ready to serve.

"RICE BIRDS" PIEDMONTESE IN WINE AND CREAM SAUCE

8 roaster boneless thigh cutlets
Salt and ground pepper to taste
4 tablespoons butter or margarine, divided
2 tablespoons chopped onion
¾ teaspoon minced, fresh rosemary or sage, or ¼ teaspoon dried
2 ounces chopped prosciutto or ham
1 cup cooked rice
4 tablespoons grated Parmesan cheese
½ cup (2 ounces) grated or diced Italian fontina or mozzarella cheese
2 tablespoons olive oil
1 cup chicken or beef broth
½ cup dry white wine
½ cup heavy cream
1 tablespoon minced, fresh parsley

Trim off and discard any fat and sprinkle chicken with salt and pepper. Place between 2 moistened pieces of plastic wrap; pound until about ¼ inch thick.

In large, heavy, oven-proof skillet over medium heat, melt 2 tablespoons butter. Add onion and ⅛ teaspoon rosemary or sage; cook, stirring occasionally, 2–3 minutes, until tender but not brown. Stir in prosciutto; cook 1 minute longer.

In small bowl, combine onion mixture, rice, and cheeses; season with salt and pepper to taste. Place 1 heaping tablespoon rice stuffing 1 inch from end of each pounded thigh. Roll up thighs into neat "packages," folding edges in over stuffing; tie packages with kitchen string.

In same skillet over medium heat, melt remaining butter with oil. Cook Rice Birds in butter-oil on all sides until lightly browned, about 8–10 minutes. Cover skillet and simmer 35 minutes. Transfer "birds" to serving platter; cut strings and keep warm.

Add broth, wine, and remaining rosemary to skillet, scraping bottom to incorporate any browned bits. Stir in cream; cook over medium heat until sauce is thick enough to lightly coat the back of a spoon. Do not boil. Return birds and any juices to skillet; cover with sauce and cook briefly just until heated through.

Arrange Rice Birds and sauce on serving platter and sprinkle with parsley.

RECIPES OF OLD SOUTH ARE TODAY'S THANKSGIVING TREASURES

Even before George Washington declared Thanksgiving a national holiday, its celebration had spread from Massachusetts Colony to all America. In the Old South, Thanksgiving could mean weeks of preparation, days of celebrating and a house that overflowed with guests. Modern times have inevitably relaxed some standards of southern hospitality, but not necessarily when it comes to setting a sumptuous table.

Here's a Carolina version of a Thanksgiving bird. It's an Oven Stuffer Roaster complete with a nest of stuffing. The stuffing is cooked outside instead of inside, so it soaks up the pan juices and develops a lightly crusted surface. It's not only wonderful eating, but an appealing presentation as well.

THANKSGIVING DAY
DINNER DELIGHT

*Roaster Nested in Sage Dressing with Sweet
Potato Puff

◆

*Creamed Giblet Gravy

◆

String Beans Almondine

◆

Creamy Cole Slaw

◆

Cranberry Salad

◆

Sour Dough Dinner Rolls

◆

Southern Pecan Pie

---

*Recipe follows

ROASTER NESTED IN SAGE DRESSING WITH SWEET POTATO PUFF AND CREAMED GIBLET GRAVY

1 whole roaster
Salt and ground pepper to taste
3 cups hot water
1 loaf (1¼–1½ pounds) day-old white bread
1 cup chopped onion
1½ cups chopped celery
¼ cup minced, fresh parsley
1½ tablespoons minced fresh sage or 1¼ teaspoons dried sage
¼ teaspoon dried thyme
2 eggs
1 tablespoon butter or margarine
Creamed Giblet Gravy (recipe follows)

Preheat oven to 350°F. Remove giblets and sprinkle inside of bird with salt and pepper. Tie legs together and fold wings back. Place roaster in roasting pan or baking dish along with giblets. Pour in 2 cups hot water. Roast 1¼ hours, basting occasionally with pan liquids.

Meanwhile, prepare dressing: tear bread into ½-inch pieces; place in large bowl with onion, celery, parsley, ¾ teaspoon salt, ½ teaspoon pepper, sage, and thyme. Mix well and set aside. After 1¼ hours, remove roaster from oven.

Reserve giblets and pour 2 cups of pan juices through strainer into a medium-size saucepan; reserve for gravy. Add water to remaining pan juices, if necessary, to bring liquid to 1½ cups. Ladle into bowl with dressing mixture; add eggs and mix until thoroughly moistened.

With hands, mold stuffing around outside of roaster to form a "nest." Brush butter over breast. Return roaster to oven; continue cooking 45 minutes to 1 hour longer or until dressing is cooked and lightly browned and juices run clear with no hint of pink when roaster thigh is pierced.

If desired, serve nested roaster from roasting pan. Or run spatula under bird to loosen it and carefully transfer it to heated platter, keeping dressing intact.

Serve with **Creamed Giblet Gravy:**

Creamed Giblet Gravy:
2 cups reserved pan juices
Reserved roaster giblets, chopped
¾ cup milk
¼ cup flour
Salt and ground pepper to taste

Chop giblets and add to pan juices; over medium heat, bring to a simmer. In small bowl, make a smooth paste of milk and flour. Whisk flour mixture into pan juices and continue whisking until gravy is thickened. Season with salt and pepper to taste.

BOURBON SWEET POTATO PUFF

6 medium-size cooked sweet
    potatoes or 1 can (40
    ounces) sweet potatoes,
    drained
¼ cup (½ stick) unsalted
    butter or margarine,
    melted
3 eggs
½ cup firmly packed brown
    sugar
¾ teaspoon ground cinnamon
¼ teaspoon ground cloves
¼ teaspoon ground nutmeg
1 to 2 teaspoons grated
    orange rind
¼ cup bourbon
1 package (10 ounces)
    marshmallows

If you have a sweet tooth like Frank, you'll love this recipe.

♦ ♦ ♦

Preheat oven to 350°F. Butter a 1½-quart soufflé dish or casserole. Peel cooked sweet potatoes. In large bowl, combine potatoes with remaining ingredients except marshmallows. With electric mixer or food processor, beat or process until fluffy. Turn mixture into prepared dish or casserole; arrange marshmallows over top. Bake 20 minutes or until marshmallows are puffed and golden.

A CHANUKAH FESTIVAL OF FUN AND FOOD

Chanukah is the Jewish holiday of remembrance, a festival of lights, and most of all, a family party that is celebrated during eight joyful days. Chanukah was first celebrated more than 2,100 years ago, following the defeat of the Syrian army by the Macabees. After driving the Syrians from Jerusalem, the Jewish temple was ceremonially cleansed. During the cleaning, a flask of oil belonging to the high priest was found. It contained enough oil to burn one night. Instead, it burned miraculously for eight days and eight nights. That is why a special eight-branch menorah (candlestick) is lit each Chanukah night at sundown, beginning with a single lighted candle on the first night and building to a full eight.

As with all Jewish holidays, traditional foods are part of the celebration. Fried and sautéed dishes have special Chanukah significance because of the oil used in cooking them. Holiday Chicken Sauté is a favorite meal in one family in which there are two small boys who still prefer fingers to forks. Their mother, a food consultant, once asked Frank what he thought of such table manners. His answer: "That's why we sell our drumsticks with built-in handles."

With most of America's Jewish settlers having come from Eastern Europe, holiday foods served in that part of the world are most popular here. For Chanukah, this means crisp, brown potato latkes (Yiddish for pancakes). Latkes are usually served with fresh applesauce and sour cream. Before the arrival of the food processor, hand grating the potatoes

---

**FAMILY CHANUKAH
SUPPER PARTY**

*Holiday Chicken Sauté

◆

*Potato Latkes

◆

*Applesauce

◆

*Fichuelas De Chanukah

---

*Recipe follows

was a traditional pre-dinner part of the ritual, with everyone taking turns at grating potatoes—and sometimes knuckles.

In Israel, fried jelly doughnuts are frequently served instead of latkes, and many Sephardic Jews (from Mediterranean countries), serve fried pastries unique to each country. Among them are Moroccan fichuelas. These crisp, honey-coated pastries are great fun to twirl in hot oil and shape into pinwheels—but beware of the little fingers near hot oil.

HOLIDAY CHICKEN SAUTÉ

SERVES 4–6

2 tablespoons vegetable oil or chicken fat
6 chicken drumsticks
6 chicken thighs
3 small zucchini, cut into ½-inch slices
3 medium-size carrots, peeled and cut into ½-inch slices
1 large onion, sliced into rings
2 tablespoons fresh lemon juice
2 tablespoons honey
1 lemon, thinly sliced
1 teaspoon salt or to taste
1 teaspoon paprika
1 tablespoon cornstarch
2 tablespoons cold water

In large, deep skillet or Dutch oven over medium-high heat, heat oil. Sauté drumsticks and thighs in hot oil until lightly browned on all sides, about 15 minutes. Remove from skillet. To pan drippings, add zucchini, carrots, and onion; sauté 3 minutes. Return chicken to skillet; Add lemon juice, honey, lemon slices, salt, and paprika. Reduce heat to medium-low; cover and cook 20–25 minutes longer or until chicken and vegetables are tender. In cup, place cornstarch; add water and blend to form a smooth paste. Stir into skillet and cook until slightly thickened. To serve, arrange chicken, lemon slices, and vegetables on large platter; spoon sauce on top.

POTATO LATKES (Potato Pancakes)

5 medium-size raw potatoes
1 medium-size onion, peeled
2 eggs
¼ cup matzo meal or flour
1 teaspoon salt or to taste
Vegetable oil for frying

Wash potatoes; remove spots or blemishes with a small knife. Peel potatoes, if desired. With hand grater or food processor fitted with steel shredding blade, coarsely grate potatoes. Transfer to large bowl; cover with cold water and let stand 10 minutes. Drain potatoes in colander, pressing out excess liquid. Using hand grater or food processor fitted with steel blade, grate or chop onion. Combine drained potatoes, onion, eggs, matzo meal or flour, and salt; mix well. (As mixture stands, more liquid will accumulate. Do not pour off liquid; stir mixture frequently to blend.)

In large skillet, heat ¼ inch oil over medium heat until hot. Drop potato mixture by tablespoons into hot oil; flatten slightly with spatula. Cook pancakes, a few at a time, until golden brown on both sides, turning once and adding more oil if necessary. Drain on paper towels. Keep cooked pancakes warm in preheated 200°F oven while others are cooking. Serve pancakes warm, with applesauce.

APPLESAUCE

5–6 medium-size tart apples
    (about 2 pounds)
2–4 tablespoons water
1–2 tablespoons sugar, to
    taste (optional)
¼ teaspoon cinnamon
¼ teaspoon nutmeg

*F*rank's normally not fond of Granny Smith apples, but he loves them cooked in this recipe.

♦ ♦ ♦

Peel apples, if desired; remove cores and seeds. Cut apples into chunks; place in medium-size saucepan. Add 2 tablespoons water, sugar if desired, cinnamon, and nutmeg. Over medium heat, bring to a boil. Reduce heat to low; cover and cook 20–30 minutes or until apples are very tender, stirring occasionally and adding more water if necessary. Remove from heat and stir until large lumps disappear and mixture is fairly smooth. If apples are used unpeeled, strain sauce in food press or mill to remove skin. Let stand until cool; refrigerate until ready to serve.

FICHUELAS DE CHANUKAH (Spiral-Shaped Sephardic Chanukah Pastries)

5 cups flour
1 teaspoon salt or to taste
2 eggs, slightly beaten
2¼ cups vegetable oil, divided
¾ cup warm water
1½ cups sugar
½ cup water

In large bowl or container of food processor, fitted with steel blade, combine flour, salt, eggs, ¼ cup oil, and ¾ cup warm water. Stir or process until mixture forms a fairly stiff dough. On unfloured surface, knead dough 5 minutes until smooth and elastic. Divide dough into 4 parts; roll each into a ball and wrap in plastic wrap. Let dough stand 1 hour for easier handling. On lightly floured surface, roll out one ball into a 9 × 18-inch rectangle. Cut dough into 6 strips, each about 1½ inches wide and 18 inches long.

In small saucepan over low heat, heat sugar in water until sugar is dissolved, stirring constantly; keep warm. In medium-size saucepan over medium heat, heat 2 cups oil to 375°F, or until small piece of dough sizzles when dropped in oil. With hand, gently lift one end of a dough strip; pierce the opposite end with a long-handled fork and twirl fork once to secure dough. Place dough, fork-end first, into hot oil. As dough fries, quickly and gently turn fork, rolling dough around to form a pinwheel. Fry dough until puffed and golden, 30–60 seconds. (Do not brown.) Slip dough off fork; remove from oil with slotted spoon and immediately dip into warm sugar mixture to coat well. Cool completely on wire rack placed over wax paper. Repeat with remaining dough.

A ROMANTIC CHRISTMAS DINNER, GEORGE AND MARTHA WASHINGTON–STYLE

George and Martha Washington made much of Christmas. They married on the twelfth night of Christmas in 1759, and from that year forward they tried to be together for the holidays. (One exception was Christmas 1776, when General Washington was busy crossing the Delaware.)

Two of the food specialists at Perdue are history buffs and they put together for Frank a Christmas menu based on "receipts" (as recipes were once called) for dishes that might have been enjoyed at Christmas dinner, two hundred years ago.

As they point out, even basic food supplies were very different two centuries ago. American waters were so abundant with crabs, oysters, shrimp, and clams, that inventive cooks tossed them into soups and spreads, baked them "potted," "scalloped" or in loaves, and used them lavishly in sauces and stuffings. The oyster stuffing included in this menu is based on a specialty of George Washington's mother. She may have

---

AN EARLY AMERICAN CHRISTMAS DINNER FOR FOUR

Potted Crab

◆

*Cornish Hens with Oyster Stuffing Mount Vernon

◆

*Sherried Pan Gravy

◆

Savory Grated-Carrot Christmas Pudding

◆

Pickled Beet Salad

◆

*"Whipt" Syllabub with Sweetmeats

---

*Recipe follows

served it with passenger pigeon—common fare in those days. Although this wild bird is extinct today, Cornish game hens make tasty, tender, modern substitutes. And it is far easier to "bag a brace" or two of Cornish hens at the local supermarket than to stalk dinner in the wild.

Early Americans weren't partial to vegetables. They tended to overcook and under season them, then serve them up as a "mess of pease." But old-time cooks did make wonderful vegetable puddings and were superb at pickling and preserving their vegetables and fruits to serve all winter long.

From the beginning, American settlers distilled spirits. Even the stern Pilgrims (who considered the celebration of Christmas pagan) drank wine and cider for their health. After a festive holiday meal, most of our founding fathers probably enjoyed a few rounds of Madeira or Port. But Thomas Jefferson's favorite holiday drink was a spicy mixture of hot ale and rum, so heat producing it was called "a yard of flannel." Frothy syllabub was thought to be suitable for everyone, even women and children, and this rich drink was a delicious accompaniment to sweetmeats, stewed fruit, cakes, or pies.

Though few would wish to return to cooking at the hearth and beehive oven, if you're smitten by the romance of the past, try serving special guests a Christmas dinner George and Martha Washington–style.

"WHIPT" SYLLABUB

SERVES 4–6

3 tablespoons dark rum or Cognac
2 tablespoons sugar
Grated rind and juice of 1 lemon
¼ teaspoon freshly grated nutmeg
1 cup (½ pint) heavy cream
Sprigs fresh rosemary (optional)
Sweetmeats (see note) or stewed fruits

In large bowl, with mixer at medium speed, beat rum, sugar, lemon rind, and nutmeg. Gradually add heavy cream, beating constantly until cream forms soft peaks. (Do not overbeat.) Cover and refrigerate until serving time.

When ready to serve, if liquids have separated, beat by hand to reincorporate. Serve Syllabub in small cordial glasses, garnished with a rosemary sprig. Accompany with sweetmeats.

Note: Sweetmeats are any dainty little confections such as stuffed dates, chocolate truffles, sugared apricots and pears, or even candied watermelon rind.

CORNISH HENS WITH OYSTER STUFFING MOUNT VERNON AND SHERRIED PAN GRAVY

SERVES 4

4 fresh Cornish game hens
Salt and ground pepper to
     taste
4 tablespoons butter or
     margarine, divided
6 oysters, shucked, coarsely
     chopped, and strained
     through a fine sieve or
     coffee filter (reserve oyster
     liquor)
Pinch ground mace
¾ teaspoon minced, fresh
     thyme or ¼ teaspoon
     dried
¼ cup chopped onion
2–3 slices day-old bread,
     cubed
¼ teaspoon salt
⅛ teaspoon pepper
1 tablespoon fresh lemon
     juice
2 tablespoons dry sherry,
     divided
Spiced or brandied fruit for
     garnish (optional)

Preheat oven to 350°F. Season hens inside and out with salt and pepper.

In medium-size skillet over medium heat, melt 2 tablespoons butter with ½ cup oyster liquor, mace, and thyme. Add onion; cook 5 minutes until onion is tender and liquid is reduced to about ⅓ cup.

In medium-size bowl, toss onion mixture with oysters, bread cubes, salt, pepper, lemon juice, and 1 tablespoon sherry.

Spoon oyster stuffing loosely into hens. Tie legs together and fold back wings.

In a small saucepan, melt remaining butter; combine with remaining sherry and baste hens with mixture. Roast hens, basting occasionally, about 1 hour and 15 minutes or until juices run clear with no hint of pink when thigh is pierced. Remove hens from roasting pan, cut strings, place on serving platter and keep warm. Pour pan juices into a heat proof measuring cup or small bowl. Skim off 2 tablespoons of clear yellow drippings that rise to the top and return to pan. Skim off any remaining yellow drippings and discard. Reserve degreased pan juices to add to gravy with broth.

If desired, serve hens garnished with spiced or brandied fruit. Serve with sherried gravy.

SHERRIED PAN GRAVY

2 tablespoons reserved pan
     drippings
2 tablespoons flour
2 cups chicken broth or water
4 tablespoons dry sherry

Place roasting pan over medium heat; add flour to reserved clear pan drippings and cook 2 minutes, stirring and scraping the bottom to incorporate any browned bits. Stir in enough combined degreased pan juices, chicken broth, and sherry to make 2 cups; simmer, stirring constantly, 2 minutes longer. Strain gravy into sauceboat.

9

CHICKEN FOR VERY IMPORTANT OCCASIONS

Show-Stopper Recipes

With the majority of the recipes in this book, I've tried to keep in mind that you are busy and have plenty of other things to do with your time besides spending it in the kitchen. I've also tried to keep the ingredients and the processes reasonably simple and I've usually had an eye on the calories and the cost.

This chapter is an exception. These recipes ignore calories, and some of them require not just minutes of preparation, but days. There are some occasions, however, that deserve showstopper recipes. Maybe your daughter is getting married? Or you're celebrating a very special anniversary? Someone important to you just got a promotion? Or you're part of a gourmet club, and you want your recipe to be at least as good as Linda's?

This chapter is the place to look for the show-stoppers, the ones that will really make people feel special, and that they'll be talking about for days to come.

GLAZED BASS DRUMSTICKS

10 chicken drumsticks, padded as illustrated below
⅓ cup flour
¾ teaspoon salt or to taste
⅛ teaspoon ground pepper
¼ cup butter or margarine
1 can (6 ounces) frozen orange juice concentrate
1 can (6 ounces) water
2 tablespoons dark brown sugar
¾ teaspoon minced, fresh oregano or ¼ teaspoon dried
½ teaspoon nutmeg

These really do look like the padded sticks a drummer would use for his bass drum.

♦ ♦ ♦

1. Remove the knobby knuckle from the end of a drumstick by giving it a good hard whack with your heaviest knife. If you happen to have a meat cleaver the job is easier.
2. Stand the drumstick on its meaty end and push the skin down to expose the tendons. Remove the largest tendons by pulling them free with a pair of clean pliers.
3. Scrape the skin and meat away from the bone to form a rounder, more compact drumstick.

In a large plastic bag combine flour, salt, and pepper. Add chicken pieces and shake to coat. In a large skillet over medium heat, melt butter. Add chicken pieces and brown on all sides, 12–15 minutes. Pour off remaining butter. In a large measuring cup combine remaining ingredients. Add orange juice mixture to skillet. Cover and cook over low heat 25–35 minutes, turning chicken several times until cooked through.

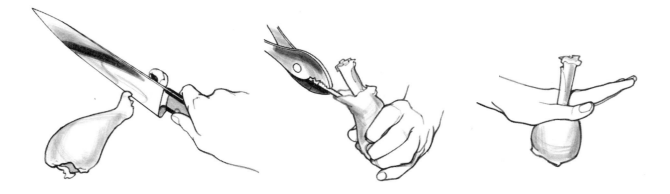

BREAST PAILLARD

1 roaster boneless breast or 1 package thin sliced boneless roaster breast
Vegetable oil
Salt and ground pepper to taste
¼ cup butter or margarine, at room temperature
2 tablespoons snipped fresh or frozen chives
1 teaspoon minced fresh tarragon, or ¼ teaspoon dried
2 tablespoons minced, fresh parsley

This is an especially attractive dish. I tried it on our indoor electric grill and since then have made it over and over again.

♦ ♦ ♦

Remove tenderloin pieces from back of breast. Place breast pieces and tenderloins between sheets of plastic wrap and pound to ¼-inch thickness to form 6 cutlets. Skip the preceding steps if using the thin sliced roaster breast. Brush with oil and season with salt and pepper. Combine butter, chives, and tarragon. Reform into a bar and freeze to harden. Grill cutlets over hot coals, a few minutes per side, rotating the chicken on the grill to form crosshatch markings. Or broil 3 inches from heat a few minutes on each side until lightly browned. Cut herb butter in slices. Sprinkle each slice with parsley and top with a butter slice. Serve immediately.

BREAST ROLL CORDON BLEU

1 roaster boneless breast
¾ cup whole milk ricotta
1 package (3 ounces) cream cheese, softened
1 egg yolk
¼ cup grated Parmesan cheese
¼ cup thinly sliced scallion
¼ cup minced fresh parsley
1 clove garlic, minced
⅛ teaspoon nutmeg
Salt and ground pepper to taste
¼ pound sliced ham
3–4 cups chicken broth

You can find another version of this on page 159, but this one is a show-stopper.

♦ ♦ ♦

Place breast halves side by side between two sheets of plastic wrap and pound to ¼-inch thickness, forming an 8 × 12-inch rectangle. In a mixing bowl combine remaining ingredients except ham and broth. Place breast smooth side down on a piece of dampened cheesecloth. Arrange ham slices over chicken breast. Spread filling over ham leaving a ½-inch border. Carefully roll breast, lengthwise, jellyroll fashion around filling. Wrap in cheesecloth, tie ends and at two or three places along length of the roll. Bring broth to a boil in a large saucepan. Add chicken and reduce heat to low. Poach chicken, covered, 35 minutes. Remove from pan and let cool. Remove cheesecloth and chill. Cut chicken roll in ¾-inch slices and arrange over lettuce or watercress

CHICKEN BROCCOLI CAKE

Sauce:
3 tablespoons butter or
    margarine
3 tablespoons flour
1½ cups milk
¼ teaspoon salt or to taste
⅛ teaspoon ground white
    pepper
⅛ teaspoon nutmeg

Filling:
3 tablespoons butter or
    margarine
2 cups broccoli, cooked and
    chopped (Once when I
    didn't have enough
    broccoli on hand, I
    rounded it out with green
    peas and it was great.)
⅓ cup grated Parmesan
    cheese
¼ teaspoon salt or to taste
⅛ teaspoon ground pepper
⅛ teaspoon nutmeg
1½ cups finely chopped
    cooked chicken
⅓ cup grated Swiss cheese
6 pancakes, each a little less
    than 7 inches wide and
    about ¼ inch thick. (The
    thicker the pancake, the
    taller the "cake." Use your
    favorite recipe or mix.)

You might think this is a very unusual dessert, but in fact, the recipe's name comes from its shape, not its taste. Although this takes a while to make, especially the pancakes, I've always felt it was well worth it every time I've made it. You can eat this with just a fork, so it's particularly good for a buffet meal when your guests are balancing food on their laps.

◆ ◆ ◆

In a saucepan over medium heat, melt butter. Blend in flour and cook, stirring for 1 minute. Add milk and cook, stirring, until sauce is smooth and thickened. Add salt, pepper, and nutmeg.

When choosing the broccoli for the filling, look for firm, compact clusters of small flower buds. If you can see any yellow flowers, the broccoli is overmature. Broccoli is at its best when the bud clusters are dark green or sage green, or even green with a decidedly purplish cast.

◆ ◆ ◆

In a saucepan over medium heat, melt butter. Stir in broccoli, Parmesan, salt, pepper, nutmeg, and chicken. (You can stop at this point the night before, but remember to bake the "cake" longer since the ingredients will be cold from being in the refrigerator.)

Preheat oven to 375°F.

To assemble "cake," butter a cookie sheet and place a pancake on it. Spread with part of the broccoli filling. Repeat layers, ending with a pancake. Pour sauce over the top and sprinkle with Swiss cheese. Bake 15 minutes (or 25 minutes if ingredients were refrigerated). Place under a hot broiler and broil until cheese is lightly browned, To serve, cut into wedges and spoon sauce over and around.

CHICKEN FONDUE I

4 skinless, boneless chicken
  breast halves
½ teaspoon salt or to taste
¼ teaspoon ground pepper
4 cans (13¾ ounces each)
  chicken broth
1 bottle (12 ounces) chili
  sauce
½ cup mayonnaise or salad
  dressing
1 tablespoon finely chopped
  onion
¼ clove garlic, minced

I haven't seen anyone use a fondue pot for a long time, but it's still a great way to serve chicken, and it's a fun and informal way to entertain. Maybe it's time to remember this once-popular way of cooking. This first version is low-calorie; the second is more traditional.

♦ ♦ ♦

Cut each breast in one-inch cubes. Sprinkle salt and pepper on chicken. Bring broth to boiling in fondue pot and keep at that temperature. Provide each guest with portion of chicken and fondue fork as well as fork for eating. Each guest cooks own chicken on fondue fork by holding in boiling broth about 1 minute, or until done. In a small bowl mix remaining ingredients as sauce for dipping after cooking.

CHICKEN FONDUE II

4 skinless, boneless chicken
  breast halves
1½ pints oil
1½ teaspoon salt or to taste
¼ teaspoon ground pepper
2 eggs, beaten
1 cup water
3 tablespoons sesame seed
1½ cups flour

Cut chicken breasts into 1-inch cubes. Bring oil to 350–375°F in fondue pot and keep at that temperature. Sprinkle ½ teaspoon of the salt and the pepper on chicken. In a mixing bowl combine remaining salt, eggs, water, sesame seed, and flour to make a batter. Provide each guest with fondue fork as well as fork for eating. Each guest cooks own chicken on fondue fork by dipping into batter and then holding in hot oil approximately 1 minute, or until done. Serve with a variety of dips. Any barbecue sauce makes a good dip. I also recommend the Dill Dip and Orange Dip, below.

Dill Dip:
(makes 1 cup)
½ cup mayonnaise or salad
  dressing
½ cup sour cream
1 teaspoon fresh lemon juice
2 teaspoons finely chopped
  onion
½ teaspoon salt or to taste
½ teaspoon dry mustard
½ teaspoon dill seed

In a small bowl combine all ingredients and stir until blended.

Orange Dip:
(makes 1 cup)
1 can (6 ounces) orange juice
    concentrate
3 tablespoons oil
1 tablespoon vinegar
1 tablespoon sugar
¼ teaspoon dry mustard
¼ teaspoon salt or to taste
⅛ teaspoon Tabasco

In a blender or food processor combine all ingredients. Blend 5 seconds or until smooth.

Note: Use leftover orange or dill dip for fresh raw vegetables such as cauliflower, broccoli, carrots, or celery.

CHICKEN KIEV

SERVES 4

4 skinless, boneless chicken
    breast halves or 1 package
    thin sliced boneless
    roaster breast
½ cup butter or margarine,
    chilled
1 tablespoon lemon juice
1 tablespoon snipped fresh or
    frozen chives
½ teaspoon salt or to taste
¼ teaspoon ground pepper
1 egg, beaten
1 cup bread crumbs
Oil for deep frying

Frank and I had this in a restaurant in Moscow back in 1988. We were there because the Soviet government had invited Frank and his CEO, Don Mabe, to give them tips on producing plumper chicken. Don's wife, Flo, and I got to go along. Frank was impressed by the knowledge and skill of the Soviet poultrymen, but he noted that their chickens' diets didn't include enough protein. The Soviet birds may have been thin, but their recipe for Chicken Kiev was otlichnii (outstanding). You've got it exactly right if, when you cut the cooked chicken, the melted butter spurts out.

♦ ♦ ♦

Place chicken between sheets of plastic wrap and pound to flatten slightly. Skip the previous step if you are using thin sliced boneless roaster breast. In a food processor fitted with a steel blade, blend butter, lemon juice, and chives; mold into four oblongs, place on waxed paper, and put in freezer. Sprinkle salt and pepper on chicken. Wrap chicken breast around chilled or frozen butter mold and secure with toothpicks. Dip in beaten egg and roll in bread crumbs. Chill again for one hour. Fry in deep fat at 350°F 8–10 minutes or until crust is golden brown. Serve immediately.

CHICKEN PAELLA PERDUE

1 chicken, cut in serving
 pieces
1 teaspoon salt or to taste
⅛ teaspoon ground pepper
1 small clove garlic, minced
8 tablespoons butter or
 margarine, melted, divided
2 cups quick-cooking rice,
 uncooked
¼ cup chopped onion
½ teaspoon paprika
1 tablespoon minced, fresh
 parsley
½ teaspoon seafood
 seasoning
2–3 filaments saffron
 (optional)
½ cup fresh or 1 can (8
 ounces) minced, soft shell
 clams
2 tablespoons clam juice
1 cup canned chicken broth
½ pound backfin crabmeat
1 cup peas
1 dozen small clams (on the
 half-shell)
1 package (9 ounces) frozen
 artichokes, cooked
1 jar (2 ounces) pimento
 strips

This is the Perdue version of the traditional paella. The authentic Spanish version takes all day to make. I've watched cooks in Spain do it. You'll notice that the saffron in this paella is optional. That's because the last time I looked at the price for it in the spice jars in the supermarket, I calculated that saffron costs more than gold dust. However, you only need to use a couple of strands of it at a time. If you don't use it, this recipe will still taste good—just different. It will also look different because saffron imparts an attractive yellow to the rice. The reason saffron costs so much is that it's made from the dried stigma of the saffron crocus. It takes 225,000 stigmas to make a pound of saffron.

◆ ◆ ◆

Preheat oven to 350°F. Place chicken in single layer, skin side up, in shallow baking dish; season with salt, pepper and garlic. Pour 4 tablespoons of the butter or margarine over chicken; cover and bake 45 minutes or until cooked through, uncovering during last 20 minutes for browning. While chicken is baking, in a large skillet over medium heat, melt remaining butter. Add the uncooked rice and onions and sauté until lightly browned. Add paprika, parsley, seafood seasoning, saffron, minced clams, clam juice, and chicken broth. Simmer over very low heat 15 minutes. In the shallow baking dish, leave ⅔ of the chicken; add the rice mixture, the crabmeat, and peas in layers. As garnish, place on top of this, the remaining chicken, all of the clams in the half-shell, cooked artichokes, and pimento. Cover and bake at 350°F 10–15 minutes to heat through.

PHYLLO-WRAPPED CHICKEN

1 cup mayonnaise
1 cup chopped scallions
2 tablespoons minced fresh
  parsley
3 cloves garlic, minced,
  divided
½ teaspoon fresh lemon juice
Pinch salt
Pinch ground pepper
1 cup butter or margarine,
  divided
12 sheets phyllo pastry
  (available in most quality
  supermarkets)
6 skinless, boneless chicken
  breast halves
Grated Parmesan cheese

Deanna Doyel, a Californian, brought these to a pot luck at my house. They were far and away the most popular food at the party that night. They're tender, flaky, delicious, and they look good. You might garnish the plate with some parsley or watercress. I've served them here to a gathering of fifty of the Perdue marketing men and women, but for variation, I cut the chicken into bite-size pieces and wrapped them individually to form cocktail-size morsels.

To make this successfully, be sure to keep the pastry sheets from drying out or they'll get brittle and impossible to fold. Work with only one sheet at a time and keep the others covered with a sheet of waxed paper, topped with a damp tea towel.

♦ ♦ ♦

In a shallow dish combine mayonnaise, scallions, parsley, half of garlic, lemon juice, salt, and pepper. In a small saucepan over medium heat melt butter with remaining garlic. Brush one pastry sheet with melted garlic butter, top with second sheet and brush again. Dip chicken breast in mixed ingredients turning to coat thoroughly. Place chicken diagonally on one corner of pastry sheets, then roll while folding in sides to make a neat rectangular package. Brush top of wrapped chicken with butter and top lightly with Parmesan cheese. Preheat oven to 350°F. Place wrapped breasts in a baking dish and bake about 35 minutes. They're a golden brown when done.

MUSHROOM SNAILS

SERVES 4 AS AN APPETIZER

½ cup butter or margarine,
   softened
2 cloves garlic, minced
4 tablespoons minced, fresh
   parsley
2 tablespoons snipped fresh
   or frozen chives
⅛ teaspoon salt or to taste
12 large mushroom caps
6 chicken livers, halved
12 ½-inch-thick slices of
   french bread, buttered on
   both sides

I'd eaten escargot (snails) in France, and thought they were expensive and overrated, but loved the garlic butter and other seasonings. One day it occurred to me that those flavorings would be delicious with the mushrooms and chicken livers that I happened to have in the refrigerator. I wrote down what I thought would be right, and then made the recipe. The verdict from my guests was show-stopping! These look lovely if by any chance you have any of the escargot serving dishes with little indentations for each snail. I'm guessing that you probably don't, so I've suggested you serve the mushroom "snails" on little rounds of sautéed French bread.

♦ ♦ ♦

Preheat oven to 400°F. In a small bowl combine butter with garlic, parsley, chives, and salt. Fill each mushroom cap with a half chicken liver. Then, top each mushroom cap with ¹⁄₁₂ of the butter mixture. Bake until filling is melted, and bubbly, about 8 minutes. Sauté slices of French bread in butter until lightly browned. Serve caps on "toasted" bread.

OLD WORLD CORNISH HENS BAKED IN SALT

SERVES 4

8 garlic cloves, unpeeled
1 bunch fresh rosemary or
   thyme, divided
4 fresh Cornish game hens
   (1¼–1½ pounds each)
Ground pepper
4 18 × 18-inch squares heavy
   duty aluminum foil
2 boxes (48 ounces each)
   Kosher salt
2½–3 cups water

This is one of my favorites. This dish looks so impressive that I can still remember the first time I saw it brought to the table, more than ten years ago. When the hostess brought the platter it looked like four chicken-shaped pieces of white pottery in the exact shape of cornish game hens, only a little larger. Our hostess had coated the cornish hens with a half-inch layer of salt, and then roasted the hens in this casing. To serve the hens, she took a small wooden mallet and gave each shell a sharp whap. Each time she did this, the shell would crack into several pieces, revealing the fragrant and beautifully-roasted game hen inside. I thought

222   THE *PERDUE* CHICKEN COOKBOOK

the hens would taste salty, but found instead some of the tenderest and most succulent chicken you could hope for.

♦ ♦ ♦

Preheat oven to 400°F. Place 2 garlic cloves and a sprig of rosemary in the cavity of each hen. Season with pepper. Fold wings back and tie legs together. Place a hen on each sheet of foil. Fold in edges of foil to form a nest with sides 1½ inches high. Leave a border of 1½ inches between hen and foil. Remove hens from nests and reserve. Place nests on heavy baking sheets. Fill each nest with a layer of salt, ½ inch thick. Return hens to nests. In a large bowl combine remaining salt with enough water to make a heavy paste. Use hands to mold salt around each hen enclosing it completely in a layer of salt approximately ½ inch thick. Bake hens 40–50 minutes depending upon their size. To serve: With a sharp knife, carefully cut around the base of each hen following its shape. Use a spatula to gently lift salt covered hens out of nests and onto platter. Decorate platter with sprigs of rosemary. In front of your guests, crack salt casings with a mallet and dust off any remaining salt. Garnish hens with sprigs of rosemary. Note: If you want to try this recipe with a 3½-pound chicken, proceed in the same manner as for the Cornish hens, using 1 box (48 ounces) kosher salt and 1½ cups water. The cooking time would be approximately 1 hour and 15 minutes.

ORIENTAL COOKOUT CHICKEN

SERVES 6–8

2 whole chickens
2 teaspoons salt or to taste
½ teaspoon ground pepper
1 cup frozen orange juice concentrate (undiluted)
4 tablespoons peanut or vegetable oil
2 tablespoons French salad dressing
3 teaspoons soy sauce
2 oranges

You need an outdoor grill with a rotisserie for this one. The sight of whole chickens wrapped in orange peel spirals, turning on a spit is really impressive. Don't let your guests or family miss this part.

♦ ♦ ♦

Rub inside of chickens with salt and pepper. In a bowl combine orange juice, oil, salad dressing, and soy sauce; rub mixture on chickens, inside and out. Peel oranges, spiral fashion, keeping skins in one strip. Cut orange segments into small pieces and place inside of chickens. Truss chickens securely with string. Place on outdoor grill rotisserie rod, securing with forked holders. Place spiral orange peels around chickens, holding in place with toothpicks. Broil on rotisserie about 1 hour or until juices run clear with no hint of pink when thigh is pierced, basting constantly with sauce.

PERDUE À LA VERTICAL

SERVES 6–8

1 whole roaster
3 ounces crumbled bleu cheese
2 cloves garlic
2 tablespoons butter or margarine
¾ cup Shittake mushrooms (if not available, use whatever mushrooms are)
1 tablespoon dry white wine
¼ teaspoon paprika

One of the really fun things about being Mrs. Frank Perdue is that people are always giving me tips on cooking chicken. Recently I met a woman in an airport in Puerto Rico who told me that my life wouldn't be complete until I tried cooking chicken on a vertical roaster. Not wanting an incomplete life, I took her advice and found that yes, vertical roasting really does have a lot going for it. The chicken cooks about thirty percent faster because the metal frame conducts heat and is in contact with the bird's interior. The bird is also juicier. The heat of the vertical roaster forces the juices outward while the heat of the oven forces them inward. The juices have nowhere to go, so instead they just stay inside, tenderizing and flavoring the meat. Vertical roasters are available in major department stores as well as in quality gourmet cookware shops.

Denis Spanek, who patented the first vertical roaster, says he's cooked at least thirty thousand birds during demonstrations and tests, and this is his favorite recipe. It's now one of my all-time favorites too, but I've felt leery about serving it to guests without knowing ahead of time that they like bleu cheese. Now I stuff one side of the roaster with the bleu cheese-mushroom mixture and omit the bleu cheese from the stuffing for the other side. Then I give our guests the choice of which side they'd like.

♦ ♦ ♦

Preheat oven to 450°F. Place roaster on its back and use your fingertips to break the skin membrane at the neck opening on each side of the breast. (See the illustration on Stuffing a Roaster Under the Skin.) Work your finger under the skin across both sides of the breast and continue along the thighs

USING A VERTICAL ROASTER

METHOD OF PREPARATION

The same easy method is used for all forms of poultry. If you're preparing poultry other than chicken, the Basic Roasting Guide* gives times and temperatures.

A. Rinse chicken inside and out and dry thoroughly. Season and place on vertical roaster as shown in Diagram 1 below. Press down onto roaster rack so top of roaster comes through neck cavity as illustrated in Diagram 2.

B. Set in roasting pan. Add ½–1 cup liquid to pan, depending on pan size. Liquid should be ⅛–¼ inch deep.

C. Roast per time and temperature in recipe.

1. Place poultry on roaster.

2. Top of ring should show.

METHOD OF CARVING

The family of Spanek Vertical Roasters perfectly positions all poultry for easy carving. You can cut any bird quickly and efficiently on the roaster, at the table, in these easy steps:

D. Remove leg and thigh—Diagram 3 below.

E. Separate leg and thigh—Diagram 4.

F. Make **V** slice under wishbone and remove—Diagram 5.

G. Peel down breast meat by placing knife on the top shoulders of bird and pressing downward—Diagram 6. Save bones for the stockpot. The degreased pan juices can be saved for extra flavoring.

3. Remove leg and thigh.

4. Separate leg and thigh.

5. Make V slice under wishbone and remove.

6. Peel down breast meat.

*Further information available from Spanek, Inc., P.O. Box 2190, Saratoga, CA 95070. Illustrations provided by Spanek, Inc.

  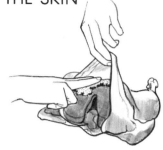

and legs. Be careful not to break the skin that's attached at the center of the breastbone.

In a food processor fitted with steel blade, combine blue cheese, garlic, butter, and mushrooms. Process, pulsating on and off, until mushrooms are coarsely chopped and mixture just holds together.

Spoon the stuffing under the skin, working over the breast, thigh, and leg areas, smoothing it evenly over each side of the bird. When the bird is stuffed, gently press it onto the vertical roaster so the metal ring at the top comes through. Set the roaster in an 8- to 9-inch cake pan and add ½ cup water to the roasting pan. Baste with a mixture of 1 tablespoon of dry white wine with paprika. This will give a rosy color to the bird and the chicken will brown beautifully. Sear 15 minutes in a 450°F oven. Lower temperature to 350°F and cook 15–18 minutes per pound.

Food Tip: Carve the bird over rice so the rice catches the drippings.

ROASTER MARINARA

SERVES 6

1 whole roaster
¾ teaspoon minced fresh
    basil or ½ teaspoon dried
Salt and ground pepper to
    taste
1½ cups homemade or
    prepared marinara sauce
    (available in
    supermarkets)
1 package (6 ounces) sliced
    mozzarella cheese

Frank is particularly fond of any recipe with tomatoes. Usually in restaurants, a menu item that's "marinara" is going to be served with a tomato-based sauce. However, according to the New York Times *food writer, Craig Claiborne,* marinara *really means "marine style" or "sailor style," and marinara sauces exist without tomatoes. In this recipe, the sauce is tomato based. I'm fond of this recipe because it looks so good.*

◆ ◆ ◆

Preheat oven to 350°F. Remove giblets from roaster. Season with basil, salt, and pepper. Place bird, breast side up, in roasting pan. Roast in oven 1¾–2½ hours. Brush marinara sauce over roaster 30 minutes before end of cooking time. Cut mozzarella cheese into long strips ½ inch wide and place in lattice pattern over breast during final 10 minutes of cooking.

STUFFED CHICKEN JARDINIERE

SERVES 6

1 whole chicken (3½–4 pounds)
2–3 zucchini (¾ pound), well scrubbed and grated
2–3 yellow squash (¾ pound), well scrubbed and grated
4 carrots, peeled and grated
1 cup thinly sliced scallions
1 large clove garlic, minced
2 tablespoons minced fresh tarragon or 2 teaspoons dried
⅓ cup grated Parmesan or Romano cheese
½ cup fresh bread crumbs (made from 2 slices low-calorie whole grain bread)
1 egg white or 1 egg yolk, lightly beaten
¾ teaspoon ground pepper, divided
½ teaspoon of salt, divided
⅛ teaspoon ground nutmeg or to taste
Yogurt-Herb Sauce (recipe follows)
Fresh tarragon sprigs, miniature zucchini, yellow squash, and carrots, (optional garnish)

I *don't know of many presentations that are more impressive than this. The price for all this impressiveness is that it's also one of the more time-consuming recipes in this book. While it's true that there is a fair amount of preparation required, the work is done in advance and not at the last minute. This recipe allows you to surprise your guests with a chicken that appears whole but slices into attractive pieces of chicken and stuffing. It's also a low-calorie and healthy recipe. You'll find directions for boning and reforming a whole chicken here, but in case you don't have either the time or desire to do it yourself, a cooperative butcher can do it for you in about five minutes.*

◆ ◆ ◆

Bone chicken except for wings and legs. Using kitchen string and a large darning needle, sew up any holes in skin and the split area near tail—chicken should form a roughly rectangular shape. Place green and yellow squash and carrots in a colander or strainer; press with back of wooden spoon or hands to remove as much liquid as possible.

In a large, non-stick or lightly greased skillet, combine grated vegetables, scallions, and garlic. Cook over low heat, stirring frequently, 6–8 minutes or until mixture is quite dry, but not brown. Remove from heat; stir in tarragon, Parmesan, bread crumbs, egg white, ½ teaspoon pepper, ¼ teaspoon salt, and nutmeg.

Preheat oven to 400°F. Sprinkle inside of chicken with remaining salt and pepper. Stuff and truss chicken, following directions for reforming a whole chicken. Brush with oil, if desired. Place on rack in roasting pan and roast 20 minutes. Reduce heat to 350°F and roast 1 hour longer or until juices run clear with no hint of pink when thigh is pierced.

Refrigerate chicken until ready to serve. Recipe can be served hot, but will slice more easily if thoroughly chilled. Serve chicken with Yogurt-Herb Sauce, garnish with herbs and vegetables, if desired.

Yogurt-Herb Sauce:
1 cup plain low-fat yogurt
1 tablespoon minced fresh
   chives
1 tablespoon minced fresh
   tarragon
1 tablespoon minced fresh
   parsley
Salt and ground pepper to
   taste

In small bowl, combine yogurt and herbs. Add salt and ground pepper to taste.

BONING AND RE-FORMING A WHOLE CHICKEN

1. On a large cutting board, place bird breast down with drumsticks turned toward you. Using a small, sharp boning knife, cut off tail. Then cut through skin down middle of backbone.
2. Keep knife close to backbone to loosen flesh, cutting around small oyster-shaped piece of meat part-way down back; leave oyster attached to skin. Just below oyster, use point of knife to locate and sever ball joint between hip and thigh.
3. Working toward neck, loosen flesh from carcass. When shoulder blade is reached, keep bone to your right and cut through joint to sever wing from shoulder.
4. Continue loosening flesh around edge of carcass until you reach breastbone. Do not try to detach this because skin is very thin at this point. Turn bird around so neck faces you; repeat steps 2 and 3. Carefully, cut through two spots where wishbone is attached to carcass.
5. When both sides of carcass and wishbone are loosened, lift carcass and cut breastbone away from meat. Cut through cartilage, but do not worry about leaving some attached to flesh. It can be

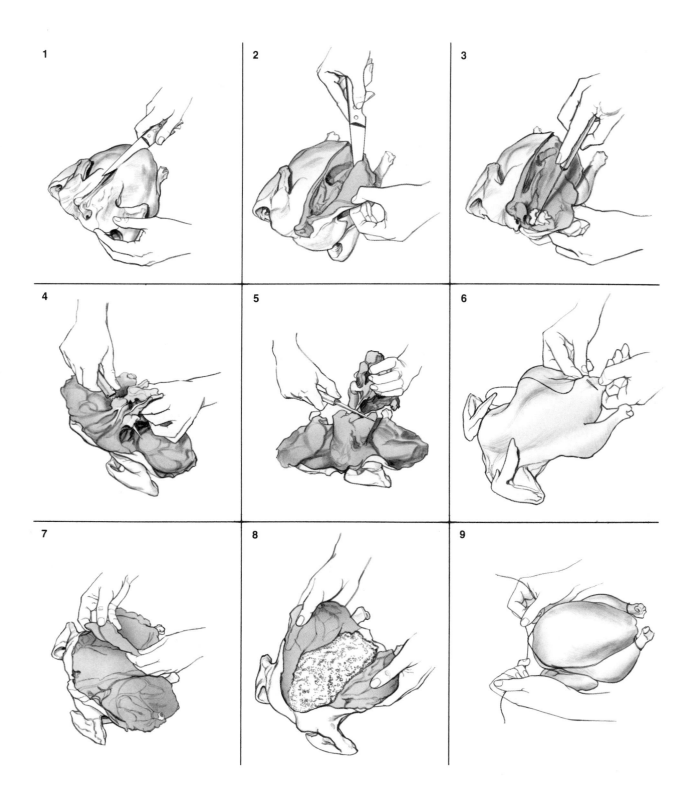

removed more easily later without piercing skin. Remove carcass and, if desired, simmer with vegetables to make a stock.

6. Using kitchen string or unwaxed dental floss, thread a large darning needle. Turn chicken skin-side up and sew closed any holes in skin. Stitch split area near tail together so that chicken roughly forms a rectangle.

7. Turn chicken skin-side down and carefully remove any remaining cartilage in breast area. Detach small breast fillets and use to cover less meaty areas near thighs. Season meat, if desired.

8. Mound stuffing down center of breast. Pull skin up on either side around stuffing and re-form chicken. Sew back of bird closed.

9. Truss bird into attractive chicken shape.

A TRIO OF SHOW-STOPPER "VEAL" CLASSICS

Chicken breasts, when pounded and flattened, make an excellent substitute for veal. And if your market has them, the thin-sliced boneless roaster breast is even better, since you don't have to pound or flatten the individual pieces. The fact is, if someone didn't tell you, and if you're not a food professional, there's a good chance that you'd have difficulty telling the difference. The muscle fibers in both meats are surprisingly similar; they're both low in fat, and neither has much collagen, the factor that makes meat fibrous and chewy. The basic ingredients in most of the "veal" dishes that follow are boneless, skinless chicken breasts. They're called "cutlets." A scaloppine is a cutlet sliced in half lengthwise.

By the way, if Frank had his way, from now on you wouldn't think of chicken breasts as an inexpensive substitute for veal. You'd think of veal as a more expensive substitute for his chicken breasts. In fact, Frank likes to say that "Anything veal can do, my chicken breasts can do better," He points out that chicken breasts are richer than veal in vitamin A, niacin, and calcium, and they're lower in calories and cholesterol. They're equal to veal in protein, and of course, they're much, much more affordable.

To make your own scaloppine, place a skinless, boneless chicken breast half on a flat surface, insert a sharp knife into the side and cut the chicken breast into two wide flat slices. Put these slices between sheets of plastic wrap and pound with a meat mallet or rolling pin to ¼-inch thickness.

CHICKEN OSCAR

8 scaloppine (about 1 pound skinless, boneless chicken breast halves) or 1 package thin sliced boneless roaster breast
¼ cup flour
¼ cup butter or margarine
1 cup cooked crabmeat
16 cooked, fresh asparagus spears or 1 can (10½ ounces), drained
1 cup chicken broth
1 cup Hollandaise Sauce (optional)

*V*eal Oscar is served in some of the finest New York restaurants. You can make this chicken version yourself for a small fraction of the restaurant cost.

♦ ♦ ♦

Dip scaloppine in flour to coat lightly, shake off excess. In a skillet over medium-high heat, melt butter. Add scaloppine and sauté for about 1½ minutes per side until lightly browned and just cooked through. Remove to serving platter. Top with crabmeat and asparagus spears. Cover and hold in 250°F oven. Add broth to skillet and cook over high heat to reduce by half. Stir frequently. Remove scaloppine from oven. Top with sauce and Hollandaise, if desired.

PERDUE PARMIGIANO

8 scaloppine (about 1 pound skinless, boneless chicken breast halves) or 1 package thin-sliced boneless roaster breast
¼ cup flour seasoned with 1 teaspoon salt and ⅛ teaspoon ground pepper
2 eggs
½ cup fine dry bread crumbs
6 tablespoons oil
1 cup homemade or prepared marinara sauce (available in supermarkets)
½ pound mozzarella cheese, thinly sliced
½ cup grated Parmesan cheese

*T*his is a little like the Austrian treatment of veal, but with an Italian accent. Serve it with spaghetti. If you don't have commercial bread crumbs handy, dry a couple of slices of bread in a 250°F oven, and then whirl in the blender or food processor. Presto! Your own bread crumbs.

♦ ♦ ♦

Place seasoned flour on a sheet of wax paper. Break eggs into a shallow bowl and beat lightly. Place bread crumbs on a separate sheet of wax paper. Dip scaloppine in flour to coat lightly, shake off excess. Dip in beaten egg, then coat with bread crumbs. In large skillet over medium-high heat, heat oil. Add scaloppine and sauté for about 1 minute per side until golden brown. Drain on paper towels. Arrange scaloppine in shallow baking dish or casserole. Cover with marinara sauce and mozzarella cheese. Sprinkle with Parmesan cheese and bake in 350°F oven 15 minutes.

PERDUE WIENER SCHNITZEL

4 skinless, boneless chicken breast halves or 1 package thin sliced boneless roaster breast
¼ cup flour seasoned with 1 teaspoon salt and ⅛ teaspoon ground pepper
6 eggs
1 cup fine bread crumbs
6 tablespoons butter or margarine, divided
2 tablespoons chopped parsley
Salt and pepper to taste
1 lemon, quartered

I had the real thing in Austria, and I don't think it was any better than this. Serve it with buttered noodles.

♦ ♦ ♦

Pound chicken between plastic wrap to flatten to ¼-inch thickness. Skip this previous step if you are using thin-sliced boneless roaster breasts. Break 2 eggs into a shallow bowl and beat lightly. Place bread crumbs on a separate sheet of wax paper. Dip cutlets in flour to coat, shake off excess. Dip in beaten eggs, then coat with bread crumbs. In a large skillet over medium-high heat, melt half of butter. Sauté breaded cutlets until golden brown on each side and cooked through, about 5 minutes total. Remove to heated serving platter. Add reserved butter to skillet and fry remaining eggs sunnyside up to desired doneness. Season with salt and pepper. Place 1 egg on top of each cutlet, sprinkle with parsley and garnish with lemon quarters.

MENU FOR THREE BEAUTIFUL GUESTS

One of Frank's most memorable commercials is "Dinner with Three Beautiful Guests." In the commercial, while Frank roasts four fresh Cornish game hens, he showers; shaves; puts on a tuxedo; chills some champagne; arranges flowers in a vase; turns on soft music; and then opens the door to greet three ravishing beauties. The commercial has been so successful that the advertising agency produced a sequel, dramatizing an actual letter that arrived at Perdue Farms' consumer relations department:

> *"Mr. Perdue, I have a complaint. I prepared four of your Cornish hens just as you did on TV. I showered and shaved just as you did on TV. I dressed as you did on TV. I chilled the wine, and laid the birds on a bed of wild rice just as you did on TV. Your advertising is misleading. No pretty girls have knocked on my door."*

People sometimes ask me if the original ad makes me jealous. Actually it's my favorite.

MENU

Quick Crisp Cornish Hens with Bacon and
Mushroom Gravy

♦

Cider Glazed Carrots

♦

Peas in Chive Cream

♦

Strawberries Romanoff

QUICK, CRISP CORNISH HENS

4 fresh Cornish game hens
Salt and ground pepper to
    taste
1 tablespoon minced, fresh
    thyme or 1 teaspoon dried
1 bunch fresh parsley
4 small bay leaves
¼ cup butter or margarine,
    melted
2 cups hot, cooked wild rice
1 lemon cut in wedges as
    garnish
Bacon and Wild Mushroom
    Gravy (recipe follows)

Wild rice is a completely different crop from regular rice. It is chewier and has a more nut-like flavor. The people who grow it refer to it as "the caviar of grains." This is a good and quick method for roasting Cornish hens but it can smoke up your kitchen. If you don't have a good fan, preheat your oven to 500°F and reduce it to 375°F when you put the hens in. Roast them 45–50 minutes instead of the half-hour mentioned in this recipe.

♦ ♦ ♦

Place rack in lower half of oven; preheat to 500°F. If you have a ventilator fan on stove, turn it on. Reserving other giblets for gravy, discard necks and livers. Season hen cavities with salt, pepper, and thyme. Trim stem ends from parsley and add 1 tablespoon to each cavity, along with a bay leaf. Tie legs together, fold back wings and place hens breast side up in a roasting pan. Roast hens about 30 minutes, basting once with butter, until skin is brown and crisp and juices run clear with no hint of pink when thigh is pierced. Remove hens from pan and skim off all but 3 tablespoons drippings to be used in gravy. Serve on a bed of wild rice; garnish with parsley and lemon wedges and pass the gravy separately.

Bacon and Wild Mushroom Gravy:

1 ounce dried wild
    mushrooms (cèpes,
    morels, or porcini)
1 cup boiling water
¼ pound bacon, diced
Giblets reserved from hens,
    chopped
⅓ cup chopped onion
¼ cup dry sherry
¼ cup flour
2½ cups chicken broth or
    water

To reconstitute mushrooms well, pour boiling water over them and allow to steep 10 minutes. Strain through a coffee filter and reserve liquid. Rinse mushrooms to remove any sand; chop finely.

In a large skillet over medium-low heat, fry bacon until crisp. Drain bacon on paper towels. Leaving 2 tablespoons bacon fat in pan, add giblets, mushrooms, and onion and brown about 5 minutes. Add to Cornish drippings in roasting pan. Whisk in sherry and flour. Cook, whisking frequently, 3–4 minutes or until flour is browned. Add bacon, reserved mushroom liquid, and broth to flour mixture. Bring to a boil, whisking frequently, and cook gravy to thicken. Serve with hens.

CIDER-GLAZED CARROTS

SERVES 4

1 pound baby carrots, peeled
2 cups apple cider
2 tablespoons butter
2 tablespoons honey
½ teaspoon salt or to taste
⅛ teaspoon ground pepper
1 tablespoon minced, fresh
  parsley

Cut larger carrots in half on a diagonal, if necessary, so that all carrots are approximately the same size. In a saucepan over medium heat, bring cider, butter, honey, salt, and pepper to a boil and add carrots. Cook 5 minutes or until just beginning to soften; remove with slotted spoon. Bring cider mixture back to a boil and cook 5 minutes to thicken glaze. Remove from heat. Two minutes before serving, reheat carrots in sauce, tossing frequently. Serve garnished with parsley.

PEAS IN CHIVE CREAM

SERVES 4

1 cup heavy cream
½ teaspoon salt and ground
  pepper to taste
1½–2 cups fresh or frozen
  peas
1 tablespoon snipped fresh or
  frozen chives

In a saucepan over medium-high heat, bring cream and seasoning to a boil and cook until thick, about 5 minutes; whisk frequently. Five minutes before serving, stir in peas and bring back to a boil, stirring frequently. Add chives just before serving.

STRAWBERRIES ROMANOFF

SERVES 4

1 quart long-stemmed
  strawberries
1 cup sour cream
½–1 cup brown sugar, sifted

Arrange strawberries attractively on four individual dessert plates. Garnish each plate with a big dollop of sour cream and a heaping tablespoonful of sugar. Dip strawberries first into sour cream, then into sugar.

ZURELLI'S SPINACH CUTLETS

For each serving:
1 skinless, boneless chicken breast half or 1 slice of the thin sliced boneless roaster breast
4 spinach leaves
1 slice provolone cheese
Onion powder
Garlic powder
Vegetable oil
Salt and ground pepper to taste

Chuck Zurelli, a butcher for one of the large supermarket chains, makes this for his customers. It's not hard to do at home and it looks professional. You may want to substitute fresh minced onion and garlic for the onion powder and garlic powder that Mr. Zurelli uses.

We all know that having sharp knives is a Good Thing, but how often do you sharpen yours? If you are like I was, once a year would be average, and once a month, would be positively virtuous. If you were to watch Chuck Zurelli at work, you'd see that in the process of butterflying chicken breasts, he runs his knife across his sharpening tool every fifteen or twenty seconds. Professionals feel it's worth their while to keep their knives very, very sharp. Now that I've tried it, I think they're right. If you're doing some serious cutting, how about a few quick strokes on your sharpening tool? It does make a difference.

♦ ♦ ♦

Take a half boneless chicken breast and butterfly it open. Or use a slice of the thin sliced roaster breast. Remove the membrane and sinews, since these can tighten unevenly and distort the look of the final product. Take four spinach leaves and layer these over the butterflied fillet. Top this with a slice of provolone cheese, cut about as thick as the pre-sliced cheeses used for sandwiches. Season with a few shakes each of onion powder and garlic powder. (Don't add salt until after it's finished cooking; salt will draw out the juices and toughen the meat.) Roll up the fillet tightly, jellyroll fashion. Fasten with a toothpick or tie with kitchen twine. Preheat oven to 350°F. Brush chicken with oil to seal in the moisture and then bake 20–30 minutes or until cooked through. Season with salt and pepper.

10

CHICKEN FOR PLANOVERS

Everyone is so busy nowadays, it's often tempting to pick up dinner at a fast food carry-out on the way home. The problem is, these foods not only dent the budget, they can short-change you nutritionally. Often they're high in the fat or sodium which many of us are trying to limit.

There are, however, ways to serve speedy meals that are also good for you. In fact, I like to think of leftover chicken as a fast food. It gives you a head start on so many recipes.

Michelle Evans, the eminent cookbook author and travel authority, likes to say that leftover chicken is the "basic black dress" of the culinary world. It's true. You can dress it up in so many ways using herbs and spices, sauces and dips, toppings and crusts. Just as a basic black dress is handy to have around, so leftover chicken is wonderful for a fast start on a number of delicious dishes.

By using leftovers, you can create fast food while maintaining control over the calories and nutrition. When you do cook, plan for leftovers by preparing extra quantities. Serve part of what you prepared immediately, and save the rest for a "planover." Then, on those days when you're short on time, use your microwave to create a meal from your store of "planovers."

TIPS FOR USING LEFTOVERS

- Know how long the food has been held at room temperature. The Department of Agriculture recommends that you throw out food of animal origin if it's been left unrefrigerated for more than two hours. I've talked with some food scientists, however, who feel that the USDA two-hour rule is unnecessarily strict. They say that except for the at-risk groups, (infants, the elderly, or those in poor health), that you can probably still use chicken that has been kept at room temperature for a little longer than two hours, maybe as long as four hours. Still, they agree that the longer chicken is kept at room temperature, the bigger the chance you're taking. Harmful organisms can multiply rapidly on food that's held in the danger zone between 40°F and 140°F. Personally, I'm in favor of being cautious.
- When refrigerating leftovers, break them down into shallow pans that aren't deeper than a couple of inches. If you fill a deep pan, for example, with lots of leftover stuffing, it could take too long for the food in the middle to cool down to 40°F.
- If you're not going to eat the leftover chicken within three days, freeze it.
- Don't store cooked chicken in the freezer for longer than three months. Label it so you can keep track of it. A California home economist friend of mine keeps a running log of what's in her freezer, marking dishes when they are removed. This reduces the search time with the freezer open, and keeps her from losing track of what's in there.
- Wrap leftovers tightly in moisture proof wrapping so as to prevent freezer burn.
- Think of ways of working leftovers into your brown bag lunches. Cold chicken makes a great lunch. Chicken soup or stew goes great in a thermos.

If you happen to be browsing in this chapter and find you want to make one of the recipes but don't have any leftovers handy, you can make some by:

1. Baking a chicken. Place whole chicken without any seasonings or coatings, uncovered in a 350°F oven for approximately 1 hour.
2. Simmering a whole chicken. Put chicken in kettle or saucepan. Add 2 cups water, salt, pepper to taste, 1 bay leaf, one onion, peeled and quartered, and 1 stalk celery, halved. Cover and simmer 45 minutes or until cooked through. Save the broth for sauces or soup bases.
3. Simmering parts of a chicken using the same recipe above. Boneless parts cook fastest: a small breast in 15 minutes, a larger roaster-size one in 20–35, and boneless roaster thighs in 40–50 minutes.

CHICKEN POTPIES REDISCOVERED

One of the best uses for leftover chicken is chicken potpies. Back in the days of the Roman empire, potpies were banquet fare, often created with surprises—even live birds—under the crust. During the time of Elizabeth I, English cooks made potpies using "chicken peepers," tiny chicks stuffed with gooseberries. By the mid-eighteenth century, an English cookbook included a sort of telescoping pie in which five birds were stuffed one inside another, then wrapped in dough.

With that history, it is not surprising that immigrants to America brought an appreciation for potpies with them. When settlers moved West, so did their potpie recipes, which they adapted to local food styles with new ingredients and seasonings. By this century, chicken potpies and "meat and taters" variations had become as American as corn on the cob. They were thrifty foods, served at the kichen table and in "home cooking" diners along country roads.

Recently, nostalgia for homespun cookery has meant a change in status for potpies. They are not only considered respectable, they're even "trendy," often appearing on the menus of fashionable restaurants. These are perfect recipes in which to use leftover chicken. If you run short of a particular vegetable go ahead and substitute whatever else looks good. In fact, you can mix and match and change the ingredients, flavorings, and toppings to suit the mood of the moment. To get you started, here are a few guidelines.

TIPS FOR MAKING OLD-FASHIONED CHICKEN POTPIES

- Potpie fillings are actually stews or creamed dishes inside a crust. If you want you can also serve fillings over rice, noodles, toast points, or pastry shells.
- To prevent a soggy bottom crust, bake 2-crust pies on the bottom shelf of a preheated oven and slit the top to allow steam to escape. For decorative slits, use a favorite hors d'oeuvre or cookie cutter. Also space dumplings, biscuits, and other toppings to allow for steaming.
- When making individual potpies, eliminating the bottom crust creates a better proportion of filling to pastry. One double-crust recipe for a 9-inch pie plate makes about 8 single-crust, 5-inch tarts. Reduce baking time by 10 minutes.
- For a different flavor in biscuits, crusts or potato toppings, crumble in a few tablespoonfuls of herbs or grated cheese.
- Potpie fillings can be prepared in advance and refrigerated, but do not pour fillings into pastry shells until ready to bake. If you plan to freeze a pie for storage, eliminate the bottom crust, sealing the top one over cooked cooled filling. Place in an airtight plastic bag or wrap tightly with heavy foil. Do not defrost before baking. Preheat the oven and add 15 minutes to cooking time.

CHICKEN HASH PIE

2 pounds (4 large) potatoes, peeled and diced
1 cup (½ pint) heavy cream, divided
6 tablespoons butter or margarine, divided
Salt and ground pepper to taste
Pinch ground nutmeg
1 cup thinly sliced scallions, white and tender green parts only
½ cup chopped celery
2 tablespoons flour
1 cup chicken broth
3 cups cooked, chopped chicken
¾ teaspoon chopped fresh thyme or ¼ teaspoon dried
Salt and ground pepper to taste
4 eggs
2 teaspoons minced, fresh parsley, optional

Grease a 9-inch pie plate or 1½-quart ovenproof casserole. Place potatoes in a large saucepan with enough water to cover. Salt to taste. Bring to a boil over high heat. Reduce heat to low and cook until tender, about 15 minutes. Drain and mash potatoes, adding ¼ cup cream, 2 tablespoons butter, ¼ teaspoon pepper, nutmeg, and salt to taste. Cover and set aside. Preheat oven to 350°F.

In large skillet over medium-high heat, melt remaining butter. Sauté scallions and celery in butter for 3 minutes. Whisk in flour and cook 3 minutes. Add broth and remaining ¾ cup cream and heat just to boiling, whisking constantly. Stir in chicken, thyme, 1 teaspoon salt or to taste, and ⅛ teaspoon pepper. Spread chicken mixture on bottom of prepared pie plate. Pipe 4 potato rings on top of pie or spread potatoes over filling and make four depressions with the back of a spoon. Bake 15 minutes. Remove from oven and carefully break eggs into rings or depressions. Sprinkle with salt and pepper, if desired, and return to oven for 15 minutes or until eggs are set to desired doneness. Garnish with parsley and serve immediately.

CHICKEN PIE

This may be one of the easiest chicken pie recipes there is. Sprinkle grated cheddar cheese over the biscuits when you want something different.

♦ ♦ ♦

2 cups cooked chicken, cut in chunks
2 cans (10½ ounces each) cream of mushroom soup, undiluted
½ cup uncooked frozen peas
2 raw carrots, sliced
2 tablespoons finely chopped onion or 1 teaspoon instant minced onion
1 tube (7½ ounces) prepared biscuits

Preheat oven to 350°F. Mix all ingredients except biscuits in 2-quart baking dish or casserole. Cover with foil and bake 1 hour. Remove foil. Place biscuits on top of mixture. Bake, uncovered, 12 minutes longer or until biscuits are brown.

CAJUN PIE

¼ pound lean bacon
Vegetable oil
3 tablespoons flour
½ cup chopped onion
½ cup chopped green pepper
½ cup fresh ripe or canned
chopped tomatoes
2 tablespoons Worcestershire
sauce
4–12 drops Tabasco (hot
pepper sauce)
1¼ cups water
1 teaspoon salt or to taste
1 package (10 ounces) frozen
succotash, thawed
2 cups cooked, chopped
chicken
8–10 ready-to-bake
buttermilk biscuits

Grease a deep 9-inch pie plate or ovenproof dish. In large, heavy skillet, over medium-high heat, cook bacon until crisp. Remove bacon with a slotted spoon to drain; crumble. Preheat oven to 425°F. Pour bacon drippings into a measuring cup and add oil to bring to ½ cup. Return to skillet and stir in flour. Cook over medium heat, stirring constantly, 5–10 minutes or until well browned. Add onions and cook 1 minute. Stir in green peppers, tomatoes, sauces, and water; season to taste with salt. Simmer until slightly thickened— 1–3 minutes; stir in succotash, bacon, and chicken. Pour into prepared dish. Place biscuits on top of filling with edges touching. Bake 15–20 minutes or until filling is hot and biscuits are golden brown.

CHICKEN TAMALE PIE (Mexican)

4 tablespoons butter or
margarine, divided
1 cup chopped onion
1 clove garlic, minced
2 cups cooked chicken, cut in
cubes
1 can (12 ounces) tomato
puree
1 tablespoon chili powder
1 cup pitted and chopped ripe
olives
½ teaspoon ground coriander
seed
3 teaspoons salt, divided
½ teaspoon ground pepper
6 cups chicken broth, divided
2 cups cornmeal

Don't be alarmed if the cornmeal mixture gets lumpy—just keep stirring and cooking and the mixture will become consistently thick.

♦ ♦ ♦

In a large skillet over medium heat, melt 1 tablespoon butter. Add onion and garlic and sauté 1 minute. Add chicken, tomato puree, chili powder, olives, coriander, 1 teaspoon of the salt, pepper, and ½ cup chicken broth. Cover and simmer 15 minutes. Preheat oven to 325°F. Bring remaining broth to a boil in large saucepan. Add remaining salt and butter. Add in cornmeal. Cook at low heat 15 minutes, stirring constantly. Line a 2-quart shallow baking dish with half of the cornmeal mixture. Pour in chicken mixture. Cover with remaining cornmeal mixture. Bake 1½ hours.

EMPANADA PIE

For the pastry:
2 cups flour
¾ teaspoon salt or to taste
6 tablespoons butter or
     margarine
2 tablespoons lard or
     shortening
About ⅓ cup ice-cold water

This is a South American version of chicken potpie. To be authentic, use the lard that the recipe calls for. If you don't choose to use lard, you'll get a reasonably similar result using butter or margarine.

♦ ♦ ♦

Pastry:

In a small bowl, combine flour and salt. With pastry blender or 2 knives, cut in 6 tablespoons butter and lard until mixture resembles coarse crumbs. Gradually stir in water until dough forms a ball; do not overmix. Preheat oven to 425°F and grease a deep 9-inch dish. Roll out ⅔ of the pastry and use to line bottom of pie plate. Pierce well with a fork. Roll remaining pastry to ⅛-inch thickness for top crust. (Pastry can be prepared ahead and refrigerated until filling is ready.)

For the filling:
2 tablespoons butter
½ cup thinly sliced onion
1 cup thinly sliced green
     pepper
1 hot green chili pepper,
     chopped (optional)
½ cup pitted green olives,
     sliced into rounds
1 cup raisins
¼ cup cider vinegar
1 cup chopped fresh or
     stewed tomatoes
1 tablespoon tomato paste
⅛ teaspoon ground cinnamon
½ teaspoon salt or to taste
3 cups cooked, diced chicken
1 egg, beaten

Filling:

In medium-size saucepan over medium-high heat, melt butter. Add onion and peppers; sauté 3 minutes or until softened. Add olives, raisins, vinegar, tomatoes, and tomato paste and cook 5 minutes. Season with cinnamon and salt; stir in chicken. Spread chicken mixture in prepared pie plate and top with pastry. Flute edges, cut decorative slits in top, and brush with beaten egg. Bake on bottom shelf of oven 30 minutes or until browned.

FANCY CHICKEN PUFF PIE

SERVES 4

4 tablespoons butter or
    margarine
¼ cup chopped shallots or
    scallions
¼ cup flour
1 cup chicken broth
¼ cup dry sherry
Salt to taste
⅛ teaspoon ground white
    pepper
Pinch nutmeg
¼ pound ham, in ¼-inch × 2-
    inch strips
3 cups cooked chicken, cut in
    ¼-inch by 2-inch strips
1½ cups fresh, or a package
    (10 ounces) frozen,
    asparagus, cooked tender-
    crisp and cut in 2-inch
    pieces
1 cup (½ pint) heavy cream
Chilled flaky pastry for a
    1-crust pie or 1 sheet
    frozen puff pastry
1 egg, beaten

In a medium-size saucepan, over medium-high heat, melt butter and sauté shallots lightly. Whisk in flour; cook 3 minutes and add broth and sherry. Heat to boiling, whisking constantly; season to taste with salt, pepper, and nutmeg. Reduce heat to low and simmer 5 minutes. Stir in ham, chicken, asparagus, and cream. Pour chicken mixture in 9-inch pie plate.

Preheat oven to 425°F. Cut an 8-inch circle from pastry, tracing around a plate as pattern. Cut pastry hearts from extra dough with cookie cutter, if desired. Place circle of dough on a cookie sheet moistened with cold water. Pierce with tines of fork, brush with egg, and decorate with cutout hearts; brush hearts with egg.

Place pastry on cookie sheet and place alongside the filled pie plate in oven. Bake 10 minutes; lower heat to 350°F and bake 10–15 additional minutes or until pastry is golden brown and filling is hot. With a spatula, carefully place pastry lid on hot filling and serve immediately.

CHICKEN À LA KING WITH BUTTERMILK BISCUITS

SERVES 3–4

2 cups cooked chicken, cut in
    chunks
⅛ teaspoon ground pepper
½ cup pimento, chopped
¼ pound small fresh
    mushrooms, sliced (1
    cup)
2 cans (10½ ounces each)
    cream of chicken soup,
    undiluted

According to food historians, Chicken à la King got its name, not from some former monarch, but from the E. Clark King family, proprietors of a fashionable resort near Manhattan at the turn of the century. The original recipe used cream and sherry and egg yolks, and was served over toast points. This is somewhat lighter and a lot easier. If you have the time and are in the mood, skip the cream of chicken soup, and instead, use a basic white sauce made with chicken broth. If you don't have your own favorite white sauce recipe, here's a quick and simple one: Stir 4 table-spoons of flour into 4 tablespoons of melted butter. Cook for a couple of minutes, but don't let brown. Slowly stir in 2 cups chicken broth. Continue stirring until thickened. Season with salt and pepper to taste.

♦ ♦ ♦

In a saucepan over low heat combine all ingredients and cook about 20 minutes or until heated through. Serve on buttermilk biscuits. You can buy them ready-to-bake in a tube, or else make them from scratch, following this recipe:

Buttermilk Biscuits:
2 cups flour
½ teaspoon salt or to taste
1 teaspoon baking powder
1 teaspoon baking soda
¼ cup shortening or butter
About ¾ cup buttermilk

Preheat oven to 425°F. In large bowl, sift together flour, salt, baking powder, and baking soda. Cut in shortening until mixture resembles coarse crumbs. Stir in just enough buttermilk so dough holds together; turn out onto a floured surface. Pat to a ½-inch thickness and cut into 2-inch rounds. Bake 15–20 minutes, or until golden.

CHICKEN AND CORN SOUP

SERVES 2–3

3 cups chicken broth
1½ cups cooked, diced, chicken
1 can (8¾ ounces) cream-style corn
1 tablespoon dry sherry
Salt and pepper to taste
1½ tablespoons cornstarch dissolved in 3 tablespoons water
1 cup watercress leaves

In a saucepan over medium heat bring broth to a boil. Add chicken, corn, sherry, salt, and pepper. Simmer 2–3 minutes. Stir in cornstarch mixture and cook, stirring constantly, 1–2 minutes, or until slightly thickened. Stir in watercress and serve immediately.

CHICKEN CHOW MEIN (Chinese)

SERVES 4–6

1½ cups cooked chicken, cut in chunks
1 can (3 ounces) chow mein noodles, divided
1 can (6½ ounces) cashew nuts, divided
1 can (10½ ounces) cream of mushroom soup, undiluted
½ cup chicken broth
2 tablespoons soy sauce

*U*sing the cream of mushroom soup puts this recipe in the category of "fast food." It's good, but if you have the time and the inclination, you'll get fresher-tasting results if you substitute your best white sauce recipe (or the one on page 245) for the canned mushroom soup. Also, if you have a choice between buying dark soy sauce and light soy sauce, remember the dark one is sweeter—molasses or caramel is added—and light soy sauce is saltier.

♦ ♦ ♦

Preheat oven to 350°F. In a baking dish combine chicken, ½ of noodles, ½ of nuts, soup, broth, and soy sauce in baking dish, mixing well. Top with remaining noodles and cashews. Bake about 30 minutes.

CHICKEN-BACON SANDWICH

SERVES 6

1 cup cooked, finely chopped chicken
¼ cup chopped celery
2 tablespoons minced, fresh parsley
4 tablespoons mayonnaise or salad dressing
2 teaspoons fresh lemon juice
¼ teaspoon salt or to taste
⅛ teaspoon ground pepper
6 slices crisp cooked bacon

*D*ifferent kinds of bread make interesting variations. You can serve the sandwiches either open-face or topped with another slice of bread. I like open-face sandwiches that the kids can decorate.

♦ ♦ ♦

In a mixing bowl combine all ingredients except bacon and spread on favorite kind of bread. Break slices of cooked bacon in half and place on top of sandwich.

HOT CHICKENWICH

6 slices hot buttered toast
1 can (3½ ounces) deviled ham
1 chicken, cooked and sliced
3 tablespoons minced, fresh parsley
1 can (10½ ounces) cream of chicken soup, undiluted and heated
Salt to taste (you may not want any since the soup and the deviled ham are both fairly salty)

If chicken has been chilled, it should be placed in 250°F oven, uncovered, for about 3 minutes. If you have the time, substitute a good homemade white sauce made with chicken broth (see the one on page 245) for the cream of chicken soup. If you don't have the time (and I bet that happens to you often!), the chicken soup shortcut is still very good.

♦ ♦ ♦

Spread deviled ham on buttered toast; sprinkle with parsley. Place sliced chicken on toast. Pour hot soup over each sandwich.

QUICK CHICKEN TETRAZZINI

1 cup cooked, diced chicken
1 can (10½ ounces) cream of mushroom soup, undiluted
1½ cups cooked spaghetti
2 tablespoons dry sherry
⅓ cup grated Parmesan cheese
Salt and ground pepper to taste (you may not want any since the soup is fairly salty)

This is even better after standing to let the flavors blend. Green beans and broiled tomato go nicely with this. If you have time, use a good homemade white sauce made with chicken broth and mushrooms (or the one on page 245) instead of the cream of mushroom soup.

♦ ♦ ♦

Preheat oven to 375°F. In a baking dish combine all ingredients and bake about 30 minutes until hot and lightly browned.

SALADS

CHICKEN SPRING SALAD

SERVES 6–8

3 cups cooked chicken, cut in chunks
1 package (10 ounces) raw spinach, washed and drained with stems removed and torn into small pieces
1 small clove garlic, minced
1 tablespoon chives, snipped, fresh, or frozen
1 teaspoon salt or to taste
⅛ teaspoon ground pepper
1 teaspoon sugar
¾ cup chopped pecans
2 apples, chopped
½ cup oil
¼ cup red wine vinegar

Spinach is an excellent source of Vitamins A and C, as well as potassium and magnesium. Dentists call raw spinach a detergent for the teeth.

♦ ♦ ♦

In a salad bowl combine all ingredients and toss lightly.

FRENCH DRESSING CHICKEN SALAD

SERVES 3–4

2 cups cooked, diced chicken
½ cup finely chopped celery
¼ cup French dressing
¼ cup mayonnaise or salad dressing
⅛ teaspoon Cayenne pepper

This is a real "fast food," perfect for when you're got a lot of other things to do besides fuss in the kitchen. It's quick and easy, but the Cayenne pepper gives it a little perk that lifts it out of the ordinary.

♦ ♦ ♦

In a salad bowl toss together all ingredients and serve on lettuce.

OLIVEY CHICKEN SALAD

2 cups cooked, diced chicken
1 cup cooked rice (⅓ cup uncooked yields 1 cup cooked)
¾ cup chopped celery
½ cup sliced pimento-stuffed green olives
¼ cup toasted slivered almonds
¼ cup thinly sliced scallions
½ teaspoon salt or to taste
¼ teaspoon ground pepper
½ cup mayonnaise or salad dressing
2 tablespoons fresh lemon juice

I like this recipe partly because it tastes good, but also because it's a dandy use for leftover rice as well as leftover chicken.

♦ ♦ ♦

In a mixing bowl combine all ingredients and serve salad on a bed of lettuce leaves.

SUNSHINE CHICKEN SALAD

3 cups cooked, diced chicken
1 can (6 ounces) orange juice concentrate
3 tablespoons oil
1 tablespoon vinegar
1 tablespoon sugar
¼ teaspoon dry mustard
¼ teaspoon salt or to taste
⅛ teaspoon Tabasco (hot pepper sauce)
1 cup chopped celery
½ cup diced ripe olives
1 medium avocado, cut in small chunks
¼ cup toasted, slivered almonds

The avocado you use in this recipe should be fully ripe, and that means it will have a slight give to it when you press it between your palms. If it has about as much "give" to it as a baseball, let it ripen for a couple of days more at room temperature. But don't refrigerate it because refrigeration puts a stop to ripening.

♦ ♦ ♦

In a blender or food processor, make dressing by blending orange juice concentrate, oil, vinegar, sugar, dry mustard, salt, and Tabasco at high speed 5 seconds or until smooth. In a salad bowl combine chicken, celery, olives, avocado, and almonds. Pour dressing over. Toss and chill at least 30 minutes before serving.

TANGY CHICKEN SALAD

2 cups cooked, diced chicken
½ teaspoon salt or to taste
¼ cup chopped celery
1 hard cooked egg, chopped
1 tablespoon sweet pickle
 relish
½ cup mayonnaise or salad
 dressing

Have you ever gotten the hard cooked eggs and the uncooked eggs mixed up in the refrigerator—and you wanted to know which was which without breaking them? Just give them a spin. The one that whirls around like a spinning top is hardcooked. The one that wobbles and doesn't spin well is still raw.

♦ ♦ ♦

In a salad bowl toss together all ingredients. Serve on crisp lettuce.

HEARTY CHICKEN SOUP
IN A HURRY

2 cans (13½ ounces each)
 chicken broth
1 cup cooked, diced chicken
1 cup cooked, high-protein
 wagon wheel macaroni or
 other pasta
1 cup frozen mixed vegetables

This is an easy soup for a beginning cook. It's also good in a thermos for a school lunch on a cold day. I can't count the number of times I've made it when I've been in a hurry.

♦ ♦ ♦

In a saucepan over medium heat bring broth to a simmer. Stir in chicken, pasta, and vegetables. Reduce heat to low; simmer 5 minutes until vegetables are tender-crisp. Spoon soup into a wide-mouth thermos jar and close tightly. Serve with crackers or lightly buttered bread.

SAUCY CHICKEN BUNDLES

2 cups biscuit mix
½ cup milk
1 cup cooked, diced chicken
¼ cup butter or margarine, melted
2 cans (10½ ounces each) cream of chicken soup, undiluted
1 can (10½ ounces) jellied cranberry sauce

This takes time but it looks good and tastes terrific. It's not a gourmet item, but it's something a young cook can really enjoy making and showing off.

♦ ♦ ♦

In a mixing bowl add milk to biscuit mix to form dough. Roll dough into a square about ¼-inch thick. Cut dough into 3-inch squares (makes about 8). In a small bowl combine chicken, butter, and 4 tablespoons of soup. Put 2 tablespoons of this mixture on each pastry square. Bring four corners of square together and pinch closed. Preheat oven to 450°F. Place on baking sheet and bake for 15 minutes. Heat remaining soup and pour over baked squares. Slice can of cranberry sauce into ¼-inch slices. With star-shaped cookie cutter, cut star from each slice of cranberry sauce and place on top of baked bundle before serving.

THE STORY OF A RARE BIRD

This part has almost nothing to do with recipes and cooking, but as I've been writing this, I've been trying to guess what you might be looking for in this book.

Clearly you wanted recipes from one of the world's premier authorities on chicken. I hope you've found this when looking at Frank's favorites.

But maybe you're also like many people who enjoy reading cookbooks almost as much as they enjoy the cooking. Many of us buy cookbooks and only try a few recipes. The real pleasure we get from a cookbook is in reading it. Knowing this, I've tried to make this book something that would be fun to read as well.

But if you live in an area where Frank sells his products, or if you've seen the PBS specials on him or read about him in *In Search of Excellence,* or perhaps read about him in some of the gossip columns, perhaps you were also curious about Frank as a person. What kind of man built a company from a father-and-son operation to one that today processes more than a million chickens a day and has sales in excess of a billion dollars a year? What is he really like?

Frank's outstanding characteristic is that he gives of himself. I've seen firsthand how important it is to him to do the best job he can for both consumers and the people who work for the company. I know how often he's set the alarm for 4:45 A.M. after being up until 1:30 A.M. so he can get a head start on work. When he's really busy with something, I've seen him get by with two hours' sleep after a month of getting only four hours.

He cares so much for the people who work for him that even during our honeymoon he made a transatlantic phone call to make sure a low-level associate's grievance was handled fairly. I'm touched by how often he visits retired associates, now in their 80s and 90s. Company functions mean so much to him that once, after we had been traveling for twenty-three hours on our return from the Soviet Union, he went straight to a Perdue Volunteer Fire Brigade Appreciation Dinner rather than going home to bed. The associates meant far more to him than his sleep. When one of the Perdue truckers needed help loading boxes, Frank worked alongside him until the job was done because Frank believed the man had a right to be home with his family.

He is generous even in the building of the company. That may seem like an unusual way to look at the work of an entrepreneur, but he is providing jobs and a quality product; he's not engaged in leveraged buy-outs and paper transactions.

Many people know that Frank Perdue is famous for his chickens, his financial success, his marketing innovations, his drive, his creativity, or even his eccentricities, but I think that his greatest success lies elsewhere. To me, true success isn't measured by what you get, but rather by what you give. The tough man who makes those tender chickens is an unusually giving man, and I feel lucky to be a part of his life.

APPENDIX I

BROILER PARTS—COOKING TIMES (minutes)

METHOD	SPLIT BREAST	BONELESS BREAST	THIGHS	DRUMSTICK	WINGS
Sautéeing	Brown 6–8 over medium-high. Simmer, covered, 15–25, over medium low.	Brown 4 over medium-high (2 per side). Simmer, covered, 6–12 over medium-low.	Brown 6–8 over medium-high. Simmer, covered, 30–40, medium-low.	Brown 6–8 over medium-high. Simmer, covered, 25–35, medium-low.	Brown 6–8 over medium-high. Simmer, covered, 20–30 over medium-low
Over Frying 375°	15–25	10–20	20–30	15–25	10–20
Deep Frying 350–365°F	10–15	8–12	12–17	10–15	8–12
Poaching	35–45	25–35	45–55	40–50	30–40
Broiling	15–25	10–20	20–30	15–25	15–25
Baking 350°F	30–40	20–30	40–50	35–45	25–35 or longer if you like them crisp
Grilling	15–25	10–20	20–30	15–20	15–25

APPENDIX II

ROASTER PARTS—COOKING TIMES (minutes)

METHOD	WHOLE BREAST	BONELESS BREAST	THIN-SLICED BREAST	BONELESS THIGH	DRUMSTICK	WINGETTE
Oven Frying 425°F	Not recommended	Cut large pieces into long strips 1½ inches thick (10–12)	1½ to 2 per side (total 3–4)	Not recommended	Not recommended	15–25
Poaching	60–70	25–35	Not recommended	40–50	60–75	55–65
Broiling	Not recommended	15–25	1½ to 2 per side (total 3–4)	25–35	Not recommended	25–35
Baking 350–375°F	50–65	20–30	12–17	35–45	60–70	50–60
Grilling	45–55	15–25	1½ to 2 per side (total 3–4)	20–35	55–65	25–35
Sautéeing	Not recommended	Cut large pieces into long strips 1½ inches thick (See Guide).	1½ to 2 per side (total 3–4)	Flatten slightly. Brown in oil, medium-high, 8–10 total. Simmer, covered, 10–15 over medium-low.	Not recommended	Brown in oil, medium-high, 6–8. Simmer, covered, medium-low 25–35.
Deep Frying 350–365°F	Not recommended	See Appendix III	See Appendix III	Not recommended	Not recommended	10–15

APPENDIX III

PERDUE CHICKEN BASIC COOKING GUIDE FOR SPLIT BREAST

DEEP-FRY	In a deep fryer heat 6–8 inches of cooking oil to 350°–365°F. Dredge chicken in seasoned flour, beaten egg and breadcrumbs, or dip in batter. Fry 10–15 minutes, until golden brown and cooked through. Drain on crumpled paper towels.
OVEN-FRY	Preheat oven to 425°F. Place ¼ cup oil in baking dish and heat for 10 minutes. Dredge chicken in coating of your choice. Oven-fry for 15–25 minutes, turning occasionally, until golden brown and cooked through.
POACH	Place chicken in simmering broth or water to cover. Immediately reduce heat to low and poach 35–45 minutes until cooked through. Allow chicken to cool in liquid if time permits.
BROIL	Season to taste with seasonings or sauce. Broil or grill 6–8 inches from heat source 15–25 minutes until cooked through.
BAKE	(350–375°F) Place breast skin side up in a shallow roasting pan. Season to taste with seasonings or sauce. Bake 30–40 minutes, until cooked through.
SAUTÉ	Over medium-high heat, brown breasts on all sides in oil or butter, 6–8 minutes. Add remaining ingredients. Cover and simmer over medium-low for 15–25 minutes, until cooked through.

PERDUE CHICKEN BASIC COOKING GUIDE FOR BONELESS BREAST

DEEP-FRY	In a deep fryer heat 6–8 inches of cooking oil to 350°–365°F. Dredge chicken in seasoned flour, beaten egg and breadcrumbs or dip in batter. Fry 8–12 minutes, until golden brown and cooked through. Drain on crumpled paper towels.
OVEN-FRY	Preheat oven to 425°F. Place ¼ cup oil in baking dish and heat for 10 minutes. Dredge chicken in coating of your choice. Oven-fry for 10–20 minutes, turning occasionally, until cooked through.
POACH	Place chicken in enough simmering broth or water to cover. Immediately reduce heat to low and poach 25–35 minutes until cooked through. Allow chicken to cool in liquid if time permits.
BROIL	Season to taste with seasonings or sauce. Broil or grill 6–8 inches from heat source 10–20 minutes until cooked through.
BAKE	(350°–375°F) Preheat oven. Place breast in a shallow roasting pan. Season to taste with seasonings or sauce. Bake 20–30 minutes, until cooked through.
SAUTÉ	Over medium-high heat, brown breasts in oil or butter for 2 minutes per side. Add remaining ingredients. Cover and simmer over medium-low heat for 6–12 minutes until cooked through, turning two to three times.

PERDUE CHICKEN BASIC COOKING GUIDE FOR OVEN STUFFER ROASTER BONELESS BREAST

BAKE	Preheat oven to 375°F. Place 2–3 tablespoons melted butter or margarine in shallow baking dish. Add breast and turn to coat with butter. Sprinkle with salt, pepper and seasonings. Bake 25–35 minutes, until cooked through.
BRAISE	Brown breast in a small amount of oil over medium-high heat, 8–10 minutes. Discard oil and add enough braising liquid (i.e., broth, wine, tomato sauce) to cover. Cover and simmer on stove or in a preheated 325°F oven for 20–30 minutes until cooked through.
GRILL OR BROIL	Place larger breast pieces between sheets of plastic wrap and pound to flatten slightly. Season and grill breast pieces over hot coals or broil 6–8 inches from heat source for 5–10 minutes on each side, until cooked through.
SAUTÉ	Cut larger breast pieces into long strips, 1½ inches thick. Over medium-high heat, brown breast pieces in oil or butter for 2 minutes per side. Add remaining ingredients. Cover and simmer over medium-low heat 6–12 minutes, until cooked through, turning two to three times.
DEEP-FRY	Cut larger breast pieces into long strips, 1½ inches thick. In a deep fryer, heat 6–8 inches of cooking oil to 350°–365°F. Dredge chicken in seasoned flour, beaten egg and breadcrumbs or dip in batter. Fry 8–12 minutes until golden brown and cooked through.
OVEN-FRY	Preheat oven to 425°F. Cut larger breast pieces into long strips, 1½ inches thick. Place ¼ cup oil in baking dish and heat for 10 minutes. Dredge chicken in coating of your choice. Oven-fry 10–15 minutes, turning two to three times, until golden brown and cooked through.
STIR-FRY	Cut into strips or bite-size pieces and use in any stir-fry recipe.

PERDUE CHICKEN BASIC COOKING GUIDE FOR OVEN STUFFER ROASTER THIN-SLICED BONELESS BREAST

BAKE	Preheat oven to 375°F. Arrange cutlets in single layer in buttered baking dish. Cover with sauce if desired. Bake 12–17 minutes or until cooked through.
GRILL OR BROIL	Grill or broil cutlets 6–8 inches from heat for 1½–2 minutes per side until cooked through.
SAUTÉ	Heat oil or butter in skillet over medium-high heat. Add cutlets and sauté for 1½–2 minutes per side until cooked through.
DEEP-FRY	In a deep fryer heat 6–8 inches of cooking oil to 350–365°F. Dredge chicken in seasoned flour, beaten egg and breadcrumbs or dip in batter. Fry 1–2 minutes until golden brown and cooked through.
OVEN-FRY	Preheat oven to 425°F. Place ¼ cup oil in baking dish and heat for 10 minutes. Dredge chicken in coating of your choice. Oven-fry for 1½–2½ minutes per side, until golden brown and cooked through.

PERDUE CHICKEN BASIC COOKING GUIDE FOR THIGHS

DEEP-FRY	In a deep fryer, heat 6–8 inches of cooking oil to 350°–365°F. Dredge thighs in seasoned flour, beaten egg and breadcrumbs or dip in batter. Fry 12–17 minutes, until golden brown and cooked through. Drain on crumpled paper towels.
OVEN-FRY	Preheat oven to 425°F. Place ¼ cup cooking oil in baking dish and heat for 10 minutes. Dredge thighs in coating of your choice. Place in hot oil and oven-fry 20–30 minutes, turning occasionally, until golden brown and cooked through.
POACH	Place thighs in enough simmering chicken broth or water to cover. Immediately reduce heat to low and poach 45–55 minutes until cooked through. Allow chicken to cool in liquid if time permits.
BROIL	Season thighs to taste with seasonings or sauce. Broil or grill 6–8 inches from heat source 20–30 minutes until cooked through.
BAKE	(350°–375°F) Preheat oven. Place thighs in a shallow roasting pan. Season to taste with seasonings or sauce. Bake 40–50 minutes, until fork tender and cooked through.
SAUTÉ	Over medium-high heat, brown thighs on all sides in oil or butter, 6–8 minutes. Add remaining ingredients. Cover and simmer over medium-low heat 30–40 minutes until fork tender and cooked through.

PERDUE CHICKEN BASIC COOKING GUIDE FOR OVEN STUFFER ROASTER BONELESS THIGHS

General Note: Rinse chicken and pat dry before cooking.

BAKE OR ROAST	Preheat oven to 375°F. Season thighs and brush with melted butter or margarine. Bake 35–40 minutes or until nicely browned and cooked through. Turn once halfway through cooking time.
SAUTÉ	Flatten thighs slightly. Season and flour lightly if desired. In a large skillet, over medium-high heat, brown thighs on both sides in a small amount of oil (8–10 minutes). Reduce heat to medium-low. Cover and simmer chicken another 10–15 minutes until cooked through.
GRILL OR BROIL	Flatten thighs slightly. Marinate or rub with seasonings. Grill thighs over hot coals or broil 6–8 inches from heat source 25–30 minutes or until cooked through. Turn, and baste with marinade or barbecue sauce if desired, three to four times during grilling.
STEW	Trim and cube thighs. Use in stew recipes.
STIR-FRY	Trim thighs and cut into thin strips. Use in stir-fry recipes.
MICROWAVE	Follow manufacturers' instructions.

PERDUE CHICKEN BASIC COOKING GUIDE FOR DRUMSTICKS

DEEP-FRY	In a deep fryer, heat 6–8 inches of cooking oil to 350°–365°F. Dredge drumsticks in seasoned flour, beaten egg and bread crumbs or dip in batter. Fry 10–15 minutes, until golden brown and cooked through. Drain on crumpled paper towels.
OVEN-FRY	Preheat oven to 425°F. Place ¼ cup cooking oil in baking dish and heat for 10 minutes. Dredge drumsticks in coating of your choice. Place in hot oil and oven-fry 15–25 minutes, turning occasionally, until golden brown and cooked through.
POACH	Place drumsticks in enough simmering chicken broth or water to cover. Immediately reduce heat to low and poach 40–50 minutes until cooked through. Allow chicken to cool in liquid if time permits.
BROIL	Season drumsticks to taste with seasonings or sauce. Broil or grill 6–8 inches from heat source 15–25 minutes, turning occasionally, until cooked through.
BAKE	(350°–375°F) Preheat oven. Place drumsticks in a shallow roasting pan. Season to taste with seasonings or sauce. Bake 35–45 minutes, until fork tender and cooked through.
SAUTÉ	Over medium-high heat, brown drumsticks on all sides in oil or butter, 6–8 minutes. Add remaining ingredients. Cover and simmer over medium-low heat 25–35 minutes until fork tender and cooked through.

PERDUE CHICKEN BASIC COOKING GUIDE FOR WINGS

DEEP-FRY	In a deep fryer, heat 6–8 inches of cooking oil to 350°–365°F. Dredge wings in seasoned flour, beaten egg and breadcrumbs or dip in batter. Fry 8–12 minutes, until golden brown and cooked through. Drain on crumpled paper towels.
OVEN-FRY	Preheat oven to 425°F. Place ¼ cup cooking oil in baking dish and heat for 10 minutes. Dredge wings in coating of your choice. Place in hot oil and oven-fry 10–20 minutes, turning occasionally, until golden brown and cooked through.
POACH	Place wings in enough simmering chicken broth or water to cover. Immediately reduce heat to low and poach wings 35–45 minutes until cooked through. Allow chicken to cool in liquid if time permits.
BROIL	Season wings to taste with seasonings or sauce. Broil or grill 6–8 inches from heat source 15–25 minutes until cooked through.
BAKE	(350°–375°F) Preheat oven. Place wings in a shallow roasting pan. Season to taste with seasonings or sauce. Bake 30–40 minutes, until fork tender and cooked through.
SAUTÉ	Over medium-high heat, brown wings on all sides in oil or butter, 6–8 minutes. Add remaining ingredients. Cover and simmer over medium-low 20–30 minutes until cooked through and tender.

INDEX